The Political Testament
of Cardinal Richelieu

The Political Testament
of Cardinal Richelieu

Introduction, Translation, and Notes by

Paul Sonnino

ROWMAN & LITTLEFIELD
Lanham • Boulder • New York • London

Published by Rowman & Littlefield
An imprint of The Rowman & Littlefield Publishing Group, Inc.
4501 Forbes Boulevard, Suite 200, Lanham, Maryland 20706
www.rowman.com

6 Tinworth Street, London SE11 5AL, United Kingdom

British Library Cataloguing in Publication Information Available

Library of Congress Control Number: 2019045556

ISBN 9781538135952 (cloth) | ISBN 9781538135969 (pbk.) | ISBN 9781538135976
(electronic)

Contents

INTRODUCTORY

Introduction

If one wishes to get into the head of one of the most famous inhabitants of the seventeenth century, one can do no better than to become familiar with the *Political Testament* of Armand du Plessis, better known as Cardinal Richelieu. He wrote it toward the end of his life, only to be read after his own death by King Louis XIII, and in this work the cardinal, who took himself very seriously, has absolutely no reason to dissimulate and every reason to justify himself not only to the king but also before God.

This is why. He had absolutely no doubt that God had created the world, that man was a sinner, that Jesus had died for his sins, and that the only sure path to salvation was through the Roman Catholic Church. But he was almost as sure that, given the corruption of mankind, the best kind of government for it was absolute monarchy, with a ruler who brooked no opposition. He was also extremely ambitious, and he wanted to serve himself.

It seemed to him, at first sight, as if these three goals were perfectly compatible. He was schooled in a tradition, the scholasticism of the medieval university, which taught him that even though the sure path to salvation lay in a collection of mysteries accessible only through the Word of God, man had also been created with a rational mind, which revelation superseded but did not displace. Thus, for example, the biblical story of how Adam and Eve fell from grace fitted right in with the corruption of mankind, which was to him all too obvious, from which it followed that kings were absolute by divine right as well as for perfectly good reasons. It also followed that anyone who had talent should not squander it.

Nothing, as a young bishop, stood in his way. Louis XIII was a boy. The government of France was in the hands of his mother, Marie de Medici, who spent most of her time with her Italian favorites, such as Concino Concini. She was peaceably disposed, and in a meeting of the Estates-General, which she was pressured into calling, the bishop attracted the queen mother's attention by speaking in favor of marrying the king to a Spanish princess, which won him entry to her council.

This auspicious beginning, however, was dealt a blow when the king, who had reached the age of fifteen, ordered the captain of his guards to arrest Concini, who was killed while attempting to resist, resulting in the queen mother's leaving the court and the exile of the ambitious bishop. It did not last. Armand du Plessis brought about the reconciliation of mother and son and worked his way back into the council, which is how he became a cardinal.

He was by disposition an authoritarian. He was horrified by the disorder into which he felt the kingdom had fallen, especially since the Reformation, as a result of which Louis XIII's father, Henry IV, himself initially a Huguenot, as the French Protestants called themselves, had decided that being accepted as king by the French, who were predominantly Catholic, was worth becoming one himself, even though he could not avoid granting toleration to his former supporters with his famous Edict of Nantes and letting them retain a number of fortified strongholds all over France.

Richelieu was also very perceptive. He had studied Louis XIII and observed that he was very dependent but also very temperamental. He did not like to be browbeaten, insulted, or shunned. This is what had prompted his violent reaction to Concini. The cardinal knew it, and he sought desperately to enroll the queen mother in accommodating the king's sensitivities. This was possible up to a point. For example, if it came to stopping duels, reforming the judicial system, stimulating commerce, or putting down the periodic revolts by the Huguenots, she could participate in the adventure. But she herself had expected that she would be able to control her son through Richelieu, and in that she was bitterly disappointed. Furious with the cardinal for having abandoned her, she began to plot against him, often using her younger son, Monsieur, as her instrument. Likewise, as Richelieu's policies turned from depriving the Huguenots of their strongholds such as the port of La Rochelle, which he succeeded in doing, to confronting the Spanish, which was much more controversial, she found support for her campaign against him in the party of hard-line Catholics, the "devout," who favored a union of the Catholic powers against the Protestants at home and abroad.

I am almost certain that if Richelieu had been the minister of a monarch like James I of England, who abhorred war and admired Spain, he would have accommodated his policies to the wishes of this king, but Louis XIII was extremely touchy about his prerogatives. The cardinal had a difficult choice. He could counsel pacifism, gratify the queen mother, and end up, if not like Concini, at least out of power, but he also had a king who was the agent of God, and Richelieu was enough of an authoritarian to discover the will of God in submission to Louis XIII. It was not easy, but, in his moral universe, serving the king in his manner was better than not serving him at all. Moderating his temper tantrums with soothing advice was better than confronting him at every turn. The cardinal had, moreover, guessed right. When, in November of 1630, Marie de Medici, backed by the hard-line Catholics, attempted to shame her son into dismissing him, it was the queen mother who had to pack her bags and go into exile in the Spanish Low Countries.

Little by little, therefore, the confrontations with Spain escalated into the subsidizing of the Lutheran King of Sweden, Gustavus Adolphus, in his war against the Catholic Hapsburgs in the Holy Roman Empire. That was not an easy step to take, and the proof of this is that almost exactly at this time, we find Richelieu beginning a detailed history of Louis XIII's reign, documented massively with the cardinal's own correspondence, in which his purpose is patently to justify himself. The task became even more imperative when, in 1634, the Hapsburgs and their allies won an impressive military victory in the Holy Roman Empire, and in the following year Richelieu went so far as to enter his king into open alliances with the Lutheran Swedes and the Calvinist Dutch against Catholic Hapsburgs both in Spain and in the Holy Roman Empire. Not only did this involvement oblige him to put aside most of his domestic reforms and impose arduous burdens on the French people, but he also prolonged a horrendous war and destroyed any lingering hope for the complete suppression of Protestantism in Europe.

There is a French saying that "whoever excuses himself accuses himself," and the proliferating folios of the detailed history of Louis XIII attest to how difficult it was for Richelieu to come to grips with his conscience. There is even further evidence of this observation, because, after almost five years of lingering warfare, in the course of 1640 the tide of war finally began to turn in favor of the French. On April 9, in Italy, the Count d'Harcourt managed to rout a Spanish army that was besieging Casale. Between June 12 and August 10, the king himself took Arras from the Spanish. On September 9 a French army relieved the Spanish siege of Turin. Suddenly, the spirits of Cardinal Richelieu began to soar. Unable to get out of an embarrassing war that neither bloody battles nor brutal sieges seemed able to end, he was all the more open to the seductions of his own wishful thinking, and he began to imagine that the Spanish would be sufficiently discouraged by three fortuitous reversals to sue for peace. Thus he put aside the compilation of his plodding history, which had reached the year 1638, to write a shorter one, not officially of the reign of Louis XIII but of the triumph of his own ministry. This is the context of the *Political Testament*.

He begins it with a "Succinct narration of the great actions of the King," with the precautionary protest that it is impossible to do everything at once, after which the cardinal proceeds to a summary of the events that he and his assistants had previously been describing in excruciating detail. But in the course of this hurried recapitulation, in which anything that had gone wrong is blamed on the cowardice or ineptitude of someone other than Louis XIII, three recurring themes leap to the eye. One is Richelieu's pride in having deprived the Huguenots of their strongholds, two is the malice of the Spanish in having obliged him to make an alliance with the Protestants, and three is his assumption that peace, for which he was even willing to give up some of his conquests, was in his grasp. All these themes are important for him, but the greatest of them is the alliance with the Protestants. No wonder! The interminable war against the Hapsburgs was weighing most heavily upon his conscience.

His justification for the war, therefore, which he had already dealt with in his previous work, merits our particular attention. He accuses the Spanish of having attempted to come to the aid of the English, who were trying to relieve the siege of La Rochelle. It is a hard sell. He has to admit that the Spanish accused Henry IV of having allied himself with the Dutch during their revolt against Spain. True enough, says Richelieu, but the Spanish started it because they supported the extreme Catholics in France both against Henry III and against Louis's father after he had legally succeeded to the throne of France, an even harder sell since the future Henry IV had led the Huguenots in their revolts even before he could lay claim to this throne! Ultimately, Richelieu has to go back to unspecified theologians who all supposedly agree that everyone has the right of self-defense.

Here, therefore, lies the entire basis of the compromise that he had made with the Sermon on the Mount. The world was too sinful for the golden rule to be applied to public policy. Any king who turned the other cheek was simply exposing himself to losing his kingdom, and once he did, how could he possibly defend the true faith? Admittedly, he was hardly the first Christian to take this position. It goes back to Saul of Tarsus telling his correspondents that they could never match up to the sanctity of Jesus, and long before the political theorists of sixteenth-century Europe had euphemized this behavior into such clichés as "reason of state" and "the divine right" of kings.

Richelieu, thus, was no revolutionary, or at least he did not think he was. He had a conception right out of the Middle Ages, in which there were different kinds of people in every society, with each kind having its specific function. The French monarchy, to him, was in complete harmony with this principle by having established three different "orders"—the clergy, the nobility, and the third estate—and Richelieu begins the body of his testament by discussing each order, what it should be, what was wrong with it, and what needed to be done to restore each to its proper place.

As to the clergy, which was the first order in the kingdom, Richelieu does not have too many complaints. He is glad to observe that the practice of giving the income from monasteries *en commende* (to nontonsured private parties) was on the decline and that the personal and moral qualities of the bishops nominated by the king were on the rise. This is not surprising in view of the fact that, at this very moment, France was in the midst of a Catholic revival and lacking in neither reformers nor saints. He is also very protective of the rights of the clergy, wishing to limit *appels comme d'abus* (appeals as if from abuse) from church courts to secular ones, and he is strongly opposed to any extension of the *régale* (the right of the king to collect the income from benefices during periods when they were temporarily vacant).

One might think, perhaps, that the cardinal at this juncture would have turned his attention to the most visible embarrassment then facing the Catholic Church in France—namely, the presence of a heretical Huguenot minority in their midst. Amazingly, he does not say a word about it, as if it had nothing to do with the business of the church. Instead, he goes off airily on what might seem to be an infinitely more tangential question—namely, the state of higher education, which in his time was almost entirely in the hands of clergy. He is appalled by the proliferation of schools and the rush of parents to enroll their children in them. He considers this dangerous for several reasons. First of all, he wants to control learning on political grounds. He has a sneaking suspicion, even if he does not admit it to himself, that all learning, not just a little, is a dangerous thing and if it falls into the hands of the masses, a babble of voices will ensue. To him, the Protestant Reformation was the most recent illustration of this phenomenon. Then there were economic grounds. If the population abounded with all sorts of sloppily trained know-it-alls, who would be left to till the soil? Reactionary as this might sound to the modern reader, it made perfect sense to the cardinal, who had no conception of the technological and scientific revolutions that were bubbling under his feet, except, perhaps, to place the astronomers on the same footing as the other potential revolutionaries. Indeed, he was satisfied to keep the educational machinery in France divided between the medieval universities and the more inventive Jesuits, hoping that neither one would get so powerful that they might threaten the state.

It would come as a surprise to any reader of Alexander Dumas that Cardinal Richelieu was a great admirer of the nobility. This would come as an even greater surprise to any amateur genealogist who could easily discover that the cardinal's mother was the daughter of a lawyer, just the kind of social climber whom Richelieu goes on to accuse of corrupting both the state and the handsome profiles of the nobility. But the reason he likes the nobility is because he considers them essential to the survival of the state. They have their privileges, but, to him, they deserve them because they are bred to shed their blood for it. True, they are arrogant and sometimes violent with their social inferiors, but he is certain that without the nobility to lead its armies, France could never have obtained the glorious peace that he is anticipating. The cardinal, therefore, earnestly advises the king to support the nobility in a variety of ways in its efforts to maintain a dignified lifestyle. What he abhors is their insistence on killing each other in duels, and even then Richelieu fears that punishing them with death, to which he sometimes resorts with great reluctance, will only redouble their courage.

Indeed, when he comes to the third estate, into which he lumps over 90 percent of the population, his biggest villains are the judges and the financiers, who are always out to limit the power of the king and, not unlike his own mother, penetrate into the ranks of the nobility. What allowed them to do it over the years, he claims, were the needs of the state in its wars, which forced the kings to institute the practice of selling offices and even permitting the purchaser to pay the *paulette* (an additional tax) if he wished to make the office hereditary. Richelieu writes at first as if he wants to abolish the practice entirely, and then his reluctance to doing everything at once kicks in. He comes up with all sorts of reasons why it may be better to leave the entire system of the venality of offices alone, or at least to postpone reform ad infinitum. We begin to think, as we follow Richelieu's hesitations, that perhaps his bark may be worse than his bite. Yes, he is prepared to behead a few great nobles and hang an even greater number of insolent peasants. But, just like Edmund Burke over a hundred years later, he is afraid of confronting deeply entrenched institutions. And for all his contempt for the ignorant multitudes, he is deeply disturbed by their suffering.

This conflict between the authoritarian idealist, the war hawk, and the compromiser with the evils of this world never emerges so clearly as in the chapter where Richelieu faces up to the eccentric character of Louis XIII. It permits the reader to imagine what it must have been like to contend with a man who could not control himself and who could swing in an instant from pangs of conscience to fits of rage against his most loyal servants. The cardinal alludes to many incidents the details of which we may never know and which only the novelist or screen writer can imagine. At the time he was writing this, in 1640, the cardinal was hoping against hope that the king had mellowed, which he probably had to some extent, but Richelieu had still one more heart-stopping crisis to overcome since, even as he was writing, Louis was developing a little too much affection for an insolent young nobleman, the Marquis de Cinq-Mars. We must keep in mind that the cardinal was speaking from beyond the grave, and still he could only strive to break through by constant reiteration and by sweetening his pills with lavish praise. We learn in the following chapter that he had been afraid, during his lifetime, to advise the king to have his private quarters swept more thoroughly. This should tell us something about an authoritarian who could convince himself to become a war hawk from fear of being turned upon by his master, while at the same time longing for a peace and being afraid to rock the boat.

Sometime in the midst of putting together the *Political Testament*, Richelieu or his assistants decided to divide it into two parts. It almost appears as if the cardinal felt he had been too general and wanted to get down to brass tacks. He repeats that the reign of God should be supreme, but this time he does not seem to be able to evade the question of what to do about the Huguenots. His advice is surprising, although it should not be if we keep his caution in mind. He concludes, even more timidly than he did regarding the heredity of offices, that any attempt to convert the Huguenots could only be done with "moderation."

In this second part, some chapters bear a resemblance to Niccolò Machiavelli's *The Prince*. At this time they were almost obligatory in a work of this type. Better to be feared than loved; go for the lesser of two evils. In one of the most striking expressions of these Machiavellian platitudes with a Richelieuian twist, he defends putting a suspect in prison without sufficient proof in order to save the state. But there are notable differences between him and his notorious model. Machiavelli feels that his Italy had fallen apart and needed to be reassembled from scratch. Richelieu was neither so desperate nor so idealistic. To him, there was nothing wrong with France that a strong hand, namely his own, could not fix. Moreover, to Machiavelli religion was simply another instrument in the hands of the lawgiver, whose efficacy for the soul, if any, was shrouded in cabbalistic interpretations of the Old Testament. To Richelieu Christianity, as the Catholic Church taught it, was the one true faith. Machiavelli wanted to go back to the ancient Roman armies, and he hated mercenaries. Richelieu found them indispensable. Machiavelli hated fortifications. Richelieu thinks they are the salvation of the modern monarchy. We are no longer in the "Renaissance," which was largely a hankering for the good old days. We are in early modern Europe, and Richelieu, in these respects, is keeping up with the times.

In any case, Richelieu seems almost in a hurry, as the peace is approaching, to get down to specifics as to what he wants to do. Thus his chapters get longer and even more repetitious as he addresses himself to the army, the navy, and the finances. Yet they are a godsend to any reader who wants an inside look at the institutions of France in the seventeenth century. His pessimistic assessment of human nature reasserts itself when he insists that the only way to preserve the peace is to maintain a standing army along with a ready reserve. Likewise, his utter contempt for any kind of assembly, whether popular or aristocratic, sounds very much like how a dean in a modern university might describe a meeting of the faculty. And his list of perfectly good reasons to go to war is long enough to gladden the heart of any Louis XIV, Frederick the Great, or George W. Bush. Still, this is the one portion of the *Political Testament* where he seems to have an inkling of what kind of changes the future had in store.

It is amazing to see how easily Cardinal Richelieu feels that France can become dominant at sea. He claims that she has a surplus of sailors, and he imagines that if the king wished to go into the business of shipbuilding, he could sell his ships at a discount to merchants who would then be eager to purchase them instead of taking the time to build them on their own. He is even certain that the Providence of God has taken care to locate France conveniently so as to separate Spain from its possessions in Europe, with the winds also conspiring to make it extremely difficult to row or sail between them. Since Cardinal Richelieu had come to terms with the corruption of humanity, it should not be surprising if he made his compromises with the root of all evil. Just as a king cannot serve God if he does not have power, no monarch can run a country if he does not have money. God continues to enter into it, because Richelieu feels tenderly for the ignorant masses who have to till the soil and pay the taxes, but once again he finds his consolation in the kind of utopia that he is hoping to bequeath to posterity. This time, surprisingly, Christian charity leads him into a modicum of economic liberalism, for he firmly believes that even the ignorant masses will not work without some incentive and that, as long as they do not get too ambitious, the lighter the taxes, the greater the taxable income for the state. Here, again, we have to keep in mind the mental universe in which he was living. Everyone has his or her place, and if they try to move out of it, the entire system will collapse. He simply cannot imagine a world in which an oligarchy of wealth can successfully run a huge state. But then, there is no reason why he should have.

It is relatively simple to determine that Cardinal Richelieu composed his *Political Testament* during the second half of 1640, but since the work has come down to us in the two texts that I have designated Text A and Text B, it is almost impossible to determine when, exactly, he made the additions to Text A that produced Text B. One thing is certain, however. His hopes kept rising as he wrote. The evidence for this comes at the end of the section on his economic reforms, where he concludes triumphantly that, instead of proposing them as his legacy, he may be able to carry them out during his lifetime. We cannot tell whether this quantum leap preceded or was prompted by two events that should at the very least have confirmed it—namely, the brewing dissatisfaction in Catalonia and in Portugal that erupted into open revolts against the Spanish monarchy toward the end of the year. In either case, by the end of the year he was exultant.

He should have paid closer attention to what he had previously observed about the stubbornness of the Spanish, because despite these cataclysmic disasters, the Spanish did not panic. In the following year, 1641, under the command of Philip IV's brother, the Cardinal-Infante, they rebounded, besieging a stronghold recently taken by the French and threatening to retake it. Richelieu too tried to keep up his spirits, but clearly the war was not going to end, and he had finished his Succinct narration a mite too hastily. So he and his collaborators picked up his narration of the great actions of Louis XIII, which, like his longer history, had reached the year 1638, and began to extend it. They even resumed the longer history. We have some fragments of the continuation of the longer history and one of the continuations of the Succinct narration, which clearly show that the scent of victory was no longer in his nostrils. About the only event he can celebrate is the death of the Cardinal-Infante, not exactly a noble sentiment. He was getting embittered, which emerges even better in other documents. His hopes for a forthcoming peace dashed, he was preparing himself and his confidant Cardinal Mazarin for a longer struggle, for which they intended to extract a higher price with which to break the will of their stubborn enemies, if that was even possible. This is why the *Political Testament* ends not with a bang but with a series of whimpers.

I cannot conclude this introduction, however, without calling attention to what Richelieu does not discuss in this work—namely, to his silences. There is no admission in this work of his cruel streak, which he cannot suppress sometimes in his treatment of other people. Only twice does he mention Louis XIII's Spanish wife, Anne of Austria, herself a victim of his barbs. Nor does he ever celebrate the birth of the king's two children, the future Louis XIV in 1638 and the future Monsieur in 1640, who, blessedly for Richelieu, relegated the first Monsieur to third place in line. Besides, it might not have gone down well to include the fathering of the two heirs by Louis XIII, who was suspected to be impotent, as among the "great actions" of the king. Likewise, there is only one passing reference, without even identifying him by name, to Father Joseph du Tremblay, Richelieu's "grey eminence," who tried to keep the devout at bay by campaigning for a redeeming crusade against the Turks. It shows, if the entire *Political Testament* were not proof enough, that the cardinal never had the remotest thought of such a project. Not a word either about the peasant revolt in Normandy in 1639, put down brutally by the Chancellor Séguier the following year.

The Manuscripts

The *Political Testament* of Cardinal Richelieu was first published in The Hague in 1688 by Henri Desbordes, a Protestant bookseller, largely as a reproach of the policies of Louis XIV. Desbordes claimed to have printed it from a mediocre manuscript written in two distinct hands, but he nevertheless advertised it as authentic and continued to publish it over the next twenty years. In the course of the following century, Voltaire, who presumed to know Richelieu better than Richelieu knew himself, ridiculed the idea that Richelieu could have written it, and all efforts to contradict him were of little avail until the late nineteenth century, when Gabriel Hanotaux came up with archival documentation that Richelieu was indeed the author. Even then the doubts continued, with Edmond Esmonin in 1937 claiming that there were seventeen manuscripts of the work and, without bothering to name them, demanded their close examination.

It was not, however, until 1945 that Louis André came out with a modern edition. It was based, in part, on an eighteenth-century copy of a manuscript that clearly preceded the Desbordes one, to which the copyist had made some significant additions from a second manuscript, which turned out to be very similar to the edition that Desbordes had published. André merely appended the additions to his edition, but to him, therefore, must go the credit for discovering that there were two versions of the *Political Testament*, which I have taken the liberty of designating Texts A and B. André, moreover, performed another signal service, which was to identify fifteen manuscripts of the *Testament* in different French archives, all of which turned out to be more copies of Text B, each with its own peculiarities.

Several difficulties remained. For all of their disputations over authorship, neither André nor any other editors of the *Political Testament* had seriously addressed themselves to the questions of when, exactly, Cardinal Richelieu wrote the work and what the differences between Texts A and B might be able to reveal about his character and policies. Moreover, none of the previous editions seem to have considered the significance of the continuation of the Succinct narration, even though this continuation was the only portion of the original manuscript that has not come down to us as a copy. My short 2005 article titled "The Dating of Richelieu's *Testament Politique*" was my feeble contribution to this historiographical tradition, and in a way the present volume is an elaboration of that article.

The need to produce a translation, however, has also required me to consult every available manuscript in order to establish the best possible text, an investigation that has led me to some rather startling conclusions. Desbordes, it will be remembered, complained about the manuscript that he had obtained as being written in two different hands, and when I got to the continuation of the Succinct narration, I observed that it was written in *three* hands and recalled that modern scholarship had already attributed them to a copyist, to Richelieu's secretary, Pierre Cherré, and to Richelieu himself. If, moreover, one considers that Desbordes was in no position to identify Richelieu's scribbles, the conclusion is clear: *the text that had fallen into the hands of Desbordes was the original manuscript in the form of a Text B!* Moreover, in my examination of the other manuscripts, I found that evolving versions of this same original Text B had been copied into sixteen other manuscripts and that Desbordes, therefore, must have been the last known proprietor of the original manuscript. On top of that, as I was working through another copy of Text B, I found that *it was entirely written in the hand of Richelieu's secretary, Cherré*, and it gave me the additional bonus of referring to Louis XIII as being "of blessed memory." Subsequently, I found that one manuscript long in the Bibliothèque de l'Arsenal, another one owned by the Médiathèque of Rennes, and a third purchased in 1955 by the Bibliothèque de l'Institut de France are copies of the first three versions that we have of the original Text B. Finally, I was able to find two more copies of Text B, one completely unknown and the other known but unnoticed, all of which combine to give us a better insight into how the original texts developed both during and after the life of Louis XIII.

It is impossible, of course, to present every minor variation in every version of the *Political Testament* while at the same time attempting a translation. I have therefore decided to get as close as I can to the original manuscript, which I have designated as OM^1 to distinguish it from the continuation of the Succinct narration, which I have designated as OM^2. To get as close as I can to the lost OM^1, I rely mainly, though not always, on the manuscript published by André, which I have designated as Text A, and for the best appearance of Text B, I rely on a careful comparison of its copies. Moreover, in order to provide the reader a sense of the major variations in Text B, which are so critical to the interpretation of this work, I have preceded and concluded them by the marker [B] in the translation and designated them as B^1 to B^{17} in the bibliography. And for those who are fascinated by historical mysteries, I am preparing to demonstrate that there is much more to this sequence of copies than meets the eye.

The Translation

Cardinal Richelieu writes in elegant and magnificently ornate baroque French, but he is also writing primarily for the benefit of a childish and disturbed soul, which forces him to be both repetitious and subservient. If I were to translate him literally, the lavishness of the style would disappear under a mountain of pompous verbiage, and if I were to translate him colloquially, the dignity of his phrasing would degenerate into slang. In this translation, I have therefore attempted to achieve a compromise between these two extremes. I have tried to retain both the feel of the ponderous syntax and the tone of colloquial conversation.

I do my best, for example, to translate French words by their cognate or at least always by the same word if possible—for example, *estimé* is always "felt," but *inconvenient*, which does not mean "inconvenient," becomes "drawback." I also try to translate synonyms consistently so as to maintain a sense of their recurrence whenever this is feasible. So, for example, *représenter*, *faire voir*, *montrer*, and *faire connaître*, which all mean more or less the same thing, I translate, respectively, as "indicate," "point out," "show," and "demonstrate." I do the same for colloquialisms and idioms, always giving each one its own English equivalent wherever feasible. So, for example, *n'oublier aucune chose* and its variations is always "do everything," *remettre devant les yeux* is always "keeping in mind," and *pas de plomb* is always "snail's pace." On the other hand, *bien* and *mal*, *heureux*, and *malheureux* I am obliged to translate variously and even with misleading consistency depending on the context. Finally, in some instances Richelieu's circumlocutions make him seem ridiculous in modern English. So *dignes de ne mourir jamais dans la mémoire des hommes* simply becomes "memorable," and I even venture to translate *se faire connaître, tells qu'ils ont toujours été* as "show their true colors." Nor will I apologize for *votre conduite fut diverse selon que les occasions le requeroyent*, which, I would suggest, is precisely what Louis XIII would have understood Richelieu to say if Joe Biden had said, "You played it by ear," to Barack Obama.

POLITICAL TESTAMENT OR MAXIMS OF STATE OF CARDINAL RICHELIEU

To the King

As soon as it pleased Your Majesty to involve me in the management of your affairs, I set out to do everything I possibly could to further your great plans for the good of your state and the glory of your person.

Since God has blessed my intentions to such a point that the virtue and good fortune of Your Majesty, which have astonished the present age, will be the admiration of future times, I felt that your glorious successes obliged me to write your history, both to keep many of these memorable events from being forgotten through the ignorance of those who could never have known them as well as I, and so that the past can serve as a rule for the future.

Soon after having had this thought, I set to work, believing that I could not begin too soon what would be the work of my life. I not only collected the materials for such a work, but, what is more, I divided it into years so that it could be published.

I admit that even though it is more agreeable to furnish materials for a history than to write it, it was also very pleasant to indicate what had only been accomplished with great difficulty.

While I was enjoying the pleasures of this work, the illnesses and the continual discomforts to which the weakness of my constitution and the load of affairs have reduced me compelled me to abandon it since it was taking too long.

Since I was unable in such straits to do what I desired to do so passionately for the glory of your person and the good of your state, I thought that at least I could not avoid, without being responsible before God, leaving Your Majesty with some memoirs of what I feel to be most important for the government of this kingdom.

Two things oblige me to undertake this work.

The first is my fear and my desire to precede you in dying.

3

The second is my fervent passion for the interests of Your Majesty, which not only makes me desire to see you showered with prosperities during my life but also makes me ardently wish to see them continue when the inevitable tribute that we all owe to nature will keep me from witnessing them.

This piece will see the day under the title of *Political Testament* because it is to be used, if Your Majesty considers it worthy, after my death for the administration and conduct of your kingdom, because in leaving it to you I am turning over to you the very best thing I can bequeath to Your Majesty when it pleases God to call me to Him.

It will be couched in the most direct possible terms, in keeping both with my character and my ordinary manner of writing and with the disposition of Your Majesty, who has always liked coming to the point as much as you have hated long speeches.

If my shadow, which will appear in these memoirs after my death, can contribute something to the regulation of this great state, in the management of which you have involved me more than I deserve, I shall be overjoyed.

To attain this end, considering how the success that it has pleased God to give to the decisions that Your Majesty has made in the past with your most faithful creatures is a powerful motive to induce you to follow the advice that I want to give you for the future, I begin this work by drawing a brief sketch of the great actions that shower you with glory and can justly be considered as the foundation of the future happiness of this kingdom.

This account will appear so trustworthy to those who are faithful witnesses to the events of your time that it will give everybody grounds to realize that the advice that I give to your Majesty has no other motive than the interest of your state and the good of your person, to whom I shall eternally be

SIRE

Your very humble, very faithful, very obedient, very passionate, very grateful subject and servant

Table

Table 7

Table 9

Chapter I

Succinct narration of the great actions of the King

When Your Majesty resolved to give me both a place in your councils and much of your confidence for the directions of your affairs, I can truthfully say that the Huguenots shared the state with you, that the great nobles acted as if they were not your subjects, and the most powerful governors of the provinces as if they had been sovereigns in their posts.

I can say that the bad example set by one and all was so harmful to this kingdom that the most orderly companies took pride in their disorder and in certain cases reduced your legitimate authority as much as possible in order to carry theirs beyond all reason.

I can say that everyone measured his merit by his audacity, that instead of feeling the favors that they received from Your Majesty at their just price, they only valued them as much as they pleased, and that the most audacious at it were felt to be the wisest and they often found themselves the happiest.

I can also say that foreign alliances were disdained, private interests preferred to the public, and, in a word, the royal dignity so far removed from what it should have been, through the deficiency of those who then had the principal direction of your affairs, that it was almost impossible to recognize it.

The behavior of those to whom Your Majesty had entrusted the helm of your state could no longer be continued without losing everything, and, on the other hand, everything could not be changed at once without violating the laws of prudence, which do not permit passing from one extreme to another without stopping.

The sad state of your affairs seemed to compel you to make hasty decisions, without choosing the time or place; yet it was necessary to do something.

The best minds did not feel that it would be possible in such uncertain times to navigate through all of the shoals without shipwreck. The court was full of people who already criticized the temerity of those who wished to attempt it, and since they knew that princes are quick to impute the bad outcome of good advice to those who give it, so few expected good results from the changes that I was supposed to make that many believed my fall assured even before Your Majesty had elevated me.

Notwithstanding all the difficulties that I presented before Your Majesty, since I know what kings can do when they make good use of their power, I ventured to promise you, with confidence in my opinion, that you would find a remedy to the disorders of your state and that in a short time your prudence, your strength, and the blessing of God would give a new look to this kingdom.

I promised you to employ all of my industry and all the authority that it pleased you to give me in order to ruin the Huguenot party, humble the pride of the great nobles, reduce all of your subjects to their duty, and raise your reputation among foreign nations to the point where it should be.

I indicated to you that in order to reach this happy ending, your confidence was entirely necessary to me and how, even though in the past all those who had served you did not have a better or surer means to acquire and to conserve it than to keep you away from the queen your mother, I would take a completely different path and would do everything I could to maintain Your Majesties in a close union, important for your reputation and advantageous for the good of the kingdom.[1]

Thus, the success that has followed the good intentions it has pleased God to give me for the reform of this state will justify to future ages the firmness with which I have constantly pursued this plan, and Your Majesty will also bear witness that I have done everything I could to keep the guile of many bad characters from dividing what, being united by nature, should also be united by affection. And if, after having been fortunate enough to resist their efforts for many years, their malice has finally prevailed, I am extremely consoled that Your Majesty has often been heard to say that when I was thinking the most about the greatness of the queen your mother, she was working to ruin me.[2]

I shall wait to clarify this matter in another place so as to stay with my subject and not to disrupt the order of this work. In 1624 the Huguenots, who have never lost any occasion to strengthen their party, surprised certain vessels that the Duke de Nevers was preparing against the Turk and subsequently formed a powerful armament against Your Majesty.[3]

---

[1] Marie de Medici (1575–1642). It becomes quite evident, if one follows the Succinct narration, that Richelieu is quite honest in claiming that he went out of his way to appease, befriend, or corrupt the creatures of the queen mother as long as they refrained from threatening his life, his priorities, or his relationship with Louis XIII. The same is evident with regard to the cronies of his brother Monsieur.

[2] See note 36 below.

[3] The "other place" is the beginning of Richelieu's *Histoire*, to which he has already referred in his preceding dedication. The Crusader was Charles III Gonzaga (1580–1637),

Even though the navy had been so neglected that you did not have a single vessel, you acted with so much skill and courage that with those that you had been able to collect from your subjects, twenty from the Dutch, and seven English skiffs, you defeated the armada that the Rochelois had put at sea, which was all the more wonderful in that this aid had only been given to you for the sake of appearances. You took by the same means the Island of Ré, which the Rochelois had unfairly seized long ago, you routed four to five thousand men that they had brought in to defend it, and compelled its commander, Soubise, to flee to Oléron, from where your arms chased him out of the kingdom.[4]

These great successes reduced these rebellious arms to a peace so glorious to Your Majesty that the most difficult to please were very satisfied by then, and all admitted that they had never seen anything like it.

The kings your predecessors had in the past received the peace rather than given it to their subjects. Although they were not diverted by any war, they lost in all the treaties they made with them, and even though Your Majesty at this time had many other occupations, you made it with them then by reserving for yourself Fort Louis as a citadel in La Rochelle and the Isles of Ré and Oléron, as well as two other strongholds, which formed no mean circumvallation.

At the same time Your Majesty protected the Duke of Savoy from the oppression of the Spanish, who had attacked him openly, and even though they had one of the largest armies that had been seen for a long time in Italy and it was commanded by the Duke de Feria, a man of intelligence, you kept them from taking Verrua, where your armies, combined with those of the Duke of Savoy, resisted the siege with so much glory that they were finally compelled to raise it shamefully.[5]

Since the Spanish had shortly thereafter taken over all the passages of the Grisons and fortified the best positions in all their valleys and Your Majesty was unable by simple negotiation to deliver his old allies from this invasion, in which these illegal usurpers had entrenched themselves all the more easily

---

Duke de Nevers from 1595. In February 1625 the Huguenot Benjamin de Rohan (1583–1642), Duke de Soubise, grabbed Gonzaga's ships in La Rochelle, while Soubise's older brother Henri (1579–1638), Duke de Rohan, led a Huguenot revolt in Languedoc.

[4] On September 18, 1625, Charles de Lorraine (1571–1640), Duke de Guise, defeated Soubise in a naval battle near La Rochelle, and the revolt was suspended by an uneasy peace between the king and the city on February 5, 1626.

[5] This was part of Richelieu's effort to keep the Spanish out of the Val Telline, discussed in the next note. For this purpose, he made an alliance with the Republic of Venice and with Charles Emmanuel I (1562–1630), Duke of Savoy from 1580, for various diversions against the Spanish. Gómez Suàrez de Figueroa (1587–1634), Duke de Feria, the Spanish governor of Milan, beat them to the punch by laying siege before Verrua in Piedmont, but the Duke of Savoy and the French Marshal de Créqui succeeded in forcing him to raise the siege.

since the Pope was favoring them in the vain hope that they gave him of procuring some advantages to the religion, you accomplished by the force of arms what you had not been able to obtain through reason.[6]

You would by this means have freed this nation from the tyranny of the house of Austria if Fargis, your ambassador in Spain, had not, at the behest of Cardinal de Bérulle, concluded, as he has since confessed to you, without your knowledge and against the express orders of Your Majesty, a very bad treaty to which you finally adhered in order to please the Pope, who claimed not to be in any way involved in this affair.[7]

Since the late king your father of immortal memory had intended to marry one of your sisters in England and the Spanish felt that they had to undermine this project and got into their head to marry one of their Infantas there, once the treaty was concluded the Prince of Wales was so ill-advised that he was willing to commit himself to the discretion of a prince who was in a position to lay down the law to him and passed incognito through France in order to marry her in Spain.[8]

As soon as we were informed of it, we negotiated in such a way that notwithstanding the incredible honors that were accorded to him in that court, where the king always gave him the right hand even though then he was not yet crowned, the marriage was broken off, and shortly thereafter the French one was negotiated, concluded, and fulfilled with conditions three times as good for the faith as had been projected in the time of the late king.[9]

---

[6] The Graubunden, or Grisons, was a canton of Swiss Protestants that also claimed sovereignty over the Catholic inhabitants of the Val Telline, which was one of the best passages from the Spanish possessions in Italy to the Austrian possessions in central Europe as well as to the Spanish possessions in the Low Countries. In 1624 Richelieu had sent a small detachment of French troops to assist the Grisons, thus giving one of the first indications about his future hostility to Spain.

[7] This was the Treaty of Monzòn, concluded by Charles d'Angennes (b. 1585), Sieur du Fargis, on March 5, 1626. He was supported by Pierre de Bérulle (1575–1629), founder of the famous seminary, the Oratory, who also served as advisor on foreign policy and became a cardinal in 1627. The pope at this time was Maffeo Barberini (1568–1644), Urban VIII from 1623. Richelieu complained bitterly that Fargis had exceeded his instructions, but in view of the continuing tensions in France with the Huguenots, it should come as no surprise that Louis and Richelieu went along with the treaty and withdrew their troops in March 1627.

[8] This was the embarrassing effort of James I (1566–1625), a great admirer of Spain, to marry his son Charles (1600–1649) to a Spanish Infanta, leading in 1623 to his futile voyage to Spain. James was so irritated at its failure that in August 1624 he went to war against Spain.

[9] The French took advantage of this fiasco and negotiated the marriage of Charles to Louis XIII's sister, Henrietta-Maria (1600–1669), which took place in Paris by proxy in May 1625. Shortly after the marriage, Charles succeeded to the throne as Charles I.

A short time later, powerful cabals formed at the court. Those who were then in charge of your brother Monsieur got him in on them at his young age.[10]

Since I am compelled regretfully to say that a very important person was imperceptibly involved with many others who inflamed her passions, I cannot deny the merit that you acquired before God and man in suppressing the scandal of her imprudent conduct by wisely covering it up.[11]

The English entered willingly into these cabals, many people in the kingdom got deeply involved; the Duke de Rohan and the Huguenot party were to act internally at the same time that the English would attack the islands and coasts of this state with a powerful naval armada.[12]

The plot seemed so well organized that few thought that the force of the plotters could be resisted. However, the capture of Colonel d'Ornano, the Duke de Vendôme, and the Grand Prior, the punishment of Chalais, and the exile of some princesses dispersed the cabal in such a way that all of its plans were without effect.[13]

Since it was not without great kindness and prudence that you consented in Nantes to the marriage of your brother Monsieur, the sincerity with which your true servants were bold enough to submit its drawbacks to you beforehand was a powerful proof of their fidelity and a sure testimony that they had no intention of fooling you.[14]

---

[10] This was the so-called conspiracy of Chalais, who paid the piper for it. Henri de Tall-eyrand-Périgord (1599–1626), Count de Chalais, was a foolish young man madly in love with the beautiful Marie de Rohan (1600–1679), Duchess de Chevreuse, one of the great schemers of all time, who wanted to get Monsieur into the council or possibly out of the country. The plotters also wanted to prevent his marriage to a French heiress, which would have tied him down. The conspiracy spread to other great nobles, like Louis's illegitimate half brothers, César (1594–1665), Duke de Vendôme, and Alexandre (1598–1629), the Grand Prior, as well as to Monsieur's governor, Jean-Baptiste d'Ornano (1581–1626). There was even talk of assassinating Richelieu and maybe even the king.

[11] He is referring to Louis's wife, Anne of Austria (1601–1666), daughter of Philip III of Spain, who had married Louis XIII at the age of fifteen in the hope of reconciling the French and Spanish monarchies. He was failing to produce an heir to the throne, much to her own embarrassment as well, and she despised Richelieu for his hostility to Spain.

[12] Charles I, who was having troubles with his parliament, was seeking to prove his own Protestant credentials by continuing the war against Spain and supporting the Huguenots in France, and he was incited in these projects the Duke of Buckingham, who was seeking military glory, as well as by Soubise, who had taken refuge in England. Meanwhile, his older brother, the Duke de Rohan, was doing his best to stir up the Huguenots in France.

[13] The plot erupted in 1626. Richelieu broke it up. Chalais was decapitated. Others were imprisoned. The Duchess de Chevreuse ran off to Lorraine.

[14] It was out of the question to decapitate the heir presumptive to the throne. Monsieur got away by marrying the heiress Marie de Bourbon (1605–1627), Duchess de Montpensier, who was fabulously wealthy.

In all of these embroilments, which seemed to weaken your power, nothing could keep you from stopping the spread of duels by the punishment of Boutteville and des Chapelles. I admit that my mind has never been more torn than on this occasion, when I could scarcely keep myself from giving in to the compassion that the misfortune and valor of these two young gentlemen imprinted in the hearts of everybody, to the prayers of the most eminent people of the court, and to the insistence of my own closest relatives.[15]

The tears of his wife touched me to the quick, but the effusion of the blood of your nobility, which could only be stopped by the shedding of theirs, gave me the force to overcome myself and to confirm Your Majesty, for the good of the state, in the execution of what everybody, including myself, hated to do.

Since it had been entirely impossible to do anything about the great preparations that the English had made for the war, Your Majesty was obliged to oppose them by force.[16] These old enemies of the state descended upon the Island of Ré and besieged Fort Saint-Martin at the very time that God decided to afflict France with the great illness which it pleased Him to visit upon you at Villeroy.[17]

This unfortunate incident and the misbehavior that Le Coigneux and Puylaurens wanted Monsieur to repeat did not keep your presence alone from resisting all the efforts of this bellicose nation, and Your Majesty had no sooner recovered than you relieved the stronghold that they had besieged, you defeated their army in a noteworthy land battle, you chased their naval forces from your coasts, and you compelled them to return to their ports.[18]

You subsequently attacked La Rochelle and took it after a yearlong siege, and Your Majesty conducted himself with such prudence that, even though you knew well that the Spanish desired neither the capture of this strong-

---

[15] François de Montmorency-Boutteville (1600–1627) and his second François de Rosmadec, Count de Chapelles (1598–1627), who thought it would be fun to have a duel in the center of Paris in broad daylight in defiance of Richelieu.

[16] See note 12 above.

[17] On June 28, 1627, in the midst of one of his confrontations with the *parlement* of Paris and just before leaving to join his army, Louis XIII began to feel ill. He had to stop at the château of Villeroy, where his condition deteriorated to the point that his intimates feared for his life, but he was gradually recovering when news arrived that on July 22 the Duke of Buckingham had attempted a landing with his forces on the Island of Ré. After convalescing for several weeks in Saint-Germain-en-Laye, Louis finally joined his army on October 12 in ample time to witness the rout and withdrawal of the English.

[18] Jacques Le Coigneux (1589–1651) and Antoine de Laage (1605–1635), Sieur de Puylaurens, were both cronies of Monsieur, who had staked their future on his succeeding to the throne. According to Richelieu, they were advising Monsieur, who had already participated in the siege, not to return to it if the king arrived there so as not to have to serve under his command.

hold in particular nor the prosperity of your affairs in general, you judged that the mere appearance of being united with them could enhance your reputation in the world and that it would be no small thing if you [made a treaty with them that] kept them from joining with the English, who were then your open enemies, which you did and which produced the very effect that you had expected.[19]

The Spanish, who had no other plan than to give you simple appearances, under the cover of which they could actually obstruct the plans of Your Majesty and the taking of this city, aroused the English as much as they could to relieve it. To this end, Cardinal de La Cueva expressly promised them that his master would not send any help to Your Majesty until you did not need it anymore and that he would withdraw it before it could do them any harm, which was observed so religiously that after Don Frederico, the Spanish admiral who had left from La Coruna with 14 vessels, learned about the defeat of the English at Ré, he refused to remain in La Rochelle for a single day on hearing the rumor that a new fleet was coming to relieve this stronghold.[20]

This assurance gave to the English the audacity to redouble their efforts to relieve it and to Your Majesty the glory of taking it with your own forces in the sight of a powerful naval armada that, after two useless battles, had the shame of seeing itself completely frustrated.[21]

And so the treachery and the ruses of Spain were without effect, and those of the English were overcome with the same blow.

During this siege the Spanish attacked the Duke of Mantua in Italy, choosing this particular time in the belief that Your Majesty could not help him.[22]

Cardinal de Bérulle and the Keeper of the Seals Marillac counseled Your Majesty to abandon this poor prince to the injustice and to the insatiable greed of this nation, which is the enemy of the peace of Christendom, in order to keep you from disturbing it. The rest of your council was of the contrary opinion, both because Spain would not have ventured to make such a decision right after having made a treaty of alliance with the English and because, even if she had made such a bad decision, she would not have been able to stop you.[23]

---

[19] La Rochelle fell on October 28, 1628.

[20] Alfonso della Cueva y Benavides (1574–1655), cardinal in 1622; Fadrique II de Toledo (1580–1634).

[21] In April and August 1628, the English made two more attempts to relieve the city. Both were then blocked by the famous dike that the besiegers had constructed across the bay.

[22] Charles Gonzaga, identified above in note 3, who in 1627 had become Charles I, Duke of Mantua, but his succession was challenged by the Duke of Savoy and by claimants supported by the house of Hapsburg.

[23] Pierre de Bérulle, identified in note 7 above. Michel de Marillac (1563–1632), Keeper of the Seals, and Marie de Medici were on one side. The members of the council who sided

It was indicated to you that it was enough that you make no declaration at all for the Duke of Mantua while you were tied down with this great siege and that this was the least you could do without committing an indignity unworthy of a great prince, who could never consent to it despite any advantage that he could gain from it elsewhere.[24]

I would be committing a crime if I did not remark in this place that on this occasion Your Majesty followed the sentiments of your heart and your ordinary practice by taking the best and most honorable option, which was so successful that a short time later La Rochelle was taken and your armies were in a position to help this unjustly attacked prince.[25]

Even though at this time Monsieur, your brother, who became a widower one year after his marriage, had planned to marry Princess Marie, he was so ill-advised that instead of favoring the Duke of Mantua, her father, he obstructed you more than your enemies by departing from Your Majesty and withdrawing to Lorraine when he should have stood with you in order to make you more powerful.[26]

This misbehavior did not keep Your Majesty from continuing the campaign that you had undertaken with such a glorious plan, and God blessed it so visibly that you had no sooner reached the Alps than you forced the passages in the heart of winter, beat the Duke of Savoy assisted by the Spanish, had the siege of Casale raised, and compelled all of your enemies to settle with you.[27]

This glorious action, which established the peace in Italy, was no sooner accomplished than Your Majesty, whose character and courage have never found repose except in work, passed without resting into Languedoc, where, after having taken the towns of Privas and Alais by force, you reduced by your firmness the rest of the Huguenot party in your kingdom to obedience

---

with Richelieu were Antoine Coiflier-Ruzé (1581–1632), Marquis d'Effiat, Superintendent of Finances, and Henri de Schomberg (1575–1632), Count de Nanteuil, Marshal of France, later Governor of Languedoc.

[24] Richelieu seems to be referring here to a *mémoire* that he presented to the king on or about April 20, 1628.

[25] See notes 22 and 24 above.

[26] Monsieur's first wife had died in 1627, and soon after her passing he had developed a passion for Marie Gonzaga (1611–1667), beautiful daughter of the new Duke of Mantua. Highly sought after, she ultimately married two kings of Poland, one after the other.

[27] Charles Emmanuel I (1562–1630), Duke of Savoy from 1580, had allied with the Spanish in an attempt to enforce his own claims to the Mantuan succession. Louis XIII himself took command of his army, and on March 6, 1629, he fought his way across the Alps near Susa and obliged the duke to change sides, so that on March 16 the Spanish raised the siege of Casale. The duke, however, proved an unreliable ally and continued to conspire against the French.

and through your clemency gave peace to those who had ventured to make war on you not, as had been done in the past, by making concessions to them that were harmful to the state but by driving their only remaining leader out of the kingdom.[28]

What is most considerable about this glorious action is that you absolutely ruined this party when the King of Spain was trying to reinforce it more than ever.

He had just made a treaty with the Duke de Rohan in order to form in this state a rebellion against both God and Your Majesty in return for one million that he was to give every year, by which means he rendered the Indies tributary to Hell. But these projects were without effect, and he had at the same time the displeasure of learning that the bearer of this glorious arrangement was dead on the scaffold by a decree from the *parlement* of Toulouse, which investigated it. Your Majesty had the pleasure of pardoning those who could no longer defend themselves, of destroying their faction, and of treating their persons well when they were expecting to be punished for their crimes.[29]

Well do I know that the King of Spain wishes to excuse such a dastardly deed with the help that you gave to the Dutch, but this defense is as bad as their cause.

Common sense demonstrates to everybody that there is a big difference between the continuation of help instituted by a project as legitimate as natural defense and a new institution manifestly contrary to religion and to the legitimate authority that kings have received from Heaven over their subjects.

The king your father only entered into a treaty with the Dutch after the King of Spain formed a league in this kingdom to usurp the crown.

This truth is too evident to be doubted, and there are no theologians in the world who can say, without going against the principles of natural reason, that just as necessity obliges anyone whose life is threatened to use every means possible to protect it, so also a prince has the right to do the same to avoid the loss of his state.

What is free in its beginning sometimes becomes necessary subsequently; nor are there any who can complain about the connection that Your Majesty maintains with these people, not only in consequence of the treaties of the late king but, moreover, because Spain cannot be considered as anything but

---

[28] Edict of Alès (Alais), of June 28, 1629, which confirmed the religious provisions of the Edict of Nantes while depriving the Huguenots of their military strongholds.

[29] This treaty of the Duke de Rohan with the King of Spain turned out to be a dead letter, but Louis XIII, after being so severe with Montmorency, pardoned all the remaining rebels. Rohan retired to Venice, from where Richelieu promptly exploited his services in order to feel out the Grisons about letting the French back into their canton.

an enemy of this state as long as it retains a part of its old domains. It is clear that since the cause that has given occasion to these treaties has not ceased, the continuation of its effect is both legitimate and necessary.

Now the Spanish are far from in the same position. On the contrary, their plans are all the more unjust so that instead of repairing the first injuries that they inflicted upon this kingdom, they augment them every day.

Moreover, the late king did not join the Dutch until they were put up as a state, and he was obliged to do so by the oppression from which he could hardly protect himself. He was not the cause either of their revolt or of the union of their provinces.

And it is not just the many times that Spain has favored the revolts of the Huguenots against your predecessors. She has wanted to unite them into a state within yours. A holy zeal has brought them to want to be the authors of such a good institution and, it is to be noted, without necessity and thusly without any reason to justify their actions other than the continuation of their old usurpations and the new ones that they plan to make, so that what is prohibited to everybody is permitted to them because of their good intentions. Having dealt with this matter at greater length in another work, I leave it to continue the chronology of your actions.[30]

Since the bad faith of the Spanish brought them once again to attack the Duke of Mantua in violation of the treaties that they had made with Your Majesty, you carried your arms for the second time into Italy, where they were so blessed by God that after gloriously crossing a river that the Duke of Savoy was defending with 4,000 horse and 14,000 foot contrary to the treaty he had made with Your Majesty the preceding year, they took Pinerolo in the presence of the Emperor's forces, those of the King of Spain, and the person and all of the power of the Duke of Savoy and, what renders this action all the more glorious, under the eyes of the Marquis Spinola, one of the great captains of his time.

---

[30] The problem here, as I discuss in the introduction, is that Henry of Navarre (1555–1610), who was a member of the French royal family, had, as a Huguenot, himself participated in rebellions again the French Crown long before he could advance any claim to the throne of France. It is true that the Spanish Low Countries had revolted against Spain and a portion of them had declared their independence in an official act in 1581, setting up what became known as the Dutch Republic, but of course the King of Spain considered them rebels. It is also true that in 1584 Philip II of Spain made a treaty to subsidize the Catholic League in France. Richelieu jumps upon the Declaration of Independence by the Dutch to justify the alliance that Henry IV, as King of France, made with them in 1605. So the question still was, if Henry of Navarre, either as a prince of the blood of France or as a king in his own right, could intervene in a civil war in France, why couldn't a king of Spain? The "other work" to which Richelieu is referring is his *Histoire*, discussed in the introduction. Ambrogio Spinola (1569–1630).

By this means you took Susa and overcame at the same time the three greatest powers in Europe, plague, famine, and the impatience of the French, of which there are few examples in history.[31]

Subsequently you conquered Savoy, chasing before you an army of 10,000 foot and 2,000 horse, which was in a better position to defend itself in mountainous country than one which had only 30,000 men with which to attack it.[32]

A short time later, the battles of Valenza [*sic*] and Carignano made your armies noteworthy in Piedmont, and the taking of Valenza [*sic*], fortified by the Duke of Savoy in order to oppose your plans, showed that nothing can resist the righteous arms of a king who is as fortunate as he is powerful.[33]

Casale was relieved, not only against the prevailing opinion of almost everybody but against the thinking of the Duke de Montmorency, who had been employed in this plan, and against that of Marillac, his replacement, who both loudly proclaimed that this enterprise was entirely impossible.[34]

The relief of this stronghold was all the more glorious in that a stronger army entrenched on the outskirts of the Milanese supplied Casale, which had been put in their hands and was protected by its walls, was compelled to evacuate it along with five other strongholds that the Spanish held in the vicinity in the area of Montferrat.

---

[31] On March 19, 1630, the Duke of Savoy did not attempt to prevent the French army, directed by Richelieu himself, from crossing the Dora Susina River and going on to take Pinerolo in Piedmont on March 23.

[32] Richelieu is referring here to the Duchy of Savoy, whose capital, Chambéry, the French easily took on May 12, as opposed to the Principality of Piedmont, whose capital, Turin, still remained in the duke's hands. The dukes of Savoy in northern Italy were caught in the middle between the French monarchy and the Spanish possessions in Italy, and their principal goal was to maintain their own independence as much as possible.

[33] The French then returned to Piedmont, where they won a battle at Avigliana, not Valenza, on July 10, 1630, shortly after which Charles Emmanuel I died and was succeeded by his son Victor Amadeus I (1587–1637), who continued the Spanish alliance. He was defeated on the bridge of Carignano on August 6, and the city fell on August 27. Valenza was in the Milanese and therefore under Spanish control.

[34] Richelieu was exaggerating. Casale was relieved after a truce arranged by the envoy of Pope Urban VIII, Giulio Mazarini, who on October 26, 1630, galloped across the field yelling, "Pace, pace!" and stopped an impending battle between the French and Spanish armies. The truce more or less confirmed the Treaty of Regensburg and restored the stronghold to the Duke of Mantua. This campaign also forced Victor Amadeus to abandon the Spanish and become an ally of the French. Richelieu is here beginning to disparage Henri II (1595–1632), Duke de Montmorency and Governor of Languedoc, who was at that moment back in France plotting to overthrow him, and Louis de Marillac (1572–1632), a favorite, along with his brother Michel, of Marie de Medici. He had mounted to the rank of Marshal of France and was also participating in the plot.

If it is known that Your Majesty almost died in the midst of this plan and that if your body was in danger, your heart was even more hard pressed.

If one considers that the queen your mother was instigated by some poisonous minds to form a powerful party that weakened you and fortified your enemies, if one also imagines that they were also receiving information that the most faithful servants of Your Majesty, whom they both feared and hated, would no longer be in a condition to hurt them, it would be impossible not to realize that God had more to do with your successes than any human prudence or force.[35]

It was then that the queen your mother made every imaginable effort to overthrow the council of Your Majesty and establish one to her liking.[36]

BIt was then that the bad characters who possessed the mind of Monsieur used him in order to do everything possible to ruin me.B

The son had promised not to marry Princess Marie, which the queen feared so much that, in order to keep him from doing it in your absence, she had her put in the forest of Vincennes, from where she only emerged through this compact, and the mother had committed herself in exchange to have me disgraced by Your Majesty and to send me away.[37]

The mother and the son had made an agreement more contrary to the state than to those whose ruin they were openly seeking, since in the present state of affairs it was impossible to make any changes in it without ruining it.

To make these promises more inviolable, they were put in writing, and for a long time the Duke de Bellegarde carried them inside his shirt to illustrate that they were next to his heart and to assure those who had made them that he would die before losing them.[38]

Never had there been such a strong faction in a state. It would be easier to report on those who had not been involved than on those who had been.

And what made your conduct on this occasion all the more marvelous is that even though I sought my own dismissal so as to please the queen, who desired it passionately, Your Majesty, who was then bereft of all other coun-

---

[35] Louis XIII fell ill on September 22, 1630, while he was in Lyon preparing for another campaign in Italy, at which point Marie de Medici made her most strenuous effort to shame him into dismissing Richelieu. By September 30, the king had miraculously recovered. On his recovery, however, he returned to Paris.

[36] It is here that Richelieu begins his description of the "Great Storm," Marie de Medici's plot to shame him into dismissing Richelieu, which terminated in the "Day of Dupes."

[37] Marie de Medici, who hated the house of Mantua, had the princess arrested and struck a bargain with Monsieur to release her and get Louis XIII to disgrace Richelieu if Monsieur would stop his flirtation. This bargain, however, did not prevent Monsieur from running off to Lorraine in September 1629, from where he was bribed back by Louis XIII and Richelieu, only to return to France to cause as much mischief as possible.

[38] Roger de Saint-Lary des Termes (1562–1646), Duke de Bellegarde, Governor of Burgundy and Bresse, superintendent of Monsieur's household, a gentleman of the old school.

cil, fell back on his own and resisted all by himself the authority of a mother, the guiles of all her adherents, and my own prayers.[39]

I speak thusly because the Marshal de Schomberg, who was faithful to you, was not with Your Majesty then, and the Keeper of the Seals Marillac was one of those who, while seconding the queen in her plans, served her against herself.[40]

Your prudence was such that by dismissing him, you delivered yourself from a man who was so full of himself that he did not approve of anything unless he had ordered it and who believed that he was justified in using whatever means his overzealousness indicated to him in order to achieve his ends.

Finally, your behavior was so wise that you accorded nothing to the queen that was contrary to your state and refused her nothing that you could not have accorded her without injuring your conscience and acting as much against yourself as against her.

I could avoid speaking about the peace that was concluded at Regensburg between Your Majesty and the house of Austria, because since it was drawn up by your ambassador on conditions that the Emperor himself recognized that he lacked the powers, it cannot reasonably be placed among your actions. But if one considers that, even though the fault of your ambassador cannot be imputed to you, just as it took no lack of kindness in order to endure it, it also took no lack of skill to repair it in some way and not to lose out on the peace so necessary to this state at a time when Your Majesty had so many preoccupations. This action will be judged as one of your greatest and, as such, cannot be omitted here.[41]

Reason and statesmanship required an exemplary punishment of the one who had exceeded his orders in such a delicate matter and on such an important occasion. But your kindness tied the hands of your justice because, even though he was the only ambassador, he had not acted alone in this affair but had an associate of a rank, which made you consider the motive for the error

---

[39] The famous "Day of Dupes" (November 11, 1630).

[40] Henri de Schomberg, (1574–1632), Count de Nanteuil was one of Louis XIII's best generals and trusted advisors. He was commanding the French armies in Italy at that time. For Michel de Marillac, see note 23.

[41] Richelieu had sent Charles Brûlart (d. 1649), prior of Léon, as his ambassador, accompanied by his confidant Father Joseph du Tremblay (1577–1638) to negotiate with Ferdinand II (1578–1637), Holy Roman Emperor from 1619, to a Reichstag (or congress of the empire) that he was holding at Regensburg. Their instruction was to weaken the position of the emperor as much as possible, but all they could come up with was a compromise treaty of October 13, 1630, that confirmed the Duke of Mantua in possession of his duchy. Much of this negotiation had taken place during Louis XIII's illness. Richelieu, under great pressure for his own survival, gave his envoys confusing orders, and when they sent him the treaty, he put the blame on them for having exceeded their instructions. I can only conclude that, as with the Treaty of Monzòn, there was a lot of posturing in this disapproval.

rather than the error itself. They were both so fearful of the outcome of your illness in Lyon that they acted based more on fear of the condition in which this kingdom might be after the misfortune of your loss than on the condition in which it was and on the orders that they had received.

Notwithstanding the bad terms of the treaty, the Imperialists were compelled to give back Mantua soon thereafter. The fear of your arms obliged them to return everything that they occupied in this duchy and what they had usurped from the Venetians and the Grisons, and after Your Majesty had admitted the troops of the Duke of Savoy into Pinerolo and into the Fort of La Pérouse to satisfy the Treaty of Cherasco, you got along so well with him that by virtue of a new treaty, these strongholds have remained in the hands of Your Majesty, to the satisfaction and to the advantage of all Italy, which will have less to fear in the future since it would see a door open through which to help her.[42]

At this time, since the dissatisfactions that the Duke of Bavaria, attached inseparably up to then to the house of Austria, had received from the Emperor and the Spanish and the fear among all the other Catholic and Protestant electors of being dispossessed of their states, just as many other princes already had been, led them privately to desire your support, you negotiated with them so skillfully that in the very presence of the Emperor, they kept a King of the Romans from being elected at the Diet of Regensburg, which had been convened for this very end.[43]

Next, in order to satisfy Bavaria, to satisfy the electors and many other princes, and to confirm them all in their decision to make the Catholic League in the Empire independent from Spain, which was usurping its leadership, your ambassadors acted in such coordination with these princes that this made it easier for them to deprive Wallenstein of the command of the Imperial armies, which caused no mean delay in his master's affairs. At almost at the same time, the influence of Your Majesty was no less evident in the North, since the Baron de Charnacé, without the title of ambassador, procured a peace between the Kings of Poland and Sweden, which many other powers had previously tried to do and failed.[44]

---

[42] It tells us a lot about Richelieu's conflicted priorities that he did not see the negotiation at Regensburg as a great success because, as he acknowledges here, his envoys did retain the Duke of Mantua in his duchy, after which, by the Treaty of Cherasco (April 6, 1631) with the Duke of Savoy, he obtained the stronghold of Pinerolo, which gave France "her door" into Italy.

[43] All the more revealing of Richelieu's whining, since the electors and other princes of the Holy Roman Empire, conveniently for France, refused to elect the emperor's son as "King of the Romans," which would have assured his succession to the Imperial throne.

[44] Most conveniently of all, the electors and princes pressured the Holy Roman Emperor into dismissing his best general, Albrecht von Wallenstein (September 13, 1630),

This peace gave occasion soon thereafter to the enterprise that the King of Sweden undertook to keep the princes of the Empire in Germany from being oppressed, and his plan was no sooner known to you than, in order to prevent the harm that the Catholic religion might receive from it, Your Majesty made a treaty with him that obliged him not to disturb its exercise throughout his conquests.[45]

Well do I know that your enemies, who want to justify their actions and to decry yours, have done everything they could to make your compact hateful. But their plan had no other effect than to reveal their malice.

The innocence of Your Majesty is all the more clear in that your ambassador only signed a treaty with this conqueror six months after he had entered into Germany, which easily proves that the compacts that were made with this prince were a remedy for the evil, so they cannot be felt to be their cause.[46] The treaties concluded, not only with this great king but also with many other princes of Germany, are all the more just because they were absolutely necessary for the survival of the Duke of Mantua, who was unjustly attacked, and for that of all of Italy, over which the Spanish had no more right than over the states of this poor prince, since they felt that whatever was convenient for them was legitimate enough.[47]

The shock that this kingdom had received from the discord that the Spanish had openly instigated in your royal family obliged Your Majesty to resort to expedients that gave you occasion to strengthen it.

Since Monsieur had left the court of France for the third time thanks to various guiles that it can truly be said were principally authored by the Spanish, and since the Cardinal-Infante had at the same time received the queen your mother into Flanders, it is easy to see that if these good neighbors had

---

when almost one year before Gustavus Adolphus (1594–1632), a Lutheran and King of Sweden from 1611, had made a truce in the war he had been waging against Sigismund III (1566–1632), King of Poland from 1587, thus freeing himself for an intervention in Germany, ostensibly on behalf of the Protestant cause. Hercule Girard (1588–1637). Baron de Charnacé, the French envoy to Sweden, had been instrumental in facilitating the truce.

[45] Gustavus Adolphus had landed in Pomerania on July 20, 1630, and immediately began to spread out over northern Germany.

[46] Charnacé, who had continued to accompany Gustavus Adolphus, signed the Treaty of Bärwalde with him on behalf of Louis XIII on January 23, 1631, which included the provision not to disturb the exercise of religion in any Swedish conquests. Richelieu, therefore, is refusing to consider his contribution to prolonging what would become known as the Thirty Years' War and thus throwing a monkey wrench into the restoration of religious unity in Europe.

[47] In this paragraph Richelieu sums up the meaning of his existence. Everything, including the salvation of his soul, is dependent upon stopping the expansion of the Spanish monarchy. The irony is that by making such a statement, he is revealing that he is not so sure about it himself.

not had some new problems closer to home, they would have carried matters further at the expense of this kingdom.[48]

It was extremely necessary to deflect the storm and to prepare, what is more, to weather it in case it could not be avoided.

Considering this, once Your Majesty could count on a powerful diversion, you imitated those who, in order to prevent being contaminated by bad air, purge their own body all the more carefully since, in their opinion, there is no better way to protect themselves from catching something.

In this situation the Providence of God was so favorable that those who inspired the queen and Monsieur against France and tried to get them to do her a great deal of harm only made them incapable of doing it, and your conduct appeared all the more admirable on this occasion so that by recalling the one and desiring the return of the other, your kindness in their regard was apparent to everybody at the same time that the effects of your justice fell upon those who had helped them to accept such bad advice.

The Duke de Bellegarde was deprived of the governorship of Burgundy and, consequently, of the keys to the doors that he had opened for Monsieur to allow him to leave the country.[49]

The Duke d'Elbeuf was similarly dispossessed of that of Picardy, which Your Majesty had given him a short time previously.[50]

The Duke de Guise, who, pressed by his pangs of conscience, had withdrawn to Italy when you recalled him to court to report on his actions, this criminal withdrawal made him lose the one with which the late king your father had honored him.[51]

Thus you were delivered from ungrateful and unfaithful governors, and provinces of great importance, such as Burgundy, Picardy, and Provence, remained in your hands and free from these troublemakers.

In the first, you placed the first prince of your blood, who desired it passionately, and by this means you carefully involved him in current affairs and gave pause to Monsieur, who, not surprisingly, feared nothing more than the institution of a person who was right on his heels.[52]

---

[48] On March 13, 1631, Monsieur and a group of followers began to make their way out of France to Lorraine, reaching its capital, Nancy, on April 28. There he secretly married the sister of the duke, and in July Marie de Medici escaped to the Spanish Low Countries, where she was welcomed by Philip IV's brother Ferdinand (1609–1641), Cardinal-Infante, their very energetic governor.

[49] See the previous note.

[50] Charles II de Lorraine (1596–1663), Duke d'Elbeuf.

[51] Charles de Lorraine (1571–1640), Duke de Guise, had been governor of Provence.

[52] Henri II de Bourbon (1588–1646), Prince de Condé, who, beginning as a Huguenot supporter of Henry IV, turned against him but eventually converted and became a close

In the second, you appointed the Duke de Chevreuse, from the house of Lorraine, to demonstrate that offenses are personal and that your indignation only extended to those of this family who had made themselves guilty by their misbehavior.[53]

You favored the Marshal de Vitry with the third, both because of his fidelity and because he was capable, with the backing of your authority and by his own nature, to equal that of his predecessor.[54]

However, the declarations that you made on these occasions and registered in the *parlement* were all the more applauded by everybody because by condemning the authors and partisans of the queen and Monsieur, you excused these two persons, who are as close as they are dear to Your Majesty, even though, in the past, under similar circumstances this would have been done quite differently.[55]

Your Majesty was then most vigilant in foiling various plans concocted on behalf of the queen and Monsieur against various strongholds in the kingdom, and you did so with such patience in these unfortunate situations that I can almost say that you did not reveal any more than you had to about their misbehavior.

However, in order to stop their spread and curtail the impression that it was permitted to undertake anything under their cover, you had the Marshal de Marillac beheaded, with all the more reason as he had been justly condemned and the state, in its present condition, required a great example.[56]

These great and unfortunate affairs did not keep you from suppressing, with as much authority as reason, certain schemes of the *parlement* of Paris that had been allowed on many other occasions, which is all the more remarkable for having been done in the heat of the dissatisfactions of the queen, Monsieur, and their supporters.

---

collaborator—in fact, almost a creature—of Cardinal Richelieu. Avaricious and an incompetent soldier, he was next in line to the throne after Monsieur.

[53] Claude de Lorraine (1578–1657), Duke de Chevreuse, tolerant second husband of the notorious Marie de Rohan, Duchess de Chevreuse.

[54] Nicolas de l'Hôpital (1582–1645), Marquis de Vitry, famous for his arrest and killing of Concini on April 24, 1617, as a reward for which he was almost immediately made Marshal of France. In 1632 he succeeded Guise as Governor of Provence.

[55] On March 30 Louis XIII issued a declaration declaring a number of Monsieur's followers guilty of treason while discretely not mentioning either the queen mother or Monsieur. Monsieur's destination was the Duchy of Lorraine, and he reached its capital, Nancy, on April 28. There he secretly married the sister of the duke and prepared his own little invasion of France.

[56] See note 73 below.

Subsequently Monsieur entered with sword in hand into France at the instigation of the Spanish and the Duke of Lorraine with the troops that these good neighbors had mostly furnished.[57]

It seemed as if the knowledge Your Majesty immediately had that he was expected in Languedoc by the Duke de Montmorency, the very prestigious governor of this province, should have diverted you from the plan that had taken you to Lorraine in order to dissuade that duke from his bad decision, but after completing what you had begun with such good planning, you had your brother Monsieur so closely followed by Marshal de Schomberg and you advanced so promptly after obtaining three strongholds from the Duke of Lorraine as a security for his word that all the efforts of those who had combined against you remained vain.[58]

The victory that the arms of Your Majesty commanded by this marshal won at Castelnaudary was also a sure sign of the blessing of God upon Your Majesty, just as the favors that you subsequently granted to Monsieur and to his dependents, when the predicament he was in would have given you occasion to treat him differently, bear ample witness to your kindness.[59]

The sincerity with which you wished to observe all the promises that were made to them at Béziers on your behalf, even though you knew for sure that Puylaurens had no other intention than to escape, under the cover of repentance, the peril in which he found himself and from which he could not protect himself in any other way, was proof enough of the noble heart of Your Majesty as well as of the inviolability of your word.[60]

The punishment of the Duke de Montmorency, which could not be omitted without opening the door to every sort of dangerous rebellion at any time and particularly when an heir presumptive to the crown was so ill-advised as to

---

[57] The *parlement* of Paris had balked at registering the declaration against Monsieur's followers, and on August 13, 1631, Louis XIII himself went to the *parlement* and ordered them to do it. Meanwhile, on June 12 Monsieur had invaded France with a little army and on August 30, he had joined it in Languedoc with one of his sympathizers, the Duke de Montmorency.

[58] Louis, however, had quickly invaded Lorraine and, by a treaty signed at Liverdun on June 26, 1632, forced the duke to let him occupy two strongholds in Lorraine for four years and cede to him an entire county in perpetuity before directing his attention to suppressing the revolt of Monsieur and Montmorency.

[59] This engagement took place on September 1, 1632. Schomberg's victory was sealed in short order by the impetuosity of Montmorency, who charged with his followers into the French camp and got himself captured.

[60] Superintendent of Finances Bullion then met with a repentant Monsieur at Béziers between September 26 and 29 with the king's offer to forgive him, including his chief advisor Puylaurens, if they would behave from then on. Monsieur signed a treaty, but on learning of the execution of Montmorency, he reneged on the agreement and took refuge with Marie de Medici in Brussels.

make himself the head of all those who were derelict in their duty, showed everybody that your firmness was equal to your prudence.[61]

This punishment also pointed out that your servants preferred the public interest to their own, since on this occasion they resisted the solicitations of many persons who were of great importance to them, and the threats of Monsieur de Puylaurens reached the point of letting them know that if Monsieur de Montmorency died, Monsieur would someday have them killed as well. The patience with which you have allowed the new monopolies that Puylaurens established in the name of Monsieur in Flanders, where he withdrew for the third time, is similar to that of a lenient father toward the behavior of one of his children who has been disobedient.[62]

That which made you endure, as long as the good of the state and your conscience have permitted it, the malice and frivolity that has repeatedly led the Duke of Lorraine to arm against you is a virtue that has very few examples in history.

If his folly had not matched his insincerity, the kindness with which you were willing, for the reparation of his second faults, to be satisfied with a few of his strongholds capable of retaining him in his duty will be found to be even more unprecedented, since there are few princes who lose the opportunity to take over a nearby state when they have both a legitimate reason and the power all together.

After so many relapses by this duke, who is your vassal, and after he had violated a promise almost as precious as your state, against his word, against divine right, and against all compacts made between men, the prudence with which you dispossessed him when his malice and his treachery could no longer be remedied in any other way is all the more admirable since, had you done it sooner, its justice might have been cast into doubt. Also, you could not have waited any longer without appearing indifferent and committing an error no less serious than if you had dispossessed another prince by violence.[63]

What more can be said about your good nature in bringing about the return of Monsieur to France for the third time, when it seemed as if one could no longer be sure of his good faith because of his various relapses and the extreme treachery of his dependents? Many felt quite reasonably that he could not return without compromising the security of your most faithful servants, and, still, they were the first to beg you to extract him from his predicament.[64]

---

[61] October 30, 1632.

[62] See note 64 below.

[63] The French finally occupied all of Lorraine in September 1633, driving out the duke.

[64] No matter how absolute Louis XIII claimed to be, he could not change the rights of succession to the French monarchy, and the idea of the heir presumptive in the hands of the Spanish was a nightmare for both him and Richelieu.

This action has few examples in antiquity if one considers the circumstances and perhaps few imitators in the future.

Since one cannot, without being extremely rash, advise Your Majesty to give Monsieur, against your own feelings, a notable addition to his appanages, the governorship of a province, and a stronghold, as was done the first time that he left the kingdom in order to bring him back from Lorraine, it took a great deal of firmness to resist for an entire year his insistence on having one on the frontier, where he wanted to retire if he left Flanders.[65]

It was no mean stroke of luck that these two decisions proved to be so successful since conceding the first stronghold was the cause of his first return and such a humane cause that it could not be abused when his dependents wanted to use it again, so that far from the refusal of the second keeping him from returning to his native country—the only place where he felt safe—this, on the contrary, is what finally obliged him to return with what he and his friends later confessed was the intention never to disturb the peace of the kingdom again.

The extraordinary benefits that Your Majesty showered on Puylaurens to oblige him to inspire his master to change his conduct are so worthy of remembrance that they cannot be forgotten in this place.

His punishment, when you learned that he was continuing to abuse your good graces, was too just and too necessary not to insert here.[66]

Posterity will note, I am sure, three important things on this subject—the entire detachment from everything except the public interest by your creatures, who had received him by your express command into their alliance and who did not fail to advise you to arrest him when the good of the state required it—the extreme prudence of having executed this action in the presence of Monsieur, who could only be delighted to see for himself that no one had anything against him—the extreme boldness to leave him at the same time with as much liberty as he had previously enjoyed purely on the grounds that since he had only behaved badly because of bad advice, the effect would cease once the cause was removed and that no sooner was he

---

[65] Monsieur was insisting on being given the governorship of a frontier province, which he could exploit for his own security. Fortunately for Louis and Richelieu, Monsieur and Puylaurens could not get along with Marie de Medici, and in July 1633 they began negotiating secretly with Richelieu. Despite Puylaurens's threats against the life of Richelieu, Louis XIII and Richelieu offered him the governorship of the Bourbonnais, large sums of money, and the title of duke and peer if he could convince Monsieur to return. The bribe worked, and on October 8, 1634, Monsieur and Puylaurens slipped out of Brussels.

[66] Puylaurens continued to scheme against Richelieu, who had him arrested on February 14, 1635, and imprisoned in the château of Vincennes, where he died mysteriously after four months in captivity.

freed of it than he would follow his own sentiments on a path contrary to the one where others had carried him.[67]

This action and many others that occurred during your reign will, I am sure, confirm the maxim that in certain situations, when it is a question of the security of the state, a manly virtue is necessary that sometimes goes beyond the rules of ordinary prudence and that it is sometimes impossible to avoid certain evils if one does not leave something to fortune or more precisely to the Providence of God, who hardly ever refuses His help when our wisdom is exhausted and cannot give us any.[68]

Besides, your conduct shall be recognized as all the more just, and those who read your history will see that Your Majesty only punishes anyone after having tried, by impressive favors, to retain him in his duty.[69]

The Marshal d'Ornano was made a marshal for this end. The Grand Prior was assured of the command of the navy until he corrupted the mind of his brother and both of them gave you cause to deprive them of their liberty.[70]

The Marshal de Bassompierre was only subsisting through your benefits when his manner of talking and acting at court compelled you to lock him up in the Bastille.[71]

The Keeper of the Seals Marillac was all the more obliged to behave until the rank to which his good fortune had raised him only allowed him to let his ambition run wild.[72]

The marshal his brother, who was appointed and promoted to an office of the crown in Verdun, had every reason by the favors he had received to avoid the execution that he so richly deserved.[73]

---

[67] In their desperate attempt to bribe Puylaurens, Louis XIII and Richelieu had also contrived his marriage to the daughter of one of Richelieu's cousins in the hope that this would stop him from causing trouble. This affair seems to have been so traumatic for Richelieu that he cannot keep himself from elaborating on it a few folios later.

[68] A candid confession of his state of mind.

[69] What follows seems more like a description of a purge.

[70] See note 10 above.

[71] François de Bassompierre (1579–1646) was a good soldier, diplomat, intimate of Louis XIII, and Marshal of France in 1622 but a little too outspoken in his loyalty to Marie de Medici. He was arrested in February 1631 and did not get out of the Bastille until Richelieu's death.

[72] See note 23 above.

[73] Louis de Marillac (1572–1632), a favorite, along with his brother, of Marie de Medici, had been governor of Verdun and risen to the rank of Marshal of France. On the "Day of Dupes," he was with his troops in Italy, where Schomberg received orders to arrest him. Tried in France by an extraordinary tribunal, he was sentenced to death and decapitated publicly in Rueil on May 10, 1632.

The various commands that the Duke de Montmorency has had in your armies, even though he was still too young to merit them, his post as Marshal of France, his free access to the person of Your Majesty, and his familiarity with your creatures should have been sufficiently great favors and privileges to keep him from running rampant to his ruin.[74]

Châteauneuf had so recently been honored with the seals before his bad behavior began to be discovered that there is reason to suspect that his intentions had been bad from the very start.[75]

However, this highest post in the judiciary to which Your Majesty appointed him against his expectations, the 100,000 crowns that you were generous enough to give him in one year, the governorship of one of your provinces, which are rather extraordinary favors for a man in his profession, were not enough to keep him from crafting his own ruin.[76]

The multifarious favors that Puylaurens rapidly received from the kindness of Your Majesty are so extraordinary that those who will learn about them will perhaps be even more astonished by his bad behavior, which is rather typical of those without merit whom fortune raises in an instant.

The pardon for his crimes that Your Majesty granted him on his return from Flanders will not be minimized by posterity; the immense sums he received from your generosity, the governorship of the Bourbonnais, the quality of duke and peer, and my alliance should have been sufficiently strong bonds to retain anyone in his duty who is capable of controlling himself.[77]

When the Count de Cramail was put in the Bastille, he had just received his recall to court as a result of being forgiven for his original faults, but this favorable treatment did not keep him from trying once more to deter Your Majesty from your original policy, whose results have been amply justified by the goodness and blessing of God.[78]

The choice of the Marshal de Vitry for Provence obliged him to live with a great deal of restraint in this great employment, which he had earned by his courage and fidelity. But his excessive greed and his insolent and haughty disposition contributed in no small part to deprive him of it and transfer him to a smaller governorship.[79]

---

[74] See notes 34, 58, 61, and 62 above.

[75] Charles de l'Aubespine (1580–1653), Marquis de Châteauneuf, who succeeded Michel de Marillac as Keeper of the Seals.

[76] He conspired with the irresistible Duchess de Chevreuse against Richelieu, who in 1633 had him imprisoned in Angoulême.

[77] See notes 65 and 66 above.

[78] Adrien de Montluc (1579–1646), Count de Cramail, Gascon gentleman, fervent Catholic, pro-Spanish. One more of the usual suspects.

[79] See note 54 above. Richelieu is getting ahead of himself here, because he is referring to an event that took place on December 5, 1636, in the château of Cannes. Vitry's dismissal

As to those who have merely been exiled from the court, what have Your Majesty and his servants not done to oblige the Duke de Bellegarde?

Your kindness and their skill had extricated him from a number of embarrassing predicaments into which the disorder of his passions had thrown him. He was a duke thanks to your favor and all the more obliged to act responsibly with Monsieur since you had appointed him to the highest post in his household.[80]

From a poor and simple gentleman, one saw Toiras in an instant become a Marshal of France, so loaded with your benefits that he received not only the best employments and the greatest governorships in the kingdom but also a gift of six hundred thousand crowns.[81]

The Fargis woman was all the more obliged to behave since Your Majesty had put her in with the queen your wife. Yet she proceeded to catch her up on all the stories that were told about you.[82]

The Dukes de Guise and d'Elbeuf have received incredible favors from Your Majesty, as everybody knows.[83]

At the same time that the Princess of Conti was busily forming her cabals at the court, she extracted a great deal from your treasury for the sale of Mouzon and Châteaurenault. But this was not enough to retain her in her duty.[84]

---

was the result of a confrontation that took place between him and his colleagues as they were making preparations for the recovery of the Islands of Sainte-Marguerite and Saint-Honoré, which the Spanish had grabbed from the French the previous year. During their dispute Vitry struck Henri de Sourdis, who was both an admiral and archbishop of Bordeaux, with a cane. Richelieu, who did not approve of marshals striking archbishops, imprisoned Vitry in the Bastille, from which he did not emerge until after Richelieu s death.

[80] See notes 38 and 49 above.

[81] Jean de Saint-Bonnet (1585–1636), Marquis de Toiras, governor of the Aunis and the Islands of Ré and Oléron, and heroic defender of Casale against Spinola, for which Louis XIII made him a marshal of France on December 9, 1630. His brothers, however, were caught up in the "Great Storm," and when Richelieu recalled him from Casale, Toiras passed into the service of the Duke of Savoy.

[82] And about Richelieu. The Fargis woman was Madeleine de Silly (d. 1639), wife of the former ambassador to Spain. She was, on the recommendation of Cardinal de Bérulle, placed by Richelieu as lady in waiting of Anne of Austria in order to spy on her. Another example of Richelieu having to employ questionable supporters! Not surprisingly, she became an intimate of the queen, even accusing Richelieu of wanting to seduce Anne. Banished from the court, Madame du Fargis took refuge in the Spanish Low Countries, while Richelieu had to resort to having her burned in effigy.

[83] See notes 51 and 50 above.

[84] Louise Marguerite de Lorraine (1577–1631), Princess de Conti. A woman of great beauty and wit, she had been a mistress of Henry IV, wife of one of his cousins, the Prince de Conti, and, after his death, mistress and secret wife of the Marshal de Bassompierre. Richelieu tried to keep her in line by having the king purchase some of her lands,

Since the exile of the Duke de La Valette, though it was voluntary and not forced, gives me occasion to put him in this category, I cannot fail to indicate how a short time previously, when he was begging Monsieur your brother and the Count de Soissons to turn your arms, which they were then commanding, against your own person, Your Majesty had honored him with the status of Duke and Peer. I cannot refrain from adding that in order to bind him more to your service, you had agreed for him to form a connection with those who were completely inseparable from it and that, in consideration of my alliance, you had granted him the succession of the governorship of Guyenne and awarded his post of Colonel General of the Infantry an increase of 30,000 livres in revenue. I can say, moreover, that the pardon for a dirty and shameful crime, confirmed on this occasion by the testimony of two unimpeachable princes, which Your Majesty was extraordinarily good enough to grant him, could not keep his weakness and his jealousy of the Prince de Condé and the Archbishop of Bordeaux from obstructing the progress of your affairs and losing a great deal of honor by missing the opportunity to take Fontarabia when the enemies could not defend it any longer.[85]

If it is a result of your singular prudence in keeping all the forces of your enemies at bay for ten whole years with those of your allies by the use of your purse instead of your sword and in going to war only when your allies could no longer subsist alone were not enough, your courage and your wisdom all together are ample proof that by keeping your kingdom at peace, you have been just like those administrators who have known just when to save and just when to spend in order to protect themselves from a greater loss.[86]

---

but after the arrest of Bassompierre, she was exiled to the Château of Eu in Normandy, where she died.

[85] Bernard de Nogaret (1592 1661), Marquis, later Duke, de La Valette d'Epernon, colonel general of the infantry, governor of Metz and Guyenne, rich, powerful, and turbulent. Despite the fact that in 1634 he married a niece of Cardinal Richelieu, in 1636 he almost joined another conspiracy against him on behalf of Monsieur, and in 1638, in the midst of the siege of Fontarabia, he refused to follow the orders of the Prince de Condé and of Sourdis, the archbishop of Bordeaux, both of whom laid the blame on him for the failure of the siege, after which, not trusting in Louis's pardon, La Valette fled to England. As with the wife of du Fargis, Richelieu could only have him tried and executed in absentia. Richelieu is getting ahead of himself here (see note 108 below), since he has not yet declared the war against Spain that preceded the siege of Fontarabia.

[86] This is the first reference in the *Political Testament* that permits us to begin determining when Richelieu wrote it. It refers the subsidizing of Gustavus Adolphus, which Richelieu, by his own recollection in his *Histoire*, attributes to April 1630. It may also refer to his subsidizing of the Dutch by the Treaty of The Hague, signed on June 17, 1630, by which Louis XIII committed himself to a subsidy of 1 million livres a year for seven years. This means, at the very least, that he was writing this section in April 1640. As to the wars, Louis XIII declared war against Spain by a herald on May 19, 1635, and in writing on June 6. There

It will no doubt seem to many people very imprudent and rash to have made various attacks in various localities at the same time, which neither the Romans nor the Ottomans ever did. However, if this is proof of your power, it is all the more so of your judgment, since this was necessary to keep your enemies so busy everywhere that they could not win anywhere.[87]

The war in Germany was not very pressing, since this part of Europe was the theater where it had been going on for a long time.[88]

Even though the one in Flanders did not have the success that might have been expected, it was impossible not to consider it as a good idea.[89]

The Grison one was necessary in order to get the princes of Italy to take up arms by relieving them of the fear of the Germans and to encourage those that they had in Germany by showing that Italy could not help the enemies they were confronting in their country.[90]

The one in Italy was no less important, both because it was the true means of involving the Duke of Savoy and also because, since the Milanese

---

was, however, no official declaration of war against the Emperor. On July 11, Louis signed a treaty in Paris with his brother-in-law, Victor Amadeus, Duke of Savoy from 1630, for a period of three years in order to attack the Spanish in their Duchy of Milan.

[87] Richelieu is quite proud that he was making history by getting France into a war that would be fought simultaneously on five fronts: Spain, the Spanish Low Countries, Italy, Germany, and what is now Switzerland, but he is ignoring the fact that if he was putting immense pressure on his enemies, he was putting even more pressure on the French people.

[88] This is Richelieu's second allusion to what became known as the Thirty Years' War, which had begun in 1618 when the Calvinists in Prague threw the officials of their Catholic king, Ferdinand, who was about to become Ferdinand II, Holy Roman Emperor, out a window and replaced him with the Calvinist Frederick V (1596–1632), Elector Palatine from 1610. Ferdinand, however, had quickly obtained the support of his fellow Catholic Maximillian I (1573–1651), Duke of Bavaria from 1597, to drive Frederick out of both Bohemia and the Palatinate. Ferdinand and Maximilian then went on the offensive with their generals, Albrecht von Wallenstein and Johan Tserclaes (1559–1632), Count von Tilly, roundly defeating the Lutheran Christian IV (1577–1648), King of Denmark from 1588, and overrunning large parts of northern Germany. The advantage kept going back and forth, with terrible suffering among the civilian population. Gustavus Adolphus seemed on the verge of victory when he died in battle in 1632. Then the advantage reverted in favor of the Catholics with a Spanish, Bavarian, and Imperial victory at Nördlingen on September 6, 1634, after which Ferdinand II concluded the Peace of Prague (May 30, 1635) with John George (1585–1686), the Lutheran Elector of Saxony from 1611, which made some concessions to the Lutherans and to which many, though not all, of the Protestant states in the Holy Roman Empire adhered.

[89] See notes 92 and 93 below.

[90] This passage is obscure. The phrasing "those that they had in Germany" seems to mean the allies that the Grisons had in Germany. This is all part of Richelieu's grand strategy. See note 47 above.

was like the heart of the Spanish possessions in Italy, this was the part that it was necessary to attack.

Besides, if one considers that Your Majesty had allies everywhere who had to join forces with you, reason required that by uniting with them the Spanish would be attacked in various places and would succumb to the efforts of your power.

It is not that, during the course of this war, which has lasted five years,[91] you have not suffered any setbacks, but this only seems to have been permitted in order to add to your glory.

In 1635 the army that Your Majesty sent to the Low Countries won a famous battle upon entering, before joining that of the States-General, and if the Prince of Orange, in command of both, did not have any success worthy of his great forces and from what should have been expected from a captain with his reputation, this was no fault of yours.[92]

Since you had put your armies under the command of this prince, it was up to him to follow the lead of your victorious army. But the lassitude of a ponderous nation could not profit from the enthusiasm of yours, which demands action rather than words and which, if it does not get it promptly, loses the advantage that its fiery nature gives it over all the other nations of the world.[93]

This same year, since the forces of the Empire crossed the Rhine at Breisach, they came so close to your frontiers that if you could not exempt them from fear, you knew how to protect them by not sparing the enemy.[94]

---

[91] This is more evidence that he is writing this in 1640.

[92] On May 12, 1635, Gaspard de Coligny (1584–1646), Marshal de Châtillon, and Jean-Armand de Maillé-Brezé (1619–1646), who was Richelieu's nephew, defeated the Spanish under Prince Thomas of Savoy (1596–1656) at the Battle of Les Avins, after which they joined with the army of Frederick Henry (1584–1647), Prince of Orange, but the victory was nullified when, on July 28, the Spanish surprised the strategic Fort of Schenk (today's Schenkenschanz), an outpost of the Dutch Republic. Frederick Henry was also the *stadtholder* (a kind of governor) in each of the provinces and captain general of the federal army in the Dutch Republic.

[93] Brother and successor of the legendary Maurice of Nassau, Frederick Henry was no mean soldier himself, but he had to concentrate on trying to retake the Fort of Schenk. Richelieu, moreover, fails to mention that Châtillon and Brezé did not get along during the campaign, a recurring theme among all his generals throughout the war.

[94] On October 9, 1634, by a treaty with Sweden, Louis XIII had already taken all the strongholds in Alsace occupied by the Swedes under his own protection, and in June 1635, the Imperialists, seconded by the Duke of Lorraine, began an attempt to recover them along with the Duchy of Lorraine. As part of this campaign, the Imperial general Matthias Gallas (1584–1647) made a brief incursion into Alsace. Though not entirely successful, it was another sobering experience for Richelieu nevertheless.

We saw Lorraine pillaged by one of the strongest armies that the Emperor had raised in a long time, and its loss was even greater, since the passivity of those who commanded your forces was the only cause.[95]

Meanwhile, the Duke de Rohan, favored by the principal leaders of the Grisons desirous of their freedom, entered openly and successfully into their country. He seized the most important passages and posts and fortified them, notwithstanding that the vicinity of the Milanese made it easy for the Spanish to come there with some help.[96]

The Dukes of Savoy and Créqui, who commanded your armies in Italy, took a fort in the Milanese and built another one on the Po, which was a hard pill for your enemies to swallow.[97]

In 1636 the cowardice of three governors of your strongholds gave your enemies the opportunity to get a foothold inexpensively in your kingdom and gain a notable advantage, which did not let you down, and, when everyone seemed to be at a loss, in six weeks you put such a powerful army in service that the entire defeat of your enemies could have been expected if those whom you had placed in command had employed it properly. Their deficiencies obliged you lead it yourself, and by the grace of God, you retook the only stronghold that was important to your state in the presence of those who had only captured it because you were at a distance.[98]

You overcame many obstructions by doing this, which were put in place by your own dependents, who, whether out of ignorance or malice, loudly criticized such a lofty plan.[99] If your siege of Dôle did not succeed, reason, which obliges everyone to do first things first, was the only cause. Your Majesty

---

[95] In regard to Lorraine, Richelieu blamed the commanders of the armies that had defended Lorraine, Jacques Nonpar de Caumont (1558–1652), Marquis de La Force and Marshal of France, for being too old, and Louis de Nogaret (1593–1639), Cardinal de La Valette, whose father and brother were known for their sympathies for Marie de Medici. Richelieu also recalled Rohan to help out against the Duke of Lorraine.

[96] After a short stay in Lorraine, Rohan traversed Switzerland with his troops, and between April and November 1635 he undertook a brilliant campaign against the Imperialists and the Spanish that gave the French the best control they had ever had over the Val Telline.

[97] From his base in Casale, Créqui entered into the Milanese, took a couple of Spanish outposts, and, in conjunction with the Duke of Savoy, spent from September 9 to October 29 besieging the stronghold of Valenza unsuccessfully. Richelieu seems to be going out of his way here to minimize the disappointing start of the war.

[98] In 1636, between July and mid-August, the Cardinal-Infante descended upon France and took the three strongholds of La Capelle, Le Catelet, and Corbie, which was even more embarrassing for Richelieu than the reverses of 1635.

[99] He is referring particularly to the efforts of Monsieur and the Count de Soissons, who were commanding an army in Champagne, to turn it against Louis XIII just as he was attempting to recover Corbie.

diverted your forces with all the more prudence since it was more important
to retake Corbie than to take Dôle.[100]

Meanwhile, since Gallas had entered into the kingdom at the head of the
principal forces of the Empire accompanied by the Duke of Lorraine with his
own, both were expelled from Burgundy with the shame of raising the siege
of Saint-Jean-de-Losne, a miserable stronghold, and the misfortune of losing
part of their artillery and such a large number of their men that out of 30,000
with which they entered in this kingdom, they left with only 10,000.[101]

In this same year, the Ticino witnessed an action in Italy that was no less
successful, in which your troops won a particularly bloody battle, and in the
Val Telline, where your enemies attempted repeatedly to come to grips with
your troops so as to expel them by force and were never able to carry out their
plan because they always kept getting beaten.[102]

In 1637 you captured two strongholds in Flanders from your enemies, and
you retook one of the ones that had been delivered to them the preceding year
by the cowardice of the governor.[103]

A third, besieged in Luxembourg, was taken soon thereafter, and your
enemies suffered as much damage from the entry of your armies into their
country as they had hoped to inflict on you in the same way.[104]

If the panic of the commander of your forces in the Val Telline and the
treachery of some of those for whose liberty you had fought made you lose,
through their cowardice and treason all together, the advantages that you
had acquired there with your forces and your reason, this year was happily

---

[100] In May 1636 the Prince de Condé entered Franche-Comté and attempted to besiege
Dôle. He failed miserably, and after three months Louis ordered him to abandon the siege.

[101] On September 18, 1636, the emperor's son, Frederick, King of Hungary, issued a
declaration of war against the French, and on October 23 Gallas, with an Imperial army
supported by the Duke of Lorraine, invaded Burgundy. On October 28 Gallas laid siege
to the small town of Saint-Jean-de-Losne, which put up a heroic defense and forced him
to withdraw back into Germany. It is hard to imagine anyone talking about the deaths of
twenty thousand men with such satisfaction.

[102] The bloody Battle of Tornavento (June 22, 1636) on the left bank of the Ticino River.
It was between the French and Savoyard army, led by Marshal Charles de Créqui (1578–
1638), Duke de Lesdiguières, and Victor Amadeus, which again attempted to invade the
Milanese, and the Spanish under the Marquis de Leganés. Both sides claimed victory, but
both armies disengaged, and the invasion failed.

[103] The Cardinal de La Valette, who had almost become a slave to Richelieu, took Cateau-
Cambrésis on June 21 and Landrécies on July 22 and recovered La Capelle on September
15, 1637.

[104] Meanwhile, Châtillon campaigned in Luxembourg from the beginning of August to the
end of October, taking a number of strongholds.

crowned by the taking of the Islands of Sainte-Marguerite and Saint-Honorat and by the relief of Leucate, which was besieged by the Spanish.[105]

By the first of these two actions, 2,500 French descended in full daylight upon an island defended by that many Spaniards and Italians, an island fortified by five regular forts, connected to each other by lines of communication that almost completely covered them by a parapet. Upon landing, your men engaged and defeated your enemies, who met them head on, and after having compelled most of them to withdraw to their ramparts, they overran them in six weeks, step by step, with as many sieges as there were forts, even though there was one with five royal bastions, so well armed with cannons, men, and everything necessary that it seemed as if they could not be attacked.[106]

By the second, a powerful army so well entrenched that there was only a single front of 1,000 *toises* on which it could be attacked, a front so well fortified that every 200 to 300 feet there were forts and redoubts mounted with cannons and flanked by infantry, was attacked at night and overrun by an army that, though smaller in number, did not fail to defeat them after many skirmishes.[107]

These two actions are so extraordinary that it cannot be said they are the results of the singular courage of the men without adding that they were seconded by the Providence and the hand of God, who was visibly on their side.

In 1638, even though the beginning of the year went badly for you in Italy, at Saint-Omer and at Fontarabia through the bad luck of the armies and the cowardice or the malice of those who commanded yours, the end put the finishing touches on the work by the taking of Breisach, captured after a long siege, two battles, and various skirmishes in an attempt to relieve it.[108]

---

[105] After recovering the Val Telline, the Grisons began to resent the dominance of the French, preferring to come to terms with the Hapsburgs and forcing Rohan to withdraw all his troops by May 5, 1637. He himself never returned to France, and Richelieu's attempt to block the passage of the Val Telline came to naught.

[106] By the "first" action, Richelieu means the combined recovery of the Island of Sainte-Marguerite, which began on March 24, 1637, and took forty-five days, and of Saint-Honoré, which took only one additional day, but Richelieu neglects to remind Louis XIII that these were two islands that the Spanish had occupied in one day on September 13, 1635, and that two of his marshals and one archbishop had failed to retake in 1636.

[107] By the "second" action Richelieu is referring to the relief of Leucate, a small town in Languedoc on the border with Spanish Roussillon. The Spanish laid siege to it on September 2, 1637, but the inhabitants held out bravely, and Charles de Schomberg (1601–1656), Duke d'Halluin, who had succeeded his father as Governor of Languedoc, raised an army that relieved it, becoming a Marshal of France for his exploit. A *toise* was exactly six *pieds* (feet)—about 1.949 meters until 1812—so a thousand *toises* would be 1.949 million meters, or a little over one mile.

[108] On October 7, 1637, Victor Amadeus of Savoy died, leaving his duchy in the hands of his wife, Cristina (1606–1663), who became regent for her son Francis Hyacinth (1632–1638).

Besides, you no sooner knew of the failure of the siege of Saint-Omer than Your Majesty went there in person, where it seemed that a disaster was to be feared. You halted the panic of your armies by ordering the taking and razing of Renty, a fortress that seriously threatened your frontier.[109]

Subsequently, Le Catelet, the only one of your strongholds that was in the hands of your enemies, was captured by force under their eyes, without their venturing to oppose the effort of your arms.[110]

The naval battle in which fourteen galleys and four ships from Dunkirk that were all hiding in the cove of Guetaria, under five shore batteries and not venturing out to sea in the face of nineteen of yours, were all burned or sunk with a loss of 4 to 5,000 men, 500 cannons, and a huge quantity of military supplies for the relief of Fontarabia, are good counterweights, not for your losses at Saint-Omer and Fontarabia, which were not great, but to the gains that you would have made by taking these strongholds.[111]

If one adds to this advantage the victory that you had previously won when your naval armada made your enemies lose fourteen great ships in the port of Los Pasajes, a great many cannons, many flags, and all sorts of munitions, if the Spanish think that this year had gone well for them, they are whistling in the dark.[112]

Finally, the combat between galleys, perhaps the most famous that has ever taken place at sea, where 15 of yours attacked that many of the Spanish and engaged them so successfully that they lost 4,000 to 5,000 men and six galleys, including one *Capitana* and two *Patronas*, if this combat were not proof enough of such a glorious action, this combat, I say, points out not only

---

Despite being the sister of Louis XIII, she, not unlike the Grisons, resented the domination of France. Also, in August 1638 the French had attempted to take Saint-Omer in the Spanish Low Countries and were driven off after a two-month siege, but the most embarrassing reversal of the year took place in September in Fontarabia, a Spanish seaport on the northern border between France and Spain. The Prince de Condé, commanding the French army besieging the town, and Henri de Sourdis, the admiral-archbishop, in one more confrontation between commanders, fell out with the Duke de La Valette, with the result that the Spanish emerged from their fortifications and routed the besiegers (see note 85 above). The only bright spot occurred in December, when Bernard of Saxe-Weimar (1604–1639), a German Protestant mercenary in French service, took the stronghold of Breisach right across from Alsace on the right bank of the Rhine, but at that point it was not clear if he had taken it for himself or for his employers.

[109] Renty was taken on August 9, 1638, in the midst of the unsuccessful siege of Saint-Omer.

[110] Left over from the year of Corbie, it was finally recovered on September 14, 1638.

[111] The Battle of Guetaria won by Sourdis on August 22, 1638 (see note 253 below).

[112] Richelieu seems to be referring to a previous engagement that took place in July 1638 when a squadron sent by Sourdis seized *four* Spanish galleons in the small port of Pasajes in the Bay of Biscay.

that your prudent conduct has been accompanied by good fortune but that the boldness of your commanders has kept pace with it.[113]

There are many things to note about this war.

The first is that Your Majesty did not enter into it as long as you could avoid it and that you did not end it before you should have. This observation is all the more glorious for Your Majesty because now that you are at peace, you have been invited many times by your allies to take up arms and have refused to do it, while during the war your enemies had often proposed a separate peace without your wanting to hear of it.[114]

Those who will learn that Your Majesty has been abandoned by many of your allies without your wanting to abandon any and that even though those who have stuck with you have failed you in various important things, you have always fulfilled your promises to them, these, I say, will recognize that you are no less successful than you are virtuous.

Well do I know that if you had not kept your word this would have tarnished your reputation, and once a great prince loses it, he has nothing left to lose. But it is no small thing, once the war is over, for you to continue to do your duty when, on various occasions, the natural desire for revenge might give you occasion to relax.

It took no less prudence than force or less self-control than arms to proceed almost alone with plans that were envisaged for the action of many.

Saxony was the first to abandon the King of Sweden, Brandenburg, the Landgrave of Hesse, many Hanseatic cities, Württenberg, Parma, and Mantua.[115]

It is true, however, that the defection of many princes of Germany, that the withdrawal from your party that the Duke of Parma was compelled to make due to the necessity of his affairs, that the death of the Duke of Mantua and the frivolity of his dowager, mother of the young duke, who was no sooner

---

[113] This engagement took place on September 1, 1638, outside Genova. It is strange for Richelieu to ignore the Battle of Lepanto of 1571 in which 168 Spanish, Venetian, Genovese, Papal and ships of other Christian states won a resounding victory over a somewhat larger number of Turkish ones.

[114] Richelieu here is fantasizing even more broadly about events that have not occurred.

[115] Not the King, but his daughter, Christina (1626–1689), queen from 1632 to 1654. See note 87 above for a discussion of the Peace of Prague and the actions of the Elector of Saxony. As to the others described in this paragraph, the Lutheran George William (1595–1640), Elector of Brandenburg from 1619, rallied to it, but the Calvinist William V (1602–1637), Landgrave of Hesse-Cassel from 1627, never could come to terms with the Emperor. The Hanseatic cities, like Lübeck and Hamburg, accepted the peace but largely managed to remain neutral. The Lutheran Ebehard III (1614–1674), Duke of Württemberg from 1628, who was driven out of his duchy after Nördlingen, was only reinstated in a portion of his lands after making a humiliating treaty with Ferdinand III.

in power than she forgot the obligations she had to France and openly turned against her, that the death of the Duke of Savoy and the recklessness of his widow, who got herself into trouble because she could not endure to be saved, it is true, I say, that all these incidents did not shake the firmness of Your Majesty and that even though they complicated your affairs, they never made you change your plans.[116]

The second remark worthy of great consideration on this subject is that Your Majesty has not wanted to protect himself from the danger of this war by exposing Christendom to the weapons that the Ottomans have often offered you. You knew full well that you had every right to accept such help, and this knowledge was still not enough for you to do something that was risky for the faith but advantageous to the peace.

The example of some of your predecessors and of various princes of the house of Austria, which pretends to be religious to God while it is actually looking out for its own interests, has been insufficient to bring you to what history teaches has been practiced many times by others.[117]

The third astonishing thing about this war is the size of the armies and the huge sums that have been spent to wage it. The greatest princes in the world have always found it difficult to undertake two wars at a time. Posterity will be hard-pressed to believe that this kingdom has been able to maintain at its own expense seven land armies and two navies, without counting those of your allies, to whose subsistence you have made no small contribution.

However, it is true that aside from a powerful army of 20,000 foot and 6,000 to 7,000 horse that you have always had in Picardy to attack your enemies, you have had another in the same province of 12,000 foot and 4,000 horse to defend this frontier.

It is true, moreover, that you have always had one in Champagne of the same number as this last, one in Burgundy of similar strength, a smaller one in Germany, another as big in Italy, and occasionally still another in the Val

---

[116] Odoardo Farnese (1612–1646), Duke of Parma from 1622, found himself overwhelmed by the Spanish in Italy and made peace with them by the Treaty of Milan on February 2, 1637. In May of the following year, the French caught the pro-Hapsburg Maria Gonzaga (1609–1660), regent for her minor son Charles II (1629–1665), Duke of Mantua since 1637, conspiring to chase the French out of Casale and turn it over to the Spanish. Moreover, in the last months of 1638 Louis XIII's sister, Cristina, the regent of Savoy, who after the death of her elder son continued as regent for his brother, Charles Emmanuel II (1634–1675), was being threatened in her position by her pro-Spanish brothers-in-law, the Cardinal Maurice (1593–1657) and Prince Thomas (1596–1656), whom we have already met at the Battle of Avins.

[117] Richelieu is quite correct in that the practice of alliances with heretics had been frequently practiced by the Byzantines, during the Crusades, and during the Spanish Reconquista, and it only became a moral issue in the seventeenth century.

Telline. And what is worthy of admiration is that most of them are designed for attack rather than for defense.

Even though your predecessors have disdained the sea to the point that the late king your father did not have a single ship, Your Majesty has not failed to have 20 galleys and 20 sailing ships in the Mediterranean in the course of this war and more than 60 well equipped in the Ocean, which not only diverted your enemies from raiding your coasts but did them as much harm as they tried to do to you.

Moreover, you have helped the Dutch with 1,200,000 livres every year, and sometimes more, and the Duke of Savoy with more than a million.[118]

The crown of Sweden with a similar sum.[119]

The Landgrave of Hesse with 200,000 Reichsthalers and various other princes with various sums, as the occasion required.[120]

Such exorbitant burdens mean that the expense in each of the five years that France has underwritten the war has amounted to more than 60 millions, which is all the more admirable in that it has been sustained without taxing the wages of the judicial officials, without touching the income of individuals, without asking for any diversion of funds from the clergy, all of which are extraordinary measures to which your predecessors have often been obliged to resort in more limited wars.[121]

Thus, 60 millions of expenses for each of these five years, 150,000 foot soldiers both for the armies and for the garrisons of your strongholds, and more than 30,000 horse will constitute a perpetual reminder to posterity of the power of this crown and of the effectiveness of Your Majesty.

If I add that these various occupations have in the meanwhile not kept you from fortifying your frontiers so perfectly that even though they were

---

[118] On April 15, 1634, the French raised their annual subsidy to the Dutch to 2.3 million livres, but these subsidies were gradually reduced once France entered the war. This was still being paid in accordance with the treaty signed in Paris on February 8, 1635, but on September 6, 1636, with the Treaty of The Hague with the Dutch, it went down to 1.5 million livres, and on December 17, 1637, with the Treaty of Paris with the Dutch, it dropped to 1.2 million. In fact the treaty signed in Rivoli on July 11, 1635, with Victor Amadeus of Savoy for the conquest of Milan from Spain provided no subsidy for him. It was not until the Treaty of Turin of June 3, 1638, with his widow Cristina that Louis XIII committed himself to a subsidy of 840,000 livres, raised by the treaty of June 1, 1639, to 1 million.

[119] The Treaty of Bärwalde gave Gustavus Adolphus 1.2 million livres per year for six years retroactively from April 1630. On March 20, 1636, that amount was renewed by the Treaty of Wismar with his daughter Christina, giving the Swedes 1 million per year for three years. On March 5, 1638, it was again renewed for 1 million per year for three years.

[120] Treaty of Wesel with the Calvinist William V, Landgrave of Hesse from 1627. It was signed on October 21, 1635.

[121] Again, we are counting from 1635!

previously open to your enemies on all sides, they can now only stare at them with astonishment, which is another outstanding service to posterity, since it will in the future be reaping as many fruits as Your Majesty has received in the past from your labors and pains.

Those who will learn from history how the great plans of Your Majesty have been met by the obstructions that the envy of your prosperities and the fear of your power have evoked from various foreign princes, by the betrayal of some of your allies, by the perfidy of your bad subjects, by an ill-advised brother from time to time, and by a mother constantly possessed by evil spirits since she wanted to deprive herself of the advice of Your Majesty and distinguish her own interests from those of the state, will recognize that such obstacles only add to your glory and that brave hearts cannot be deterred from the difficulties that they meet.

Moreover, if they consider the natural frivolity of our nation, the impatience of the soldiers who are unaccustomed to fatigue, and finally the weakness of the instruments that you have had to use on these occasions, of which I am the first, they will be compelled to admit that nothing has compensated for the deficiencies of the tools as much as the craftsmanship of Your Majesty in using them.

Finally, if they keep in mind that by overcoming all these obstacles you have managed to conclude a peace, in which the deficiencies of some of your allies and your affection for them made you return some of your own conquests, it will be impossible for them not to realize that your kindness is equal to your power and that your prudence and the blessing of God march in lock step.

There, Sire, have been the actions of Your Majesty up to the present, which I shall consider to have been entirely concluded if they are followed by a period of tranquility that gives us the means of showering your state with all sorts of benefits.

In order to do this, it is necessary to consider the various orders of your kingdom, the state as a whole, your person who is responsible for its conduct, and the means that you must use to acquit yourself worthily, which requires nothing more in general than to have a good and faithful council, consider its advice, and follow the guidance of reason in the government of your states, which is what the rest of this work is all about, treating each of these matters individually in various chapters, subdivided into various sections in order to be absolutely clear.

Chapter II

Reforms of various orders of the state

FIRST SECTION

[B]Which indicates the bad state of the Church at the beginning of the King's reign, the state it is now in, and what it is necessary to do to set it right[B]

One could write entire volumes on the subject of the various orders of this kingdom. But my end not being that of many others, who are satisfied with discoursing at length about all the parts of a state without considering whether or not the public will draw some utility from their reasoning, I will limit myself to indicating in a few words to Your Majesty what is most important in order to procure the advantage of all your subjects in their various conditions.

When I remember that I saw in my youth gentlemen and other laymen possess by subterfuge not only most of the priories and abbeys but also parishes and bishoprics, and when I consider that in my first years, there was so much licentiousness in the monasteries and convents that in those days only scandals and bad examples were to be found where just the opposite should have been expected, I confess that I draw no little consolation from seeing that these disorders have been so absolutely banished in your reign that subterfuges and disorders are rarer now than legitimate possessions and genuine religion were then.

To continue and augment this blessing Your Majesty can do no better, in my opinion, than to take particular care to fill the bishoprics with persons of merit and exemplary life, to give abbeys and other simple benefices for which you have the right of nomination only to persons of recognized integrity, to exclude from this favor those who lead too loose a life for a saintly profession that ties men particularly to God, and to make an example by punishing the scandalous.

Many other expedients for the reform of the clergy could be proposed. But providing that Your Majesty will observe these four conditions and treat the respectable people of this profession favorably, you will do your duty and make clergy of your state either what they should be or, at least, so prudent that they will work at it. I must, in this regard, indicate to Your Majesty how you must watch out not to be deceived in judging the capacity of the bishops. One might be learned, perhaps considered capable, who, besides knowledge, also requires zeal, courage, vigilance, piety, charity, and energy all together. It is not enough just to be an honest and respectable man to be a good bishop, but being good for oneself, it is also necessary to be so for others.

I have often feared that persons from aristocratic families might be less committed to their duty and less disciplined in their life than others.

Many, who fear the same thing, feel that doctors who combine a good life and low birth are more fit for such employments than those of higher extraction, but there are many things to consider in this regard. To have a bishop to one's liking, he should be learned, zealous, and of good birth, because the authority required in such posts is only found in persons of quality. But since it is difficult to find all these qualifications in the same person, I shall venture to say that, presupposing good morals, which have to be considered more than anything else, leadership, which ordinarily goes right along with them, is to be preferred to learning, since I have often seen very learned people who have made very bad bishops and poor administrators because of their low extraction and poor upbringing, which, in keeping with their birth, approaches avarice, while the nobility, which has virtue, often has a particular desire for honor and glory, which produces the same effects as the love of God, so that it cohabits with the brilliance and generosity commensurate with such a post and knows better how to act and interact with people.

It is necessary above all that a bishop be humble and charitable, that he be learned and pious, courageously firm, and zealous for the Church and for the salvation of souls.

Those who seek bishoprics from ambition or interest in order to make their fortune are ordinarily those who endeavor to solicit in order to obtain by persistence what they cannot hope for from their merit, so they cannot be chosen, but those who are called by God to this state, which is recognizable by the difference in their lifestyle, learn the ecclesiastical way of life in seminaries, and it would be very useful if Your Majesty were to declare that you will only choose those who have spent a good deal of time after their studies in performing such functions in seminaries, which are the places established to learn them, it not being reasonable for the most difficult and important craft in the world to be undertaken without having been learned, seeing as how it is not permitted to do the least important and the most menial without several years of apprenticeship.

After all, the best rule one can follow in making this choice is not to have one at all but to choose learned people sometimes, less scholarly and more noble persons at other times, young people on certain occasions, and old ones in others, depending on which people in these various categories will be found proper.

I have always kept this in mind, but, as careful as one has been to do it, I admit that I have sometimes been mistaken. It has been very difficult not to be with decisions that are all the more difficult since it is impossible to penetrate into the souls of men or to control their unpredictability.

Often they have no sooner changed their class than they change their disposition or, rather, than they uncover what they had previously dissimulated in order to achieve their ends.

While such characters live in poverty, they have no other care than to give the appearance of all sorts of good qualities that they do not have, and when they attain what they desire, they make no effort to hide the ones that they have always had.

However, if one applies the precautions that I propose to choices that one makes, even if they would not always succeed, one will be sufficiently relieved before God, and I venture to say that Your Majesty will not have anything to fear, provided that by obliging those who will be chosen with the condition that they reside in their bishoprics and establish seminaries there for the instruction of their clergy and visit their flocks as they are obliged by the canons, you give them the means of performing their duty successfully.

I speak this way, Sire, because this is now entirely impossible because of the schemes that the officials of Your Majesty are always perpetrating upon their jurisdiction.

Six things are primarily to be desired so that the souls that are committed to them receive all the assistance from them that they must expect.

Three depend on your own authority, one simply from Rome, and the two others from Rome and from your authority together.

The first three are the regulation of appeals as if from abuse, that of privileged cases, and the suppression of the *régale* demanded by the *Sainte-Chapelle* of Paris from most of the bishoprics of this kingdom until those whom Your Majesty nominates have sworn their oath of fidelity.

The 4th is a rule in the number of verdicts required by canons for the punishment of a crime committed by a clergyman, so that the criminals cannot in the future escape punishment that they deserve because of the length of the formalities that are practiced.[122]

And the two others, which depend on the sovereign authority of the Church and yours together, are the exemptions of chapters and the right of various holders of benefices and laymen to nominate curates.

---

[122] See the fifth section of this chapter.

SECOND SECTION

On appeals as if from abuse[123]

I do not undertake here to clarify the origin of appeals as if from abuse as something that is absolutely necessary to know. Providing that this evil can be remedied, it is not important to know when it began.

Well do I know that it is so difficult to know the true source of this practice, which the Attorney General Servin used to say that if he had known the author of such a good regulation, he would have built a statue to him.

However, there is every reason to believe that the foundation of this custom came from the confidence that clergymen had in royal authority when, since they were being mistreated by the refugee antipopes Clement VII, Benedict XIII, and John XXIII in Avignon, they had recourse to the reigning king Charles VI so as to be relieved of the extraordinary annates, pensions, and subsidies that were often imposed upon them.[124]

The complaints of the clergy of France led the king to issue an ordinance that prohibited the execution of the rescripts, mandates, and bulls that the popes might conceive in the future against the freedoms and liberties that the Gallican Church enjoyed.

This order gave occasion to the first schemes of the king's officials against the ecclesiastical jurisdiction.

However, this was no sooner done than their fear of being harmed by it instead of being helped led the king to suspend its execution for some years. Subsequently the continuation of the harassments to which the holders of benefices were subjected made him reinstate it for a number of years, after which it was finally suppressed by King Charles VII at the beginning of his reign because of various abuses that were committed in its execution.[125]

Their bad experience with such an order obliged the clergy to tolerate, at least for a while, the treatment that they were receiving from the officials of the court of Rome.

But finally, the accumulation of the exactions that were imposed upon them compelled them to assemble in Bourges in 1438 in order to consult over the means of liberating themselves. This assembly, famous for the number and merit of the prelates who were there, carefully studied the various evils from which the Church was suffering and judged that the best remedy that could

---

[123] *Appels comme d'abus*, which I translate as "appeals as if from abuse," were appeals from ecclesiastical courts to civil ones, or even vice versa.

[124] Clement VII (1378–1394) and Benedict XIII (1384–1424) were antipopes, and John XXIII was an antipope in Rome from 1410 to 1415 until deposed by the Council of Constance. Charles VI (1368–1422) was King of France from 1380 until his death.

[125] Charles VII (1403–1461) was King of France from 1422.

be applied was to receive the decrees of the Council of Basel, which reduced almost everything to the common and canonical law and prohibited all the officials of the court of Rome from undertaking anything against the clergy.[126]

Subsequently it formed a pragmatic out of the decrees of this council, which it resolved to execute under the good pleasure of the king, whom they beseeched to protect it.[127]

The king, adhering to the supplications of the clergy, expressly issued an ordinance to his royal judges to have its pragmatic observed religiously, and this is how the evil from which the Church now suffers in this kingdom from the enterprises of the officials of the king came back to life after beginning in the reign of Charles VI and how the *parlements* have taken the occasion to appropriate jurisdiction over most of what belongs only to the tribunal of the Church of God.

The royal judges had already begun to appropriate to themselves the jurisdiction of what belongs only to the Church, claiming that the bull of Martin V issued in the year 1439 had given it to them.[128]

It was thus very easy to attribute to themselves what had initially only been given to them, to the exclusion of their subordinate judges, and to extend beyond their jurisdiction, on this pretext, what had initially only been given to them, since they had only their inferiors to deal with on this point.

In the institution of the first order issued to remedy the infractions of the pragmatic, the appeals did not take place. Those who obtained rescripts or mandates against common law from the court of Rome were punished on the mere complaint of the plaintiff without investigating the foundation of the case.

This 1st regulation never had the name or the goal or the effect of appeals as if from abuse. Subsequently, time in combination with power, which just like fire attracts everything to itself, transformed such an order, instituted for the conservation of the common law and the liberties of the Gallican Church against the schemes of Rome, into appeals as if from abuse, whose disorder entirely nullifies the ordinary jurisdiction of the French prelates and of the Holy See all together. Well do I know that in order to authorize their practice, the most skillful supporters of the *parlements* can say that since the prelates at Bourges had beseeched the king to have his officials keep the Holy See from violating the pragmatic, they had plainly given him the right to oppose the

---

[126] Council of Basel (1431), a council extremely critical of the papacy in the heyday of the conciliar movement in the Church.

[127] The Pragmatic Sanction of Bourges (1438), one of the high points in the late Middle Ages in the efforts of regional churches to limit the authority of the Holy See.

[128] Martin V (1369–1431), pope from 1417, issued the bull *Quod antidota* in 1418 just to the contrary.

violations that they themselves might commit, along with jurisdiction over the verdicts that they impose day in and day out in their tribunal.

But here one can apply the proverb that you only get what you pay for, and it is absolutely certain that this was the last thing the Gallican Church had intended to do at Bourges.

It had recourse to the king against the schemes of Rome since there was no tribunal on this earth superior to the Holy See and only the secular princes, who are protectors of the Church, can stop the disorders of the officials in Rome, whereas the enterprises of bishops can be remedied by their superiors, who will see to it.[129]

Finally, whoever gives his friend weapons for his defense does not do this in order to kill him. The *parlements* could never claim that the protection that the prelates in Bourges sought from the king gives his officials the right to appropriate their jurisdiction.

This word draws its origin from the practice of prosecutors and lawyers, who, since they were accustomed to practicing in the *parlement*, also gave this name to the recourse of the clergy

However, since evils get worse with the passage of time, the plan of the *parlements*, which they had kept under their hats, began to come out in the open during the last century in the reign of Francis I, who is the first to have always used the term appeals as if from abuse in the ordinance of 1539.

Many who realize the bad effect of this custom will think perhaps that it would be advisable just to abolish it. But I feel that such a change would do more harm than good and that this procedure is only dangerous if it is abused.

Whatever may be the foundation for what is now practiced, it is certain that when it was established openly, this was done only in order to stop the schemes of the ecclesiastical judges against the royal jurisdiction. Subsequently, not satisfied with stopping violations of the ordinances of the kingdom, which cover a lot of matters beside jurisdictions, it has been extended to the Holy Canons and to the decrees of the Church and of the Holy See and finally to all sorts of matters, which the laymen claim is an infringement of the police power, which they maintain belongs to the officials of the prince.[130]

It could reasonably be asked that the effect of this remedy be restricted to its original limits, which had no other extent than the limits of the royal jurisdiction, which was sufficiently regulated by the ordinance of 1539. But in

---

[129] This statement provides the key to Richelieu's conception of the relationship between the secular and spiritual arms. Since the secular arm is stronger, only it can exercise the responsibility of maintaining order within the spiritual one.

[130] *Lésion de police*, which I translate as "infringement of the police power," appears to be an attempt by royal officials to interfere in the name of the king with civil contracts that they considered to infringe on the royal authority.

order to eliminate any pretext of infringement by the officials of the prince so that they cannot claim plausibly that it is impossible for them to enforce the ordinances because of the schemes of the Church, I feel that you can consent to appeals as if from abuse if the judges base their ruling directly upon the ordinances, which is the only way in which Charles IX and Henry III, by article 59 of the Ordinance of Blois, wants them to do it, and that, on this pretext, they are not extended to the violations of the canons and to the decrees, especially since many of the ordinances, and particularly the capitularies of Charlemagne, often recapitulate those of the Church.[131]

Well do I know that it would be awkward to make the jurisdiction of the ordinances as exact as I would like without there being some disorder regardless of the regulation that is made. But if the king's officials are willing to follow his intentions, the order that it may please him to institute will easily serve as their rule.

The claim of the *parlements* that when the ecclesiastical judges rule against the canons and decrees, of which the kings are the executors and protectors, it is up to them to correct the errors of their verdicts is in effect a scheme so devoid of any appearance of justice that it is completely unbearable.

If the entire Church ruled against the canons and decrees, it might be said that the king, who is the protector, could and should sustain them by the extraordinary power emanating from his authority.[132] But since, when a judge has ruled incorrectly his verdict can be voided and amended by his superior, the officials of the prince cannot, without committing a sacrilege and without a manifest abuse, want to replace those who are particularly consecrated to God, and when they do this before the Church has given its final verdict, their scheme is devoid not only of justice but also of any appearance of it.

The intentions that the *parlements* still have to transfer the entire spiritual and ecclesiastical jurisdiction to the tribunal of the princes on the pretext of their secular police power is even more destitute of any apparent foundation. However, there is not a single presidial court or royal judge who does not presume to set the time for processions, the hour of important masses and of many other ceremonies under cover of the public interest. Thus, the tail wags the dog, and instead of the cult of God marching at the head and giving the law to all civil activities, this will only take place as long as the secular officials of the princes will permit it.

Well do I know that the miserable justice sometimes administered by those who exercise the ecclesiastical jurisdiction and the duration of the formalities prescribed by the canons give a specious pretext to the schemes of the royal

---

[131] Charles IX (1550–1574), King of France from 1560, Henry III (1551–1589), King of France from 1574, Charlemagne (742?–814), King of the Franks from 768, Emperor in 800.
[132] Richelieu reveals himself again! See note 129 above.

officials. But this is not reasonable because one drawback cannot justify another, but both need to be corrected, as I hope to point out later on.

I would be glad to pass over in silence the other pretention of the *parlements*, which is to invalidate any judgment made against their decrees, to which they want to give the same force as ordinances, if I was not obliged to point out that all they want to do by this intolerable scheme is to make their authority equal to that of their king.

The harm that the Church receives from such schemes is all the more unbearable since it absolutely keeps the prelates from doing their duty. If a bishop wants to punish a clergyman, the cleric immediately escapes his jurisdiction by an appeal as if from abuse. If the bishop, in making his visitation, issues some ordinances, they are immediately kept from taking effect because, even though in matters of discipline the appeals are purely procedural, the *parlements* make them suspensive against all reason.

Finally, it may truly be said that the Church is in chains and that even if its ministers keep their eyes open, their hands are tied, so that they can see what is wrong, but they cannot do anything about it.

What consoles me in this crisis is that what on this subject is impossible for the Church will be easy for Your Majesty, since the remedy for these disorders depends entirely on your will.

The 1st thing that it is necessary to do to avoid them is to order that in the future the appeals as if from abuse will no longer be accepted except in case of an egregious affront to the royal jurisdiction and an evident violation of ordinances coming exclusively from the secular authority of kings and not from the spiritual one of the Church.

Given this ordinance, in order to have it observed religiously, Your Majesty must issue a regulation that contains six things, by which means you will keep both the Church and those in the *parlements* from their schemes.

The 1st provision of this regulation must require that in the future all appeals as if from abuse must be sealed with the great seal of the *parlement* of Paris, and as to the others whose distance from your court obliges to make use of the small seal, they can only be sealed if three senior lawyers confirm the abuse with their own seal, submitting to a fine if they are overruled.

The second must declare that any appeal launched in matter of discipline will be suspensive and not procedural.[133]

The third must be that the abuse in the complaint be specified both in the notification of appeal and in the verdict that will intervene in it, which is all the more necessary because it has often happened in the

A similar remedy was practiced fifteen years after the pragmatic sanction in order to

---

[133] The other way around.

past that even though there was only one deficiency in the form or on one point in the verdict, when the *parlements* rule that there is an abuse, the verdict is reversed on all the provisions even though it only needs to be reversed on one of its circumstances, which is usually not even an important one.

The fourth must constrain the *parlement* to put appeals as if from abuse at the top of their calendar and to decide on them prior to all others in order to avoid delay, which is most often desired by those who are just trying to avoid punishment for their crime or to elude their ordinary judges, for it is not reasonable to deprive the public of the ecclesiastical courts and to turn their principal officials into plaintiffs before jurisdictions inferior to their own.

stop the usurpations by secular judges of ecclesiastical jurisdictions. It was ordered that whoever wished to obtain briefs from the chancellery in order to oppose rescripts and briefs from the pope was obliged to specify exactly how they claimed that the pragmatic sanction had been infringed

The fifth will impose upon the *parlements* the necessity to fine and to condemn to pay fines and court costs all those who have for any reason whatsoever lost their appeals and to send them back to their judges, which is all the more necessary since without this remedy every criminal will be able to avoid his ordinary jurisdiction by launching an appeal as if for abuse without reason.

Now, since the best ordinances and the most judicious regulations are often disdained by those who should observe them most religiously and the license of the sovereign courts often carries them to the point of violating or amending your orders just as they please, in order to make sure that Your Majesty is obeyed on this important point, reason demands that to these five provisions you add a sixth, which will be a powerful remedy in order to compel your officials to do their duty on this subject, just as appeals as if from abuse are excellent for keeping the ecclesiastical judges from abusing theirs in the exercise of their jurisdiction. This remedy simply requires that you permit your clergy to appeal from you to yourself by proceeding to your council when the *parlements* fail to observe your orders and regulations.

This is all the more reasonable in that in order to suppress the schemes of the ecclesiastical judges, they would be going before a tribunal inferior to theirs by its nature, whereas by appealing to your council in order to stop the *parlements*, they would be going before a tribunal of the same kind and yet unquestionably superior.

Even those who envy the liberties of the Church will have nothing to complain about since, instead of making it independent of the secular power, they are making it one step less dependent.

Finally, it would be all the more advantageous to Your Majesty that while keeping the power of the Church within its proper limits, you will reduce that of the *parlements* to its right size, which is prescribed to them by reason and by your laws.

And, aside from ordering your council to employ your authority on this subject to impede the schemes of all your subjects and particularly those of your judicial officials, Your Majesty will be careful to fill it not with people whose presumption and pressure are their principal claims to fame but with persons from your entire kingdom chosen purely for their merit. You will have the satisfaction of seeing that those who refuse to restrain themselves will be compelled to do so by force until, before long, they become accustomed to restraining themselves voluntarily.

THIRD SECTION

On privileged cases

Those who consecrate themselves to God by attaching themselves to his Church are so completely exempt from the secular jurisdiction of princes that they can only be judged by their ecclesiastical superiors.

Both civil and divine law clearly establish this immunity, civil law in that it has been recognized by all the nations, divine law by the authority of all the authors who have written about it prior to the modern jurisprudence of the last century.

The Church has retained its possession until the disorder in the administration of justice has given the secular officials grounds to take it over.

For 30 years this distinction between privileged cases and common crimes was unknown in the Church. Common crimes include all the offenses that belong in common law to the ecclesiastical tribunal by universal consent.

Since it has itself recognized that the misfortunes of the past kept it from suppressing with its own force a great many disorders among those who were under its jurisdiction, in order to eliminate all grounds for complaint against the impunity for crimes that were committed under the shadow of its authority, the Church itself resolved to empower the secular judges to intervene in certain cases called privileged in its jurisdiction, because they could only take them over by virtue of the particular privilege that they had been accorded for this purpose.

It is necessary to note in this regard that the cases that are deemed privileged everywhere else are not the same as those that are claimed to be such in France.

The first can be reduced to two, namely, premeditated murder and blatant apostasy, which leads the clerics to abandon the ecclesiastical life and stop wearing its garb in order to live scandalously in the world, whether by taking up arms or by engaging in some other activity completely contrary to their profession.

The second were only a few at the beginning, when the pragmatic sanction was instituted, and there were only two: carrying arms and the infringement of a royal safeguard, but more were added soon thereafter.

Any violation of the pragmatic sanction was felt to be a privileged case. That of concordats was subsequently put in the same category.[134]

The checking of certifications by a royal judge has also been found to be of the same kind. Rapes, highway robbery, perjury, counterfeiting, treason, and all major crimes are deemed to be of the same nature by the *parlements*. Finally, if you listen to them, all the offenses of the clergy, even misdemeanors, will fall under privileged cases, and there is no longer such a thing as a common crime.

The crimes recognized as privileges in every state are such by the consent and by the common opinion of the entire Church, and many of those that are such in this kingdom are only such because of the abuse and the schemes of the royal officials.

They have even more boldly attributed to themselves jurisdiction over all the misdeeds of clergymen, which, since the canon law requires three concurring verdicts for the condemnation of offenses, it is very difficult to punish even the most flagrant ones and impossible to do it speedily.

Even though this pretext is plausible and it requires the reform of the formalities observed in the administration of ecclesiastical justice, nevertheless the old legal experts have never condoned such schemes.

And it is useless to say that these crimes, which make the clergymen unworthy of their profession, also deprive them of their immunities, since, by this same reasoning, one would have to infer many false and harmful decisions by those who employ it.

The only conclusion that can be drawn from the delays and disorder that is noted in the administration of ecclesiastical justice is that it has to be straightened out and that, just as clergymen are obliged to do it, kings must also maintain them in the immunities that God has wanted to attach to his Church.

In order to satisfy these two obligations of the Church, one must remedy, by measures that we shall propose later on, the unbearable delays of the three verdicts required by the old canons and be so prompt subsequently in punishing the crimes committed by those who are under its power that no sooner is a scandal noticed than it is punished.

And the king, by issuing a declaration that expresses one by one all the privileged cases besides the carrying of arms, the infringement of a royal safeguard, the verification of certifications, and blatant apostasy as explained

---

[134] The Concordat of 1517 of Francis I (1494–1547), King of France from 1515, with the Holy See, which completely negated the Pragmatic Sanction by giving the King of France the right to nominate bishops and abbots with papal approval.

above, as well as highway robbery, counterfeiting, and every other kind of treason, must absolutely prohibit his officials from hearing any kind of case until the accused are sent to them by ecclesiastical judges, and if they contravene this order, their crime is immediately followed by their punishment.

Now, because justice demands that every offense be thoroughly investigated before thinking about its punishment and kings cannot personally sit in judgment on all their subjects, Your Majesty can satisfy this obligation by ordering his privy council to receive the complaints against the officials of whatever status they may be who contravene this regulation and to punish their schemes severely, in which case the Church will be satisfied and all the more careful to administer justice on behalf of its prince.

FOURTH SECTION

On the *régale* claimed by the *Sainte-Chapelle* on all the bishoprics of France

By letters patent of the year 1453, Charles VII granted this favor to the *Sainte-Chapelle* to replace the remainder of the donations that Charles V had given them both for the repairs of the entire building and for the *Sainte-Chapelle*[136]

Even though the canons of the *Sainte-Chapelle* of Paris maintain that the *régale* was given to them by their founder, Saint Louis,[135] it is nevertheless true that the first donation that has been found is from Charles VII, who gave them for three years only the right to enjoy the revenue from the vacant bishoprics that were subject to the *régale*; the duration of this favor having expired, he renewed it for three years and then for four more, all on condition that one-half of the money would be used for the maintenance of choirs for their services and the other half for repairs to the stained glass, for ornaments, and for the nourishment of the children in the choir, under the direction of the *Chambre des Comptes* in Paris.

On the death of Charles VII, his son Louis XI granted this same favor to the *Sainte-Chapelle* for the duration of his life, which seemed so extraordinary at the time that the *Chambre des Comptes* was only willing to verify his letters for nine years.[137]

---

[135] Louis IX (1214–1270), King of France from 1226, the only French king ever canonized.
[136] For Charles VII, see note 125 above. Charles V (1338–1380), King of France from 1364, managed to recover many of his father's losses during the first stages of the Hundred Years' War.
[137] Louis XI (1423–1483), "the Spider," from 1461, one of France's least lovable kings.

Subsequent to the reign of Louis XI, his successors, Charles VIII, Francis I, and Henry II, each continued this same favor during his lifetime.[138]

Charles IX went further and accorded to the *Sainte-Chapelle* in perpetuity what his predecessors had only accorded it for a limited time.[139]   By the edict of February 1565

The intention of these princes is worthy of praise because they gave up a right that belonged to them for a good cause. But the fashion in which the *Sainte-Chapelle* has used it could not be worse because instead of limiting themselves to what had been given to them, they have tried on this pretext to subject all the bishoprics in France to the *régale*.

The *parlement* of Paris, which claims sole jurisdiction over the *régale*, has been so blinded by its own interests that it has not hesitated to subject even the bishoprics that have recently been united to the crown to this servitude   The Bishopric of Belley
and to leave no doubt in the minds of the lawyers that the *régale* stretches as far as the kingdom does.

This scheme was too obvious to succeed, and it gave occasion to the churches that were found to be exempt from this right to refuse to recognize the jurisdiction of this tribunal and for the king to recall all such cases to his council.

The extension of this right to all the bishoprics of this kingdom is a claim so ill founded that, to realize how unjust it is, it is only necessary to read a deed whose original is in the *Chambre des Comptes*, which begins with the words *Dominus Rex* etc., which Judge Le Maître has had printed, and which contains a list of the bishoprics that are subject to the *régale* and those that are exempt.

Formerly, it was commonly thought that beyond the Loire river, there was no *régale*. Kings Louis the Fat and Louis the Young exempted the Archbishop of Bordeaux and his suffragans. Raymond the Count of Toulouse granted the same favor to the bishops in Languedoc and in Provence, which was subsequently confirmed by Philip the Fair, and Saint Louis granted the *régale* of all Brittany to the dukes of the country by his treaty with Pierre Mauclerc, which demonstrates that he did not give the *Sainte-Chapelle* the ordinance when he founded it.[140]

---

[138] Charles VIII (1470–1498), King of France from 1483. For Francis I, see note 134 above. Henry II (1519–1559), King of France from 1547.

[139] For Charles IX, see note 131 above.

[140] Gilles Le Maître (1499–1562). Louis VI the Fat (1081–1137), King of France from 1108. Louis VII the Young (1120–1180), King of France from 1137, husband of the famous Eleanor of Aquitaine. Raymond VII (1197–1249), Count of Toulouse from 1222, repentant supporter of the Albigensians. Philip IV the Fair (1268–1314), King of France from 1285. Richelieu then backtracks to Saint Louis, who in 1234 signed a treaty with Pierre Mauclerc (1187–1250), Duke of Dreux, then regent for the Duke of Brittany.

The ordinance *Dom. Episcopus alicujus Episcopatus ubi Rex habet regalem*[141]

Philip IV in his Philippics of the year 1302 uses these words: *in aliquibus ecclesiis regni.*[142]

Philip VI in his ordinance of 1334 speaks in this manner: "to the bishoprics in which we have the *régale.*"[143]

Louis XII in his ordinance of 1499, cited by Chief Justice Le Maître: "We have prohibited and prohibit all our officials, as well as archbishoprics, bishoprics, abbeys, and other benefices to which we have the right of *régale* or of guardianship, to interfere under penalty for sacrilege."[144]

Pasquier, in Book 3 of his *Researches*, Chapter 13.[145]

The late king Henry IV, by article 14 of his edict of 1606: "We only intend to enjoy our right of *régale* in the same fashion as our predecessors, and we have done so without extending it to the detriment of the churches which are exempt from it." And since this good prince believed that the *parlement* thought differently, he suspended all cases about the *régale* for one year by letters of the 6th of October 1609.

The present king, who has inherited his piety as well as his kingdom, declared, by article 16 of his ordinance of 1629, that he only wishes to enjoy the *régale* as in the past, and since the clergy complained that this terminology was not clear enough, His Majesty had this precisely written reply given by his commissioners that the ordinance was in reference to that of 1606, so that its terminology was sufficient to demonstrate that he did not intend to enjoy the *régale* any more extensively than he had used it in the past.

---

[141] "When a Bishop in a diocese where the king has the *régale.*" This document in sixteenth-century Gothic script from the *Chambre des Comptes* is now in the Bibliothèque Nationale de France, *Manuscrit Français.* 4429, fols. 11–13, undated. Richelieu or his assistants seem to have copied it out of Gilles Le Maître's *Traité des régales*, first published in 1567, or out of Pasquier's *Recherches*, cited in note 145 below. The fact that this is an incomplete sentence supports the observation made in 1947 by Louis André that this chapter was never entirely revised.

[142] For Philip IV, see note 140 above.

[143] Philip VI (1293–1350), king from 1328, first king of the house of Valois, loser of the battle of Crécy.

[144] Louis XII (1461–1515), king from 1498,

[145] Etienne Pasquier (1529–1615) was a presiding judge in the *Chambre des Comptes* of Paris. His *Des recherches de la France* began to appear in 1560 with Book I, more books being added in subsequent years. His study of the origins and development of the *régale* does indeed appear in Book III, but in Chapters 35 to 38. He cites the *Dom. Episcopus* ordinance in Chapter 37.

The ordinance *Dominus Rex* uses these words: "*consuevit capere regaliam.*"[146]

Philip IV, in his ordinance of 1302, says, "*Regales quos nos et predecessores nostri consuevimus percipere.*"[147]

And the Philippic of the year 1334: "Just as the kings our predecessors, because of the royalty and nobility of the crown of France, have used and been accustomed to be in possession and seizure." And since then, all the kings in their ordinances have only spoken of the custom and of their possession.

Many other bishoprics, such as Lyon, Autun, Auxerre, and various others, are so obviously exempt from this subjection that there is no doubt about it.

The ordinances issued from time to time clearly demonstrate that the kings have never claimed that the *régale* took place in all the bishoprics, and this truth is so evident that Pasquier, attorney for the king in the *Chambre des Comptes*, is compelled to admit that whoever maintains this doctrine is more of a flatterer than a French legal expert: these are his very words.[148]

The ignorance, or rather the cowardice and the self-interest, of some bishops has in no small measure contributed to the present embarrassment of the bishops in this kingdom since, in order to avoid being prosecuted themselves, they have not hesitated to accept a receipt from the *Sainte-Chapelle* for what they did not actually pay to it.

Their fear that if they challenged its right before judges who were on its side they would be found guilty led them to commit this error, which would have disastrous consequences if your Majesty were not there to bail them out.

Since common law demands that the fruits of a benefice be reserved to its successor, one cannot do otherwise without a lawful title over them.

However, there are not any that establish as clear a claim as kings have to dispose of it as they please, so that to justify it, it is necessary to have recourse to customary law.

This truth is so certain that all the ordinances issued on this subject refer only to their old possession.

Now, since it is easy for sovereign powers to find excuses to attribute to themselves what does not belong to them, and since what was originally an

---

[146] "The king . . . customarily limits the *régale*." This ordinance dates back to c. 1400. Once again, a rapidly inserted phrase.

[147] "The *régales* that we and our predecessors are accustomed to impose."

[148] Pasquier begins Chapter 35 of Book III of his *Recherches* by admitting that no one knows exactly when the kings of France obtained the *régale* but then goes on to insist that they have always had it, so Richelieu is stretching Pasquier's point beyond all credibility.

unjust usurpation may sometimes be deemed legitimate by virtue of its possession, it seems that one may reasonably doubt that the crown can claim a legitimate title on behalf of sovereigns.

But since I have decided not to question the rights of Your Majesty but merely to regulate them so that they do not affect the salvation of souls, without wanting to dig deeper into the origin and the basis of *régales* that I assume to be valid, I will merely attempt to clarify what the *Sainte-Chapelle* claims by virtue of the concessions that it has received from your predecessors and to propose the remedies that it is necessary to apply to the abuse that is made by the enjoyment of such a favor.[149]

It often happens that a bishop from a poor family who is rich in all the qualities that the canons and piety can desire remains unable for two or three years to do his duty since the payment of his bulls to which the concordats have obliged him often involves an entire year of his revenue, while this new duty deprives him of another, so that if one joins to these two expenses what it is necessary for him to spend in order to purchase his ornaments and the furniture that he needs in order to maintain his dignity, he will often find that three years go by before he can earn enough to feed himself, with the result that many either do not go to their bishoprics or do not live there respectably and cannot sustain the reputation that they need in order to care properly for their flock by their charity as well as by their words.[150]

It sometimes also happens that in order to avoid this drawback they borrow so much that they begin to engage in shady practices in order to repay their debts, and those who do not stoop so low are unable to repay their debts to the dismay of their creditors.[151]

The remedy for this evil is as easy as it is necessary, since it merely consists of annexing the *Sainte-Chapelle* to an abbey with revenue equal to what it can draw from this institution.

It might perhaps be said that it will not be easy to clear up this whole matter because this company will balk at revealing what it prefers to keep hidden. But if you order it to justify within two months out of its books how much it was receiving prior to the perpetual concession of Charles IX, under threat of losing its privilege, this perfectly legal procedure will clearly show on what basis it is necessary to compensate for the favor it has received from your predecessors.

---

[149] By this admission, Richelieu seems to refuse to provide any explanation regarding the origins of government other than tradition.

[150] Compare with the first section of this chapter, where Richelieu displays comparatively less sympathy for these pious souls.

[151] Or can't he help but confirm that his sympathy is skin-deep.

Well do I know that this chapter will claim that one must consider the revenue that it receives from the *régale* at the present time. But since it is certain that they were no sooner assured of the perpetuity of this favor than they extended it to various bishoprics that are exempt, it is clear that the date that I propose is the right one.

If Your Majesty does this, you will procure at little expense an incredible benefit to your Church by means of which souls can more easily receive the nourishment that is so necessary to them and that they must expect from their pastors.

If, subsequently, you continue in your decision, as you have been doing for a long time, not to impose any pensions upon the bishoprics, which is absolutely necessary, you will have done everything in your power to keep the poverty of the bishops from keeping them from doing their duty.

FIFTH SECTION

Which treats of the reform of the three concurring verdicts required by the canons for the punishment of clerics

It is common knowledge that the day-to-day running of the Church can and must often be changed in the course of time.

In the purity of the first centuries of Christianity, some institution may have been good that is now very harmful.

Since time, which is the father of all corruption, has made the morality of today's clergymen different from what it was in the good old days, it is certain that instead of so many years in which the zeal of prelates made them as severe in the punishment of crimes as they are at present loose and negligent, it is certain, I say, that instead of a time when delays in the procedures of ecclesiastical jurisdiction were not to be feared, they are now very harmful, and reason does not permit them to be continued. This consideration makes it absolutely necessary to abolish the procedure prescribed by the canons, which requires three concurring verdicts for the conviction of clerics.[152]

The long-standing use of this procedure, the source of all impunity and consequently of the disorders in the Church, obliges it to reform itself on

---

[152] The requirement of three concurring verdicts stems from Canon 3 of the Council of Sardica (today's Sophia), held around 343 in the midst of the Trinitarian controversy. It was apparently intended to keep the dispute from spreading and was subsequently interpreted as requiring three concurring decisions by ecclesiastical judges before a litigant could launch an appeal to a higher court.

this point in order not leave the secular judges with any pretext to follow the opinion of some theologians who have not hesitated to say that it is better to resort to an incompetent judge than to put up with the disorder. It is impossible to eliminate the jurisdiction of archbishops, primates, and the Holy See, but inasmuch as it often happens that six or seven verdicts are given before three concurring ones are found, this drawback can be remedied by ordering that the verdict of judges delegated by the Pope, on appeal by the primate, or of the archbishop will be definitive or sovereign, and so that this last decision can be obtained promptly and that the zeal of the Church is apparent in its good administration of justice, it would be appropriate, instead of running to Rome for every single case that it is necessary to decide, for it to please the king to join his clergy and obtain from the Holy See the authority to appoint qualified persons in all the provinces of the kingdom to judge definitively all the appeals made to their tribunal.

This proposal cannot be distasteful to Rome because the Concordat obliges the Pope to delegate judges *in partibus*[153] to decide the cases that come up. The only difference will be that since every case now has to be pursued individually in order to obtain the said judges, they would then all be in place for the decision of all the cases in the kingdom, which would facilitate the punishment of the crimes of clergymen and remove any pretext by the *parlement* to interfere, as it does in the jurisdiction of the Church, and by the clergymen of any subject for complaint.

Thus those who are enemies or envious of her immunities will have to shut up in the future, and her faithful children who have hesitated to speak in her defense up to now will speak boldly and proudly on her behalf against her oppressors.

Well do I know that the Holy See will fear that if the delegates are appointed as I propose, they can eventually become dictators, but by changing them from time to time, which I feel is appropriate and necessary, this drawback is not to be feared, and if one continues to obtain from Rome the notifications of appeal in each case, which can be endured, the rights of the Holy See will remain intact without any diminution.

It will perhaps be said that it will be just as time-consuming to obtain new appointments of judges from Rome for each crime that is committed as it is to get a notification of appeal sent to the appointees. But there is a great difference, since it is certain that one of the principal abuses that impedes the punishment of the crimes of clergymen is that the appellant usually obtains from Rome remission to whatever judge in France he pleases through collusion with his bankers.

---

[153] "abroad."

SIXTH SECTION

Which treats of exemptions

An exemption is a dispensation or relaxation of an obligation that one has to obey his superior. There are different kinds, some of right, some of fact.

Exemptions of right are those that one has enjoyed through the concession of a legitimate superior, who gives them for a specific reason.

Exemptions of fact are those that are possessed without legal title but simply since time immemorial.

Whereas the first kind of exemption is approved by canonists as coming from a legitimate authority, the last, which in itself is not legitimate, is not always condemned by them because they presume *"Quid est quod sine privilegiis potest acquiri consuetudines immemoriali,"* say the Canons[154] that those who enjoy this privilege since time immemorial have formerly obtained bulls that gave it to them, even though they cannot show it.

There are three different exemptions for places.[155] The first is that for monasteries for begging monks, which the bishop does not visit, even though he is received solemnly when he goes there, so that he can maintain order there and perform all the episcopal functions whenever he likes.

The 2nd is for all other places where they are not received and cannot perform any episcopal functions unless they declare that this is without prejudice to the rights and privileges of the said places. The abbey of Marmoutiers, that of Vendôme, and many others are in this category.

The 3rd is of certain territories over which the bishop does not have any jurisdiction, even over the civilians, over which only those who possess such an exemption have any jurisdiction and power, which is commonly called *lex diacesana*: diocesan. The abbeys of Saint-Germain-des-Pres, of Corbie, of Saint-Florent-l'Ancien, of Fécamp, and many others are in this category over all their territory, the monks exercising all the episcopal authority by themselves.

They give dispensations from bans, decide to issue notices, publish jubilees, set dates for celebrations when authorized by Rome, benefices are transferred

---

[154] "What is without a privilege can acquire it by immemorial custom."

[155] There was obviously quite a debate in the fashioning of the *Political Testament* about whether to use any kind of marginal notes, for after experimenting in the text that has come down to us as B³ with integrating them into the body, it was decided to put some of them back! This decision created some confusion because the copyist of B⁴ and other copyists took the paragraph beginning "There are three different exemptions" and moved it seven or eight (depending on the copy) paragraphs ahead in the text, a fatal misstep that either Cherré or his copyists failed to rectify until they got to the text that has come down to us as B¹⁰, and even after that Cherré in B¹¹ himself was not sure where to put it and proceeded to place it in a marginal note. I am, in the interest of authenticity, keeping this text in its original order as it appears in our Text A.

in their name, they even claim they have the right to choose whatever bishop they like to ordain priests without permission of the bishop of their diocese.

Finally, they issue permissions to be ordained by whatever bishop they please. Such is the exemption of the chapter of Chartres, by virtue of which the bishop can neither enter into the church nor visit the Holy Sacrament and Holy Oils without signing an act by which he promises to preserve all the privileges of the church.

These persons are so exempt from the jurisdiction of their bishop that when a canon has just committed a crime, the chapter gives him judges to try him, and if there is an appeal of the judgment, they proceed to Rome in order to have judges *in partibus* because this church *ad Sanctam Ecclesiam admissa nullo medio pertinet.*[156] They publish indulgences, they exercise their jurisdiction over some one hundred parishes, and they appeal all their verdicts to Rome. They organize all the big processions. The same is true of Saint-Martin of Tours.

Four kinds of persons in the Church are primarily exempt: archbishops who are primates, the bishops of archbishoprics, the monks and monastics of the bishops, and the canons of the bishops and archbishops.

Such exemptions vary. Some are personal exemptions, and the others exempt their places of residence in different ways.

It has only been sixty years since the Archbishop of Rouen has shaken off the yoke of the Primate of Lyon and has made himself Primate of Normandy.

Previously the archbishops were subject to the primates, to whom the popes would send the pallium in order to exercise power and authority over the metropolitans. Subsequently, those of France, with the exception of those of Tours, Sens, and Paris, have managed by a bull or by decree not to belong to the primates.

Some bishops have also gotten themselves exempted by the Pope from the jurisdiction of their archbishops.

The Bishop of Puy is exempt from the Archbishopric of Bourges, as are many others. They must, however, appear at the principal councils that the archbishop holds. Saint Gregory of Tours exempted a hospital, a church, and a monastery from the jurisdiction of the Bishop of Autun at the request of Queen Brunhilda and her grandson King Theodoric. Crotbert, Archbishop of Tours, exempted the monastery of Sainte-Marthe from his jurisdiction.[157]

Monks are almost all exempt from their ordinary jurisdiction, and their right is founded on the concession of the bishops themselves or on that of the popes. Their oldest exemptions, which they were granted 7 to 800 years ago, come from bishops and

---

[156] "belongs directly to the Holy See."

[157] Brunhilda (c. 547–613) was a Visigoth queen who married a Merovingian king of the Franks and ultimately became regent for her grandsons, Theodoric II (587–613), King of Burgundy, and Theudebert II (586–612), King of Austrasia, as well as for her great-grandson. She died by being tied to the tail of a wild horse. Crotbert (d. 931), Archbishop of Tours.

archbishops. But all those that they have obtained since that time have been granted by popes in order either to keep the bishops from disturbing their solitude or to protect them from being mistreated by some of the bishops, who were ostensibly mistreating them.

The last ones to exempt themselves from their superiors were freshly appointed canons. They were so tightly tied to their bishops that they could not do anything without their permission, and the greatest crime they could have committed at this time was to withdraw their obedience.

Many have felt that all their exemptions come from antipopes or that they are patently suborned or simply founded on immemorial possession. But it is very certain that there are some that precede the schisms and more authentic than those that derive their force by virtue of antipopes. Some are accorded by the most legitimate ones, or following concessions by the bishops or transactions with them, or on their own in order to protect the canons from being mistreated by them. In order to get to the bottom of this matter and to tell the good exemptions from the bad ones, it is necessary to study individually the bulls that authorize them.

A letter of Alexander III given to the chapter of Paris proves that popes have granted exemptions.[158]

Others are those that have been granted by the popes prior to the misfortune of the schisms and still others that have been given since end of the schisms.[159]

Those of the first kind must be considered as good and valid. But since such bulls are exemptions from common law, which is always repugnant, it is necessary to examine them carefully so as not to miss their point, since it is certain that many can be put forward as bulls of exemption when they are simply previously obtained bulls of protection that accorded some particular privileges but not an exemption from the ordinary jurisdiction or bulls that only empower chapters to exercise a jurisdiction inferior to that of the bishops, similar to that of the archdeacons in certain dioceses, who have the right to excommunicate, place under interdict, or order public penance, even though they are still subject to the jurisdiction of the bishops.

As to the bulls of the second kind, since they are null and void from the illegitimacy of those who have issued them, particularly from the constitution of Pope Martin V issued at the Council of Constance, which invalidates all bulls obtained during the schisms, no one can honestly make use of them contrary to the common law.

The exemptions of Sens, Paris, Bourges, Bordeaux, Limoges, Meaux, Auxerre, and Le Mans were obtained from antipopes.[160]

---

[158] Alexander III (1100/1115–1181), pope from 1159.

[159] Richelieu is referring to the "great" schism of 1378, which was healed by the Council of Constance in 1417.

[160] Richelieu fails to mention that two of these antipopes, Clement VII and Benedict XIII (for part of his antipontificate), were recognized as popes in France.

Those of the 3rd kind have been granted either to serve as new exemptions or to confirm preceding ones.

The first must be considered null, because they either are completely contrary to the decree of Martin V or have been surreptitiously obtained, such as those of the *parlements* of Paris and Toulouse against the chapters of Angers and Cahors.

Since the second have only been conceded in order to confirm an old right that has never been found to be valid, they must, in the mind of any dispassionate person, be without effect.

The exemptions of Auxerre, Noyon, Orléans, Châlons, Angers, Poitiers, and Lyon are founded on concessions of bishops or transactions made with them.

It remains to be seen if the exemptions founded on simple concessions by the bishops or by transactions and arbitration decisions intervening on this subject against them or their chapters are good and valid.

If bishops are never permitted to alienate their properties without obvious reason, even less can they renounce their spiritual authority without great harm to the Church, which, by this means, sees its members separated from their head and the rule by which it survives changed by confusion into its ruin.

This principle makes the nullity of transactions, compromises, or arbitration decisions very evident, because one cannot compromise or trade what one is not free to dispose of. If there are some authors who feel that one can traffic in spiritual things, all make an exception of certain ones, of which this kind of subordination is first and foremost, and in fact the titles of this nature are so invalid that even if they were confirmed by the popes, this would not be sufficient to deprive the successors of the bishop of their supremacy, of which they have been deprived in one of the 3 fashions specified above.

Since reason demonstrates that none of these ways can prevail against the common law, it also shows that the bulls that are simply confirmative of the above-stated concessions, transactions, or arbitration decisions give no right to those who want to use them because they cannot have any greater force than their supposed foundations.

One point only remains to be examined: namely, whether the custom and the old possession of the chapters is valid enough as a title against the authority of their bishops to make the Church endure the evil of the exemptions.

Frustra quidem qui ratione vincuntur nobis opponent quasi consuetudo maior sit veritade aut non fuerit in spiritualib. sequendum, si milius fuerit a spiritu sancto revelatum Cypr.[161]

Custom is an extremely misleading rule. Bad ones, even though very old, are universally condemned, and all those that are against the common law and overturn an order established by ecclesias-

---

[161] "In vain some oppose us with the superiority of reason, as if custom were greater than truth and should be followed in spiritual things as if it were better than the revelations of the Holy Ghost." Saint Cyprian (c. 200–258) to his brother in 256. *Epistolae* LXXIII c. 12.

tical constitutions must be held as such and cannot be a reliable foundation of a right, even less in canon law than in civil, seeing as the institutions of the Church derive their origin from a surer principle. And thusly one must decide the proposed difficulty by saying that custom must serve as title for what can be possessed by common law, but never when the possession violates it, in which case it is completely useless if it is not accompanied by a title that is so valid that it is exempt from all suspicion, from which it follows that since common law subjects all canons to their bishops, there is no custom powerful enough to exempt them from this subordination.

It is impossible to imagine the various evils caused by the exemptions. They overthrow the order that the Church has established in conformity with reason, which demands that inferiors be subject to their superiors. They ruin the harmony between the head and its members. They authorize all sorts of violence and leave many crimes unpunished, both of the persons of the privileged ones and of the libertines who seek refuge in their shadow.

There are two means of seeing to this evil: either by abolishing all these exemptions or merely by controlling them. Well do I know that since the 1ˢᵗ expedient is the most extreme, it is the most difficult. But since it is not impossible, I do not fail to propose it to Your Majesty, who has always taken pleasure in doing what your predecessors have never ventured to try. I do not, however, feel that it is appropriate to use it in regard to the exemptions enjoyed by the monks and monasteries.

With various bishops, each with his own ideas, spread out in different dioceses, the uniformity of thought that must prevail requires that they be governed by a single head, and on this foundation I maintain boldly that it is as necessary to maintain them in the possession of the legitimate exemptions that they enjoy as it is just to investigate the validity of their bulls, which they sometimes exaggerate beyond all reason.

But I insist that one can abolish all the other exemptions all the more profitably since the common good is sufficient to dismiss the private interests on this occasion. It is enough for something to be just to decide to do it, and one is obliged to undertake it when it is entirely necessary.

Since the Church has survived up to now without the change that I propose, I do not suppose that it is absolutely necessary, but I repeat that it would be extremely useful since the bishops would no longer have any excuses if they failed to do their duty.

To utilize this 1ˢᵗ means, all that is necessary would be for His Holiness to revoke the exemptions and privileges in question, while empowering the bishops to exercise their jurisdiction over their chapters and over all other exempted persons with the exception of those I have said above. A bull to this effect, accompanied by a declaration from Your Majesty certified in your *parlements* and in your great council, would break the chains that tie the hands of the prelates of your kingdom and makes them responsible for the disorders of their dioceses, with which they can hardly cope now.

Capitula cathedralium et aliorum majorum ecclesiarum illorum personae nullis exemptionibus, consuetudinibus, sententiis, juramentis, concordis fieri si possint I quominus a suis episcopiis et aliis majoribus praelatis per se ipsos solos vel illis quibus sive videtur adjunctis juxta canonicas sanctiones toties quoties opus fuerit visitari, corrigi et emendari etiam autoriate apostolica possint et valeant. Ses. 14, Cap. De refor.[162]

In my opinion, this bull would be very easy to obtain since it is given its openings by the Council of Trent, which categorically declares that the chapters and canons cannot by virtue of some exemptions, customs, possessions, verdicts, oaths, and whatever conventions there may be, keep themselves from being visited, corrected, and punished by their bishops or other persons deputized by them. And even if this expedient will not be liked in Rome, where even useful changes are often hated and where the slightest opposition usually blocks the best things, if Your Majesty enforces the council's decree on this subject, you will not need any new expedition.

Well do I know that this remedy will be disapproved by the *parlements*, in whose minds custom and practice often prevail over any kind of reasoning. But after having foreseen and considered all the obstacles that may be met, I venture to say that it would be much better to overcome them than to be stopped by any attempt that may be made to get Your Majesty to change his mind, all the more so because by restoring things to the common law, you would be returning them to their nature, and it is sometimes good for sovereigns to be bold on certain occasions that are not only just but whose importance cannot be put into doubt.

ISIDORE[163]

"Saepe per regnum terrenum celeste regnum profecit ut qui infra Ecclesiam positi contra fidem et disciplinam Ecclesiae agunt vigore principium conterantur."[164]

---

[162] The text is corrupt and badly cited. It should read, "*Capitula cathedraliaum et aliorum majorum ecclesiarum, illorumque personae, nullis exemptionibus, consuetudinibus, sententiis, juramentis, concordis quae tantum suos obligent auctores, non etiam successores, tueri se possint, quo minus a suis episcopis et aliis majoribus praelatis per se ipsos solos, vel illis, quibus sibi videbitur adjunctis, juxta canonicos sanctiones, toties quoties opus fuirit, visitar,i corrigi et emendari, etiam aucctoritate apostolicos, possint et valeant,*" which I translate as "The chapters of the cathedrals and all major churches and their personnel cannot, by any exemptions, customs, verdicts, oaths, agreements that only oblige themselves, or their successors, protect themselves so that they cannot be visited, corrected, and punished in accordance with the canonical sanctions, not only by their bishops and principal prelates but also by their deputies as well as apostolic authorities as often as they so wish." Session 14, Decree Concerning Reform, Chapter 4.

[163] Isidore (c. 560–636), Bishop of Seville, who presided over the Council of Toledo in 633.

[164] "Sometimes the heavenly kingdom comes to the aid of the earthly one so that when those who are placed under the authority of the Church act against the faith and the dis-

The canons keep their titles so well hidden that it is impossible to consult them without authority from the king. Often they even claim that they do not have any. This is what Peter du Bois and Peter the Venerable complain about loudly.[165]

The Ordinance of Orléans, Article 11: "All canons and chapters, both secular and regular and of cathedral and collegial churches, are equally subject to the archbishop or bishop of their diocese without being able to claim any privileges of exemption in regard to visitation and punishment of crimes, notwithstanding objections or appeals whose jurisdiction we have evoked to our privy council."[166]

Even though the utility of these two expedients, which are actually a single one, should ensure their approval, nevertheless my fear that the difficulty of their execution will render them useless makes me pass on to the second, which consists of naming commissioners, bishops, canons, and monks, who, along with deputies of the council and of the *parlements*, demand all the privileges and exemptions of the churches for evaluation so that those that are found to be legitimate can be retained and those that are not can be withdrawn and abolished. There is all the more of an opening for the practice of this expedient, since the Ordinance of Orléans, issued during the reign of Francis II, has a specific article for the regulation of exemptions.

If, subsequently, the Pope chooses to give each metropolitan and each judge who is deputized the power that we have proposed above to regulate by the authority of the Holy See what the bishops can still not do by themselves because of the exemptions that will remain in their force and vigor, and if Your Majesty orders his council to investigate the disputes that will arise on this subject, you will immediately eliminate all the evils that such privileges cause.

---

cipline of the Church, they are restrained by the power of the prince." Fourth Council of Toledo 633. *Isidorus lib. 3, Sentencia de summo bono* c. 53, incorporated into *Decretum* XXIII v. 20 or *Liber sententiarum*.

[165] The reference appears to be to Pierre du Bois (c. 1250–c. 1321), propagandist for Philip IV against Boniface VIII and the whole world. Pierre le Vénérable (1092–1156), reforming prior of Cluny.

[166] The Ordinance of Orléans of 1560 was issued during the reign of Francis II (1544–1560), King of France only from 1559 to 1560. It was one of the three great ordinances issued by the monarchy following meetings of the Estates-General or of an Assembly of Notables during the tumultuous sixteenth century, with all sorts of good intentions but rarely with much effect. An evocation meant that the lower courts, including the *parlements*, were obliged to surrender their jurisdiction to the council of the king.

SEVENTH SECTION

On the right of various clergy and other laypersons to nominate curates

It remains to speak of the evil that comes from bishops not being able to appoint most of the curates, which the clerical patrons or lay persons in their dioceses have the right to nominate.

Year 441.[167] The clergy began to enjoy this right of patronage at the Council of Orange, where it was ordered that the bishops who would have churches built in another diocese would have the right to put in priests as they wished, as long as they were approved by the bishop of the diocese.

Chap. 18, *Novel.* 123, in 541.[168] The same right was also given by Justinian to lay persons who wanted to found chapels, which they even obtained subsequently in regard to the monasteries that they founded.

The letter of Gregory to Secundinus of the year 598 proves this point.[169] The 9th Council of Toledo extended the right of patronage still further to parish churches, permitting the founders to nominate the curates, so that the negligence of the bishops in maintaining the foundations did not discourage the founding of any new ones.

Initially this right was lost when the founders passed away. Justinian, Gregory, and Pelagius extended it to their children. Finally, under Charlemagne, it passed to the heirs, whoever they may have been, which has continued up to the present. This right, which is praised by many fathers of the Church and confirmed by various councils and especially that of Trent, must be considered holy and inviolable by virtue of its long-standing authority, founded on the canons of the fathers and the councils, and for its utility to the Church, in whose favor many foundations are made in order to acquire, by this means, the right to nominate to them.[170]

But when I keep in mind that necessity is not a law and that since what was once good because of the devotion of the founders is now so bad because of the corruption of their heirs, who have neither their zeal, their virtue, nor sometimes even their religion, that it is impossible to continue it without imperiling

---

[167] This makes it the First Council of Orange rather than the Second.

[168] Justinian (c. 482–565), emperor from 527. The date of the novel should be 546. Gregory the Great (540–604), pope from 590.

[169] The Ninth Council of Toledo took place between November 2 and 24, 665. Secundinus was the bishop of Tauromenium in Sicily.

[170] Pelagius II (520–590), pope from 578, not to be confused with the famous (or infamous) holy man Pelagius (c. 390–418), champion of free will against predestination.

the salvation of many souls, I venture to say boldly that there is no excuse for tolerating such a dangerous disorder without being responsible to God.

Many will think that the best remedy for this evil is to eliminate its cause entirely. But when I consider that what is bequeathed for a fee, that is to say, for the transfer of one's own wealth, cannot be legally possessed without fulfilling the conditions under which it has been given and that the fathers of the Council of Trent, who in investigating abuses did not think about changing it, I am stuck, and I do not see how a private individual can prudently propose such a remedy. It is better to have recourse to a milder means, previously proposed by the Council of Trent, even though it *Sess. 2, Chap. 8, de refor. Item Sess. 24* of the same chapter.[171] has not pursued it. This is that the synod appoints some examiners, by whom all candidates to benefices with a cure of souls be carefully examined for their capacity and integrity, and they can subsequently propose two or three of the most capable to the possessors of the curateships that fall vacant for them to choose and present their preference to the bishop.

Well do I know that this expedient revokes the liberty that the patrons possess today in France. But since, while restricting it, it still leaves it to them, and it prevents the appointment of incompetent persons to be curates, it must be accepted, and all the more willingly, in my opinion, since by remedying this evil in the presentation of curates, the order of the council is observed, it will make it more difficult for archbishops to designate priests whom their subordinates have rejected, and since the council demands that the examiners be obliged to render account of all their actions to provincial councils, it also does not allow the archbishops to go beyond their jurisdiction without a cause that is so just that it cannot be put into doubt.

EIGHTH SECTION

On the reform of monasteries

After such just regulations as the above ones, it behooves the piety of Your Majesty to authorize, insofar as you can, the reform of monasticism. Well do I know that those that have been attempted in our time may not have turned out as they should have, but it is well worth giving it a try, seeing as doing a little bit of good is still doing good, and this is what God wants of you. It is very true that I have always thought, and still do, that it would be better to make some moderate reforms that bodies and souls can comfortably survive than to

---

[171] The reference is incorrect. Richelieu is again referring to Session 14 of the Council of Trent, this time "Decrees Concerning Reform, Chapters 1, 3, 12 and 13."

undertake some strict ones that the loftiest souls and the strongest bodies can hardly endure. Moderate things have a way of being stable and permanent, but it takes extraordinary grace to keep forcing nature.

It should also be noted that reforms of monasticism in this kingdom must be different from those in other countries, which, since they are free from heresy, require deep humility and exemplary simplicity from their monks, whereas doctrine is entirely necessary in this kingdom, in which the ignorance of the most virtuous monks in the world may be as harmful to certain souls, which need their erudition, as their zeal and their virtue are useful to others and to themselves.

I must say in passing on this subject, and particularly in what concerns the reformation of convents, that resorting to elections and particularly to triennial ones instead of appointment by the king is an expedient that does not always work.

Given the weakness of this sex, the guiles and the factions that get a foothold are so great sometimes that they are intolerable, and on two occasions I have seen Your Majesty compelled to revoke them once you had put them in so as to restore things as they were.[172]

Just as it behooves the piety of Your Majesty to work on the reform of the old orders, it also behooves your prudence to stop the excessive number of new monasteries that are being established every day.

It is necessary in doing this to disdain the opinions of certain minds who are as feeble as they are devout and more zealous than they are prudent and who believe that the salvation of souls and of the state depends on something that is harmful to both.

Thus, while one would have to be either malicious or blind not to see that religious orders are not only useful but necessary, it would take a fanatical zeal not to realize that too much is too much and that it could reach the point of being disastrous.

What is done for the state is done for God, who is its basis and its foundation. Both reforming the established houses and stopping too many new ones from being instituted is agreeable to God, who likes everything to be in order.

---

[172] It is extremely interesting that in his disparagement of womanhood, Richelieu does not mention his arrest on May 15, 1638, of Jean Duvergier de Hauraine (1581–1643), Abbot of Saint-Cyran and spiritual counselor of the nuns of the convent of Port-Royal, who was also an intimate friend of Cornelius Jansen (1585–1638), the Bishop of Ypres in the Spanish Low Countries, who had celebrated France's declaration of war against Spain by publishing his *Mars gallicus* (1636), a scathing denunciation of Richelieu's foreign policy. Richelieu must have thought that he had merely nipped a run-of-the-mill troublemaker in the bud, whereas the combination of Saint-Cyran and Jansen with the nuns of Port-Royal and their supporters came back to haunt the Catholic Church and the French monarchy over the next two centuries.

NINTH SECTION

On the obedience that is owed to the Pope

The order that God wants to be observed in all things gives me occasion here to indicate to Your Majesty how princes are obliged to recognize the authority of the Church, to submit to its holy decrees, and to give them their entire obedience in what concerns the spiritual power that God has placed in their hands for the salvation of souls, but just as it is their duty to preserve the honor of the popes as successors of Saint Peter and vicars of Jesus Christ, they must not yield to their schemes if they come to extend their power beyond its limits.

If kings are obliged to respect the dignity of the Supreme Pontiff, they are also obliged to conserve the power of their crown.

This truth is recognized by all theologians, but there is no little difficulty in distinguishing the relationship between these two powers.

In this matter, one must believe neither the jurists, who ordinarily measure the power of the king by the shape of his crown, which is as endless as it is round, or those who go all out for Rome from an excess of zeal.

Reason demands that both sides be heard so as to resolve the difficulty by persons so learned that they cannot be misled by ignorance and so frank that neither the interests of the state nor those of Rome can overpower their reason.

I can truly say that I have always found both the doctors of the faculty of Paris and the most scholarly monks among the religious orders so reasonable on this subject that I have never seen in them any hesitation to defend the just privileges of this kingdom. Moreover, I have never noticed in them any special affection for their native country that might prevail over those of the Church.

On such occasions, the opinions of our fathers must be of great weight. The most dispassionate historians and authors of every age must be carefully consulted in this situation, in which nothing could be worse than weakness and ignorance.

TENTH SECTION

On letters

Ignorance, which, as I have just indicated, is sometimes harmful to the state, gives me occasion to speak about letters, one of the greatest ornaments of states, and I must do it in this place, since they are justly in the empire of the Church insofar as all sorts of truths are naturally related to the first of all, the sacred mysteries to which the eternal wisdom has wanted to consign the ecclesiastical order.

Since the knowledge of letters is entirely necessary in a republic, it is certain that they must not be taught indiscriminately to everybody.

Just as a body that had eyes all over it would be monstrous, so would a state all of whose subjects were scholarly. One would see less obedience, while pride and presumption would abound. The commerce of letters would absolutely banish that of goods, which fills states with riches, it would ruin agriculture, the true wet nurse of the people, and it would quickly empty the breeding ground of soldiers, who grow better in the rough soil of ignorance than in the purity of the sciences. It would, finally, fill France with tricksters more prone to ruin families and to disturb the public peace than to do any good for states.

If letters were squandered on all sorts of minds, one would see more people capable of creating doubt than of resolving it, and many would be more prone to opposing truth than to defending it. It is for this reason that politicians want more masters of the mechanical arts than teachers of the liberal ones in a well-ordered state. I have often seen, for the same reason, Cardinal du Perron campaign strongly for the elimination of some of the colleges in this kingdom. He wanted to have four or five eminent ones established in Paris and two in each major city in the provinces. He added, to all the considerations that I have made, that it was impossible to find enough people in any age to fill a multitude of colleges, whereas if one settled for a small number, one could fill them with worthy individuals, who would keep the pure fire burning in the temple and who would transmit the sciences in their perfection without interruption.[173]

It seems to me, when I consider the great number of people who profess to teach letters and the multitude of children who are instructed, that I see an infinite number of sick people who, since they are desperate for some pure and clear water in order to get well, are overpowered by such a strong thirst that they drink indiscriminately whatever is handed to them, which is most often impure and in poisoned glasses, thus only increasing their thirst and their sickness.

Finally, from this great number of colleges, indiscriminately established everywhere, two evils occur. One, which I have just indicated, from the modest capacity of those who are constrained to teach, since it is not possible to find enough eminent individuals to fill the chairs, the other from the lack of aptitude for letters by those whose parents make them study without considering the inclination of their minds because of the convenience they find in

---

[173] Jacques Davy du Perron (1556–1618), raised as a Huguenot and very learned, converted to Catholicism and helped to convert Henry IV, who as king nominated him to be a cardinal, which he became in 1614. He was a patron of a number of bishops, including Richelieu, especially during the Estates-General of 1614.

it, from which it comes that almost all those who study remain with a mere smattering of letters, some from lack of capacity, others from bad instruction.

Although this evil is very great, the remedy is easy, since all that is needed is to reduce all of the colleges in the smaller cities to three or four small classes sufficient to draw the youth out of abject ignorance, even disturbing to those who devote their lives to arms or to trade.

By this means, before children are destined to any status, two or three years will disclose the bent of their minds, after which the good ones, who will be sent to the big cities, will be all the more successful because of their aptitude for letters and because their instruction will be in better hands.

Having thus seen to this evil, much greater than it seems, it is still necessary to protect oneself from another, into which France would doubtless fall if all its existing colleges were in the same hands.

The universities claim that they will be extremely wronged if they are not left with the exclusive right to teach the youth.

The Jesuits, on the other hand, might not be unhappy perhaps to be the only ones employed in this function.

Reason, which must decide all sorts of disputes, cannot permit molesting an old possessor about what he is entitled to possess, and also the public interest cannot allow a body, commendable not only for its piety but also as celebrated for its doctrine as that of the Jesuits, to be deprived of a function that it can perform with great utility for the public.

If the universities were the only ones to teach, it is to be feared that they would eventually return to their former pride, which would in the future be as harmful as it has been in the past.

If, on the other hand, the Jesuits had no competition in the instruction of the youth, not only might one fear the same drawback, but one might have just cause to fear many others.

A company that conducts itself, more than any other has ever done, by the laws of prudence and that gives itself to God without depriving itself of the knowledge of the things of this world lives in such harmony that it seems as if a single mind animates its body; a company that is submitted by a vow of blind obedience to a perpetual chief must not, following the laws of good policy, have much authority in a state where any powerful community must be feared. If it is true, and it is very certain, that one is naturally pleased to advance the ones from whom one has received the first instructions and that parents always have a particular affection for those who have performed these duties for their children, it is also true that one should never commit the entire education of young people to the Jesuits without exposing oneself to giving them a power all the more suspect in states where all the posts and ranks of importance would be filled with their ideas and where those who had at an early point obtained an ascendancy over minds often retain it for a lifetime.

If one adds that the administration of the sacrament of penitence gives this company a second authority over all sorts of persons, which is no less powerful than the first, if one considers that in these two ways they penetrate into the most secret movements of hearts and of families, it will be impossible not to conclude that they must not be left alone in the ministry in question.

These reasons have been so powerful that we have not seen any state up to the present that has wanted to leave the empire of letters and the entire instruction of their youth to this company alone.

If this society, good and simple in itself, aroused the suspicions of the Archduke Albert, one of the most pious princes of the house of Austria, who only acted on the orders of the council of Spain, yet did not fear to exclude it from certain universities where it was established in Flanders and to oppose the new institutions that it wanted to create throughout Flanders, if it gave certain republics grounds to keep their domination away entirely, albeit too strictly, the least one can do in this kingdom is to restrain it somewhat, seeing that it is under a perpetual and foreign chief and, moreover, subject and always dependent on princes who seem to have no greater ambition than the humiliation and ruin of this crown.[174]

Just as in matters of faith all the Catholic states in the world have only one doctrine in what concerns it, there are often many others that have basic maxims that make them need theologians who can on certain occasions defend opinions that have always been received and have been preserved by a transmission without interruption, who are independent of any suspect power, and who have no dependence that deprives them of their liberty in things that the faith has left up to everybody.

History teaches us that the order of Saint Benedict was formerly so absolutely master of the schools that there was no teaching anywhere else and that it declined so absolutely in science and piety all together in the tenth century of the Church that it was called "miserable" as a result. It also teaches us that the Dominicans subsequently had the same advantage that these good fathers had been the first to possess and that time deprived them of it, like the others, to the great detriment of the Church, which then found herself infected with all sorts of heresies. It also teaches us in the same way that letters are like birds of passage, which never remain in the same country, and thusly political prudence demands that one try to prevent this drawback, which, since it has happened twice, must reasonably be feared a third time and apparently will

---

[174] Albert (1559–1621), governor with his wife, Isabella, of the Spanish Low Countries between 1598 and 1621, who in 1609 managed to bring about the Twelve Years' Truce with the rebellious northern provinces and strengthen the Spanish hold over the southern, while letting up a bit on the persecution of Protestants in the South.

be avoided if this company has its competitors in the profession of letters. All parties are dangerous in matters of doctrine, and nothing is so easy as to form a new one under the pretext of piety, when a company finds itself obliged to do so in order to subsist.

The history of Pope Benedict XI, against whom the Cordeliers, annoyed by the perfection of poverty, which was the source of revenue to Saint Francis, got aroused to the point that they made open war upon him not only in their books but also with the armies of the Emperor, who oversaw the rise of an antipope to the great harm of the Church, is so striking an example that it is not necessary to say more.[175]

The more loyal a company is to its leader, the more it is to be feared, particularly by those whom he does not favor.

Prudence obliges not only keeping anyone from disturbing the state but also that no one have the power to do it, because power often gives birth to the will.

Also, since the weakness of our human condition requires a counterweight in all things, and since this is the foundation of justice, it is more reasonable that the universities and the Jesuits teach as they like, that competition sharpens their virtue, and that the sciences will be all the more secure in the state since they are consigned into the hands of two guardians, so that if one loses this sacred trust, it will be found elsewhere.

ELEVENTH SECTION

Which proposes the means of controlling the abuses that are committed for graduates in obtaining benefices

Since it is to be feared that all sorts of minds are attracted to letters, and it is desirable that only the best ones succeed, Your Majesty could do nothing more useful for this end than to impede the abuses that are committed in the distribution of benefices, which must be given to those who are worthiest as a reward for their labors.

One would have to be the enemy of letters and virtue to raise any doubt about this right.

---

[175] Not Benedict XI (1303–1304) but John XXII (1316–1334), Avignon pope who condemned the Conventional Franciscans (Cordeliers), whom the Holy Roman Emperor Louis of Bavaria protected. In 1328, while in Italy, he contrived the election of the antipope Nicolas V. This is one case in which Voltaire did manage to catch Richelieu in an error of fact.

The Council of Basel ordered that one-third of all benefices should be conferred upon masters of arts, degree holders, and doctors of medicine, canon law, and theology who had attended a recognized university for a given period. By the Concordat made between Leo X and Francis I, it was decided that the graduates would enjoy the vacant benefices for one-third of each year, namely, the months of January, April, July, and October[176]

The Council of Basel and the concordat made between Leo X and Francis I subsequent to the Lateran Council establish it too clearly to think about it, and it would be necessary to be too perverse and unreasonable not to want to correct such great abuses as the fraudulent interchanges, fake resignations, the guiles of the conferrer, the authority of the holders of indults who are more powerful than the graduates, and by the industriousness of those who owe their degrees only to their purse, this privilege, far from being the price of virtue, is now only the result of the guile and skullduggery of those who are as ignorant of letters as they are learned in trickery.

The real remedy for this evil, in conformity with the Holy Canons, is for doctors and holders of degrees in theology to be preferred to those who hold the same degrees in other faculties, for theologians who hold the same degree, those who have been preaching the Word of God or theology, to be placed before the others, for the doctors and holders of degrees in law to have the same advantage over simple masters of arts, and that, among the last, those who have been teaching the longest be preferred, for no one to receive his master of arts and degree in civil or canon law except from the universities where he has studied, and for no one to be given a master's degree unless they have completed their entire course in philosophy, nor any degree in civil or canon law unless they have studied three full years in law schools and have defended their theses at the required times.

If this order is carefully observed, one will certainly see the value of letters prized and ignorance no longer hidden under their cloak.

If, subsequently, Your Majesty frees those who have become famous through letters from the persecution of the concessionaries, you will make it so the many will redouble their labors in order to receive the praise that they deserve.

---

[176] An extremely inaccurate reference to a portion of Session 23 of the Council of Basel, which took place on March 26, 1436, and concerned itself exclusively with the number and qualifications of cardinals. It would appear, therefore, that this annotation was inserted by memory. The refence to the Concordat of Bologna is to Rubric III "*Des Collations*," which, however, reserves one-third of the benefices to the graduates, not one-third of each year. Giovanni de' Medici (1475–1521), Pope Leo X from 1513.

TWELFTH SECTION

On the right of indult

Since the right of indult draws its origin and its force from a lost bull of Pope Eugene addressed to Charles VIII, whoever wants to examine it thoroughly would find that its foundation is not too solid, because reason demands that things that are not verifiable and those that are not true be put in the same category.[177]

Well do I know that since Paul III wanted to please the presidents and other judges of the *parlement* of Paris who were opposing the verification of the concordats, he gave them power to appoint to both monastic and nonmonastic benefices. Well do I know that the Chancellor of France, as the

This bull was sent to King Francis I in the year 1538

non creditur referenti nisi constet de relato[179]

head of this company, received a similar privilege by this same bull. But if one considers that this bull claims to draw its authority from the one by his predecessor that is lost, this consideration has no force, since legal experts clearly teach that hearsay evidence cannot be trusted.[178]

The less certain the foundation of this privilege, the more unbearable it is.

Even though this right is personal, that is to say that it has only been given to the person of the officials specified by the bull of Paul III, it now passes on to the widow and heirs as private property. And even though this favor has only been granted to them for the legitimate use of their children or some of their friends or relatives worthy of the benefices to which they are appointed, those who obtain these benefits by virtue of these indults are often compelled, against all laws, human and divine, to resign them to whomever they please, abusing this privilege to the point that often those who do not wish to become accomplices to this crime can only avoid it by another, which makes them guilty of simony before God.

The weak foundation of this favor and how badly it is abused could give Your Majesty legitimate grounds to abolish it, which could be all the easier since all that would be needed for this end is to re-

Ipsa mutatio consuetudinis etiam quae adjuvant utilitate novitas perturbat[180]

fuse in the future to all holders of indults your letters of nomination, without which they cannot lay claim to any benefice. But since experience demonstrates that an existing evil is sometimes better than a troublesome innovation,

---

[177] Eugene IV (1383–1447), pope from 1431.

[178] Paul III (1468–1549), pope from 1532, convener of the Council of Trent.

[179] "If the author is not credible, neither is the repetition."

[180] "Whoever changes customs only raises new problems."

Your Majesty must be satisfied with issuing a new regulation that those who want to enjoy this favor cannot abuse it in the future as they have in the past.

If you keep the same official from nominating to many benefices, if you ensure that those presented for nomination cannot be appointed without your ordering that they pass a good and impartial examination.

If you order that their letters of nomination carry in precise terms that the benefices to which they are nominated will really be for them and that they cannot be compelled to resign them to anyone whatsoever and that if it is discovered that they have lent their name as accomplices, aside from not ever being eligible for a benefice again, they may be punished for their crime.

If, subsequently, you prohibit the transmission of this personal right to heirs, the enforcement of this regulation will ensure that your officials will not be deprived of the favor that your predecessors have obtained for them, and learned men will thrive during your reign from being liberated from such a vexation.

One could also not permit the officials who have nominated someone by an indult to substitute another in his place if he should die before taking office.

Chapter III

On the nobility

FIRST SECTION

Which proposes various means of advancing the nobility so that it can subsist with dignity

After having indicated what I consider to be absolutely necessary for the reestablishment of the first order of the kingdom, I pass to the second and say that it is necessary to consider the nobility as one of the principal nerves of the state, capable of contributing much to its conservation and to its reestablishment.

It has been for some time so overwhelmed by the great number of officials that the misfortunes of the age have raised to harm it that it has great need of being sustained against the schemes of such people. The opulence and the pride of the ones overwhelm the needs of the others, who are rich only in courage, which leads them to employ their life willingly for the state, from which the officials draw the substance.

Just as it is necessary to sustain them against those who oppress them, it is necessary to take particular care that they do not treat those who are below them as they are treated by the officials.

It is a fairly ordinary deficiency of those who are born into this order to use violence against the people, to whom God seems to have given arms for earning their livelihood rather than for defending it.

It is very important to stop the spread of such disorders through continual severity, so that your weak subjects, even though they are unarmed, have as much security under the shadow of your laws as those who have weapons in their hands.

Since the nobility has shown in the war happily concluded by the peace that it has inherited the virtue of its ancestors, which gave Caesar grounds to praise them to the sky, it has to be disciplined so that it can acquire its original reputation once again and preserve it and so that the state will be well served.[181]

---

[181] The words "Il est besoin de la discipliner" must have been in the original manuscript in order for this paragraph to make sense; though they do not appear in our Text A they do appear in all our copies of Text B.

Since those who are harmful to the state are not useful to it, it is certain that the nobility that does not serve it in war is not only useless but burdensome to the state and can, in this case, be compared to a body that supports paralyzed arms like a weight, which is a burden upon it instead of a relief.

Just as gentlemen deserve to be well treated when they behave well, it is necessary to be severe with them if they fail to fulfill the obligations of their birth, and I do not hesitate to say that those who degenerate from the virtues of their ancestors and fail to serve the crown with their life and limb, as the laws of the state require, deserve to be deprived of their birthright and reduced to bearing a part of the load of the people. Since their honor should be dearer to them than their life, it would be a lot better to punish them by depriving them of one than of the other.[182]

Taking the life of persons who expose it every day for the simple illusion of their honor means a lot less to them than taking their honor and leaving them with their life, which is condemning them to a perpetual torment.

If everything must be done to maintain the nobility in the true virtue of their fathers, nothing must be forgotten to preserve it in the possession of its wealth.

Just as it is impossible to find a remedy for every evil, it is very difficult to put forward a general way to achieve the ends that I propose. The various marriages that are made by every family in this kingdom, whereas in other countries often only the eldest son gets married, are a true cause for the rapid ruin of the most powerful houses. But if this custom impoverishes individual families, it strengthens the state, whose force lies in the multiplicity of strong arms, so that instead of complaining about it, it is necessary to rejoice in it and, instead of changing it, merely try to give those children the means of subsisting with the purity of heart that they draw from their birth. It is necessary, for this end, to distinguish the nobility that is at court from the one that remains in the countryside.

The one that is at the court will be notably relieved if the unbearable expense for the luxuries which have been introduced there little by little is reduced, since it is certain that such a regulation will be as useful to them as all the pensions that they receive.

As to the one that is in the countryside, even though it does not receive much relief from this order because it is too poor to be so lavish, it does not fail to feel the effect of this remedy, which is so necessary to the state that it cannot avoid its ruin without it.

If Your Majesty adds to whatever regulation it will please you to apply to this disorder the establishment in the provinces of a company of men-at-arms

---

[182] For more evidence of Richelieu's mixed feelings toward the nobility, see the Second Part, Chapter IX, Fourth Section.

and a similar number of light cavalry in the provinces paid on conditions to be specified later, you will provide considerable means of subsistence to the nobility that is not so well-off.

If, subsequently, you suppress the sale of governorships of the kingdom and of all military positions for which this order already pays enough with its blood.[183]

If you practice the same thing in regard to the posts in your household, instead of all sorts of people being admitted by the simple use of their purse, entry will be closed in the future to all those who do not have the good fortune to be of noble birth. Your Majesty will choose those with this advantage on the basis of their merit, and the entire nobility will profit from such a good regulation.

Instead of gentlemen being unable to rise to posts and dignities without ruining themselves, in the future their loyalty will be all the more assured since the more they are favored, the less they will owe it to their purse and to that of their creditors, who never allow them to forget how much they owe them for rising in this way.

If, moreover, your kindness extends to favoring their children, who will be worthy of it by the requisite knowledge and piety, with some of the benefices you have at your disposal, this order will be all the more grateful to you since, by relieving it of a part of the load that overwhelms them, you truly give them the means of maintaining their houses, since the sustenance and preservation of the best often depends on those who, by embracing the ecclesiastical profession, often consider their nephews as their children and find no greater joy than in raising some of them with enough learning and virtue so that they can be invested with some of their benefices.

Many more things could be put forward for the relief of the nobility. But I will perish the thought after having considered that even though it would be very easy to write about them, it would be very difficult and perhaps impossible to put them into practice.

SECOND SECTION

Which treats of the manners of stopping the spread of duels

There have been so many edicts against duels without having had any success up to now that it is difficult to find any sure means of stopping the course of this craze.

---

[183] Note that at this point, Richelieu is contemplating the elimination of the sale of offices, a position that he changes in the next chapter.

The French have such disdain for their lives that we have learned from experience that the most severe penalties have not always been the best for stopping their frenzy. They have often felt that there was all the more glory in violating the edicts, since this extravagance would point out that their honor was worth much more to them than their life and that they were much more willing to lose the conveniences of this world than to die out of grace with God, without which they would be miserable in the next. The fear of losing their posts, their possessions, and their liberty has had more effect on their minds than that of losing their life. I have done everything I can to find some remedy that might cure this dangerous evil.

I have often held consultations to discover, since it is permissible for the king to allow two individuals to fight in order to avoid a battle, he might not also approve of some combats in order to avoid the many duels that occur every day. I was figuring that by this means one could very likely protect France from this frenzy that causes it so much harm, seeing as by giving those who had some justification the hope of obtaining permission to fight, each one would willingly submit to judges deputized to investigate their case, which would apparently impede the misfortune of duels, since there are few quarrels that cannot be settled peacefully.

I added, in keeping with this thought, that formerly many duels had been permitted in this kingdom, and this had also been practiced in other states.

I felt that one could by this means abolish the barbaric custom by which any man who feels offended can procure his own justice and find his satisfaction in the blood of his enemy. But after having read and reread everything that the best authors say on this matter and reflected at length upon such an important subject, I have found, with the advice of the least delicate and most resolute theologians of our time, that since kings are established to preserve their subjects and not to lose them, they cannot expose their lives without some public utility or particular necessity, so that they could not permit individual combats exposing the innocent to suffering the penalty of the guilty, seeing that since God is not always obliged to render reason victorious, the appeal to arms is uncertain, and even though some permissions have been granted in various states and even with the consent of some particular churches, they have been abusive, which appears quite evident since the universal Church has finally prohibited them and condemned them under very great penalties. I have recognized that there was a great difference between having two individuals fight in order to avoid a battle and end a war and having them fight in order to avoid duels.

The first is permitted because nature teaches us that a part must expose itself for the whole, and reason demands that the particular must expose itself for the general, because aside from this expedient having always been practiced, examples of it are found in the Holy Scriptures, and its effect is safe and sound, in that whatever the outcome of such a duel may be, it saves the life of a great numbers of persons who can serve the public on other occasions.

But it is not the same for the second, which is illicit by its nature in that instead of certainly saving the general by taking a chance for some individual and thus protecting against a greater evil by a lesser one, it exposes individuals for no good reason.

This means is even less acceptable because instead of stopping the spread of duels, it is capable of augmenting their popularity in that the nobility is so blind that many feel that asking to fight in this way would seem like looking for an excuse not to fight and would make it a point of taking a shortcut to demanding reason for their insult just to give proof of their courage.

In 1609 the late king wanted to try this means with all the circumstances that could enforce it. He deprived of their possessions, their posts, and their life those who fought without having obtained permission. But this was useless, and this is what has obliged Your Majesty, after having had the same experience at the beginning of his reign, to have recourse by his edict of the month of March 1626 to another remedy, which has been all the more effective in that since the penalties are moderate, they are more striking to those who care less about their life than about their possessions and their liberty.[184]

Now, because the best laws in the world are useless if one does not enforce them inviolably, and because those who fall into this kind of fault often use so many guiles in order to suppress the evidence that it is almost always impossible to convict them, I do not hesitate to tell Your Majesty that it is not enough to punish challenges and duels as proved by the letter of your edicts, but when there is notoriety without proof, you must have the delinquents arrested and imprison them at their own expense for more or less time according to the circumstances of their offense. Otherwise, the ordinary negligence of your prosecutors general in investigating, the leniency of your *parlements*, and the corruption of the age, which is such that everyone feels as honored to help those who have fought to disguise their crime as a true gentleman would be ashamed to conceal the theft of a thief, would render your edicts and your efforts useless.

It is in such a case that only extralegal action can have your laws and your ordinances observed. This is one of those occasions when your authority must go beyond formalities in order to maintain order and discipline, without

---

[184] Edict of February 1626, which mandated the death penalty for duels in which one of the participants died or the seconds also dueled. It was registered in *parlement* on March 24, 1626, but did little to discourage the practice until Richelieu began enforcing it more vigorously, as he did the following year. See note 15 above.

which a state cannot subsist, and give your officials the means to punish according to the formalities, since it is very likely that the cause and the proof of a crime will be found more easily when the guilty are under arrest than if they are entirely free to suppress the evidence.

If, subsequently, Your Majesty orders that encounters will be considered as duels and will be punished as such until those who will have engaged in them will have turned themselves in voluntarily as prisoners and are acquitted by verdict, you will do everything that can probably be done to stop the spread of this frenzy, and your care to preserve the lives of your nobility will make you the master of their hearts and will oblige them to be so loyal that they will pay with interest in whatever employments they will be favored.

Chapter IV

On the Third Order of the Kingdom

To treat of the third order of the kingdom methodically and to see clearly what is necessary in order to support it in the state that it should be, I shall divide it into three parts:

The first shall contain the body of the officers of justice.
The second that of those who handle the finances.
The third, the people, who carry almost all the burden of the state.

FIRST SECTION

Which touches in general on the disorders of justice and examines particularly if the suppression of the sale and heredity of offices would be a good remedy to such evils

It is much easier to recognize the deficiencies of justice than to prescribe the remedies. There is no one who does not see that those who are instituted to administer it equitably all around have tipped the scales so far to one side to their own advantage that there is no more counterweight.

The disorders of justice have reached such a point that they cannot continue. I would enter into the details of these disorders and into the remedies that can be applied to them if my knowledge both of the present holder of the highest post in the judiciary and of his plan to purify it as much as the corruption of mankind will allow did not oblige me to be satisfied with only proposing certain general remedies to Your Majesty in order to stop the spread of the principal disorders.[185]

In the opinion of most people the best one consists of suppressing the sale and heredity of offices and of giving them free of charge to persons of recognized competence and integrity so that their merit cannot even be denied by the envious.

---

[185] Pierre Séguier (1588–1672), chancellor of France from 1635. He had just suppressed the peasant revolt in Normandy.

But since this is not something that may be done at this time, and it will be difficult to put this expedient into practice at any other that there may be, it would be useless to propose the means to attain this end.

When one will want to undertake this plan, some will undoubtedly be found that cannot now be foreseen, and those that one could prescribe now would no longer be in season when one wanted to get to work. However, even though it is almost always dangerous to be in the minority, I cannot help but say boldly that in the present state of affairs and for the foreseeable future, it is better, to my way of thinking, to continue the sale and heredity of offices than to change this institution entirely.

There are so many drawbacks to be feared from such a change that even though elections to benefices are older and more canonical than nominations by kings, still the great abuses that cannot be kept from being committed in them make the use of nominations more bearable as being less subject to bad consequences.

Also, even though the suppression of the sale and heredity of offices is both reasonable and legal, since the inevitable abuses that would be committed if the distribution of posts that are dependent on the will of kings were consequently dependent on the favor and on the guile of those who happened to be the most influential at the time, this renders the fashion in which they are now filled more tolerable than the one that has been utilized in the past because of the great drawback that has always been associated with them.

One would have to be blind not to realize the difference between these two options and not to wish for the suppression of the sale of offices with all one's heart, assuming that in this case the posts were distributed purely in consideration of virtue. But it is impossible at least not to realize that in such a case, the guiles of the court will prevail over reason and favor over merit.

Nothing gave the Duke de Guise more means of becoming powerful in the league against the king and his state than the great number of officials that his influence had introduced into the principal posts of the kingdom, and I have learned from the Duke de Sully that this consideration was the most powerful motive that brought the late king to the institution of the annual payment and that this great prince was thinking less about the revenue that he could draw from it than about his desire to protect himself from similar drawbacks, and even though the finances meant a lot to him, reason of state was more powerful on this occasion.[186]

---

[186] Henry I de Lorraine (1550–1588), Duke de Guise, leader of the Catholic League during the War of the Three Henrys. Maximilien de Béthune (1560–1641), Duke de Sully, Huguenot supporter of Henry of Navarre, later his finance minister. The *droit annuel*, or "annual payment," also known as the *paulette*, was a tax that permitted officeholders to sell offices that they had purchased or pass them on to their beneficiaries or heirs.

When instituting a new republic, one could not, without committing a crime, fail to prohibit the sale of offices, because in such a case reason demands that the most perfect laws that humanity can endure be instituted. But prudence does not permit doing the same in an old monarchy, whose imperfections have become a habit and whose disorder has become a useful part of the order in the state.

It is necessary, in this case, to succumb to one's weakness and prefer a moderate rule to a more austere one, which might not be so appropriate because it would shake things up too much.

Well do I know the old saying that whoever buys justice wholesale can sell it retail. But it is still true that an official who puts the greatest part of his wealth into a post will think twice before losing all his net worth and that in such a case the price of the offices is no small warranty of the loyalty of the officials.

Complaints against the sale of offices have been common in every period of the monarchy. But even though they have always been acknowledged as reasonable in themselves, the disorders that caused them are still tolerated on the assumption that we are not up to such high standards.

It would be necessary to be ignorant of history not to know that some of its writers do not even spare Saint Louis and have blamed his reign because from his time on posts were not given free of charge, and they condemn his successors because under them the sale of offices was already so public that it was leased out, and they make the memory of the great king Francis odious because he was the first who was in such great need that he made a regular business out of it, which has continued up to the present.

I admit that it is a great misfortune for this prince to be the author of these bad institutions. But perhaps he would not be so blamable if one understood the reasons that constrained him to do it.

His realization that individuals sold his favors without his knowledge and the importance of the great affairs with which he was overwhelmed made him believe that there was no better or quicker way to extract some wealth voluntarily from his subjects than to give them some honor in return for money.

The late king, assisted by a very good council in a profound peace and a reign exempt from necessity, added the institution of an annual payment to the sale of offices. It is to be presumed that he did not do it without great consideration and without having foreseen, as much as human prudence may permit, the consequences and the results, and it is a sure thing that what is done by princes, whose conduct has been judicious, cannot reasonably be changed if experience does not demonstrate its harm and if it is not clearly seen that one can do better.

Disorders that have been instituted because of public necessities and have entrenched themselves for reasons of state can only be remedied with time. It is necessary to bring minds around mildly without passing from one extreme to another.

An architect who is skillful enough to repair an old building and reduces it to better proportions without tearing it down merits more praise than one who completely demolishes it and constructs a brand-new edifice.

It would be difficult to change the established order for disposing of offices without disheartening those who possess them, in which case it is to be feared that instead of their having in the past been of great use in holding the people to their duty, they would in the future contribute more than anything else to corrupting them. It is sometimes prudent to dilute medicines in order to make them more effective, and the orders that are most reasonable are not always the best, because they are sometimes not proportionate to the bent of those who must execute them.

Instead of the suppression of the sale of offices and heredity opening the door to virtue, it would open it to solicitations and to factions and would fill the posts with low-born officials, often better loaded with Latin than with wealth, from which many drawbacks would ensue. If one could enter into these posts without money, commerce would be abandoned by many people who would be dazzled by the splendor and dignity of these offices and rush to their ruin instead of enriching their families by trade.

Besides, it is common knowledge that the weakness of our age is such that people prefer to let themselves go wild rather than acting reasonably and that instead of being guided by justice, they are carried away by their furor.

The experience of the past must make us fear the future, not only because the past has always pointed out that the most influential often win their case over the virtuous, but because the prince and his close confidants can only evaluate people by the judgment of some third party, often they cannot keep from taking a shadow for a body.

Low birth rarely produces the qualities necessary to magistrates, and it is certain that the virtue of a person from a good family has something more noble than what is found in a person of lowly extraction. The minds of such people are ordinarily difficult to mold, and many are so touchy that they are not only unpleasant but harmful.

The first are to the second like trees that, since they are planted in good soil, bear better fruit than those that are not.

And thusly, far from needing to condemn the sale of offices because it excludes many persons of low estate from posts and offices, on the contrary this is one of the things that makes it more tolerable.

Wealth is a great ornament for dignities, which are so elevated by external brilliance that one can boldly say that between two persons of equal merit, the one who is better off is preferable to the other, since it is certain that a poor magistrate must have a powerful soul not to be tempted by the consideration of his own interests. Also, experience teaches us that the rich are less subject to being bribed than others and that poverty compels an official to be more mindful of his pocket money.

It will be said, perhaps, that if these drawbacks oblige to endure the sale of offices, at least it is true that the annual payment should be suppressed because it makes the offices overpriced and keeps persons of virtue from even attaining them with their money.

The late king foresaw this evil and had some precautions inserted in his edict on this subject capable of preventing this by exempting from the annual payment the posts of first presidents, prosecutors, and attorneys general and, moreover, reserving to himself the offices that are attached to them whenever they should fall vacant by previously paying to the heirs of their possessors the price of their estimated value.

These precautions proved as harmful as they were necessary, and, to be frank, the evils that the annual payment causes presently in the state do not proceed as much from its nature as they do from the imprudence with which the amendments that this great prince had added have been removed. If the edict had remained in its original purity, the offices would never have reached the exorbitant price at which they sell now. The changes that have been made have been as harmful as they would have been innocent if it had been left as it was, and, thusly, it is more necessary to correct the abuse than to change the institution.

The repeal of the annual payment would oblige the old officers to retire from their posts just when their experience and maturity should make them more capable of serving the public. However, it is appropriate for there to be both old and young officers, because just as the prudence of the first can be very useful in guiding the others, the vigor of the young is necessary to wake up and stimulate the old men.

If my goal in this work were to gain the approval of the people rather than to merit their goodwill by making myself useful to the state, I would maintain that it is necessary to suppress the sale of offices and the annual payment altogether. Everyone is so convinced that these are two sources of the disorders in the kingdom that public opinion would celebrate me without considering whether or not I merited it.

But since I know that whoever tries to acquire a reputation by reforms that are more in conformity with the rigor of the laws than they are proportionate with the forces of the state is only looking out for his own interest and has no excuse for such vanity, this is not only blameworthy but criminal, and in this case his ill-conceived cares do as much harm to the public as someone else's negligence and malice.

I would be very wary about doing this. There are too many drawbacks in the repeal of these two edicts to venture to conclude that it is appropriate to do it.

If they open the door to ignorance and to vice, as it is ordinarily supposed, I do not hesitate to say that they should not be tolerated. But when I consider that if persons without the proper qualifications are admitted into these offices, this is the fault of the prosecutors general who investigate their background and morals and of the companies that, as judges of their capacity and virtue, do not reject them when they do not have the required qualifications, so I can only say that the remedy for this evil consists more in observing the ordinances than in abolishing the sale of offices and the annual payments, which are not its cause.

It will be said, perhaps, that if judicial offices were not sold, justice might be offered for free. But as long as the costs are limited, this is not so bad.[187]

Well do I know that, strictly speaking, the only cost for the administration of justice is paid by the law-abiding and that obliging those who go to court to pay money compels them to pay a second time for what they have already paid for by their innocence. This custom is nevertheless so well entrenched that even though specie is by nature spicy, no one would venture to complain about what is spent at the courthouse, and whoever proposed to abolish it would expose himself to being laughed at.[188]

There are some abuses that it is necessary to endure from fear of falling into worse ones. Other ages and occasions will open our eyes to those that could not be tried in this one without shocking the state.

All the above reasons and many others duly considered, even though the sale and the heredity of posts is not canonical, even though it is to be wished that merit had always been the only price of posts and virtue the only qualification that could transmit their succession to the heirs of the officials, instead of concluding in favor of changing these two arrangements, the present constitution of the state obliges me to say three definitive things:

The first is that, if the sale of offices were taken away, the disorder that would come from the solicitations and machinations by which the posts would be filled would be greater than what arises from the liberty of buying and selling them.

The second, that if heredity alone were abolished, aside from the reduction that this would bring about every day in the price of the offices that would fall vacant, this would make the returns from the Incidental Investments almost completely disappear, and by this means a dirty trade is introduced that

---

[187] Richelieu wants to discourage people from going to court.

[188] Richelieu is making a pun here, since *épices*, or "spices," were bribes, court costs, or a combination of the two.

would give occasion for a great many people of little merit to partake in the favors that the king would intend for the officials, and we would go back to the evil from which the late king had wanted to protect the state when, by the establishment of the *paulette*, he prevented the great nobles in the kingdom from acquiring at his expense all sorts of dependents who would serve them at any given time to do harm to the public interest.[189]

The third is that, since men are not always sufficiently virtuous to prefer merit to favor, it is better to leave the sale of offices and the annual payment than to abolish these two institutions, difficult to eliminate all at once without disrupting the state.

But I add that it is absolutely necessary to lower the price of offices, which has risen to such a point that it is impossible to endure. If any advice is worthwhile, this is it, for its advantage is evident and its execution is very easy because it requires nothing more than to return to the edict on the annual payment as it was first instituted.

In this case, if the offices are reduced to a reasonable price, which will not exceed one-half of what the aberration of the mind has now brought it to, and if the king is free to pay it to the heirs in order to dispose of new posts as he wishes, far from any damage being done to the state, I venture to repeat that it will receive many advantages from it.

Besides, one can reduce things to this point without giving the interested parties anything to complain about, since it is easy to reimburse them for the evil that they have done to themselves by various means that I will not now specify, because if they were revealed, they would lose their force when one wanted to put them into practice.

SECOND SECTION

Which proposes the general means that can be practiced to stop the spread of the disorders of justice

Next, before finishing this chapter, it only remains for me to say what I have already said to Your Majesty on the subject of the 1st order of your kingdom.

If you show that you value of the officials of justice whose reputation is untarnished, if you do not look kindly upon those who are without merit and have only reached the magistracy by means of their money, if you deprive entirely of your favor and punish those who are derelict in their duty and sell justice to the detriment of your subjects, you will do everything

---

[189] "Incidental Investments" is the best translation I can come up with for *parties casuelles*, which was the section of the treasury that collected the "annual payment," or *paulette*.

that can usefully be done for the reform of this body, which, along with the ecclesiastical order, depends more on those who administer it than on laws and regulations, which are useless if those who are in charge of executing them do not have the will to do it.

Even if the laws were deficient, if the officials are respectable people, their integrity would be capable of making up for the fault, and no matter how good they may be, they would be entirely fruitless if the magistrates neglect to execute them, all the more if they conspire to prevent their use depending on their passion and their disorders, since it is difficult to be wise and young all together. I cannot avoid remarking, subsequently to what I have said, that in order to reform justice, it is of no small importance to enforce the ordinances on the subject of the age at which the officials can be appointed.

One could not, in my opinion, be more exact or, consequently, more severe toward the prosecutors general who fail in their obligation to watch out that the candidates do not mislead the judges on this subject or evade, by hook or by crook, the good intentions of the prince.

Aside from that, by this salutary strictness one would protect oneself from the evil of immaturity, which is not small, or that of ignorance, which is the source of many others, since the officials would be unable to rush, as they do at present, to their admission and would study harder instead of being idle, which hardly ever happens until after they get what they want.

I must not omit in this regard that it would even be absolutely desirable to curtail the practice of certain professors who train the young like parrots by teaching them to repeat what they do not understand and who only render them capable of deceiving the public by deceiving themselves.

Such people are similar to fencing masters, who are only good for instructing men on how to ruin themselves and keep them from learning the true exercises of soldiers, which are only learned the hard way in the army.

Getting rid of the ones and the others would be of no little use. But since this is easier said than done, I prefer here to condemn the fathers who allow their children to be instructed in this manner and to induce them not to commit such a crime against their own flesh and blood rather than to beg Your Majesty to enact new laws on this subject, which would no sooner be promulgated than a thousand ways would be found to circumvent them.

Twenty years of continual experience that I have acquired in the administration of public affairs oblige me to note that even though it would be desirable that the permanent companies, which are absolutely established to dispense justice to all and to prevent and regulate all the disorders in this kingdom, would perform their duty so well that it would not be necessary to have recourse to extraordinary courts in order to do the same thing, it is nevertheless so difficult to hope for the best on this subject that I dare to say that in order to keep this great state in the law and order without which it cannot flourish, one could do nothing more appropriate than to send chambers of justice into the provinces from time to time, composed of councillors of state and masters of requests carefully selected to avoid the snares of the *parlements*, who create difficulties about everything, so that this body can hear the complaints that may be made against all sorts of persons without exception of their rank and see to it.[190]

Well do I know that the sovereign courts would not look kindly on such an institution. But since it is impossible for them not to recognize that a sovereign is not obliged to allow them to be negligent and that reason demands that he compensate for their deficiency, I do not hesitate to say that it is better on such an occasion to acquire their esteem by his keeping to his obligation than to conserve their good will by neglecting the public interest.

Now, because it is impossible to send such companies to all the provinces at the same time and one of this nature, composed of the same or different officials, will suffice for all of France, I think it will be very useful to send well-chosen councillors of state and masters of requests often to the provinces not only to perform the function of intendant of justice in the capital cities, which might do more for their vanity than for the public good, but to go everywhere in the provinces to investigate the conduct of the officials of justice and of the finances, see if the taxes are raised according to the ordinances and if the receivers are not committing any injustice by mistreating the people, see how they are carrying out their tasks, learn how the nobility is behaving, and stop the spread of all sorts of disorders and especially the violence of those who, since they are rich and powerful, oppress the weak and the poor subjects of the king.

THIRD SECTION

Which indicates how important it is to keep the officers of justice from infringing on the authority of the King

After having indicated what must be practiced and how easy it would be to make the officials of justice what they must be in regard to private individuals, I could not abstain, without committing a crime, from proposing what it is necessary to do to keep a body as powerful as this from being harmful to

---

[190] This statement may appear puzzling, given that Richelieu only reentered the council of Louis XIII in 1624 and certainly could not have made it two years after his death. However, he is counting his return to public life from 1620, when he brought about the reconciliation of the king with his mother, Marie de Medici.

the state as a whole. It seems as if there is much to say on such a subject, but three words will be enough if I put forward that it is only necessary to limit the officials of justice to rendering it to the subjects of the king, which is the only end of their institution.

The wisest of your predecessors have taken this to heart, and they have not regretted it. Your Majesty has followed their example for as long as I have had the honor of serving under you, and, indeed, this is so important that if one loosened the reins of these powerful companies, they could never again be kept within the limits of their duty.

If one were to follow the sentiments of those who are as ignorant in the practice of governing states as they presume to be learned in the theory of how to administer them, and who are capable of neither making solid judgments on the conduct of public affairs nor issuing decrees about them that are beyond their bent, it would be impossible to keep the royal authority from being ruined.

As nothing that weakens royal authority must be allowed to these great companies, it is prudent to tolerate some of their other deficiencies.

It is necessary to sympathize with the deficiencies of a body that, since it has many heads, cannot always be of the same mind and, since it is being pulled every which way by its members, can often not even be brought to know what is good for them.

No one can approve of their behavior when they get carried away with some disorder, but while it is reasonable to condemn it, it is difficult to remedy it because in these great companies the bad are always more numerous than the good, and even if they were all wise, there would still be no assurance that the best sentiments would be in the majority since their decisions are inconsistent even if they have the best of intentions.

It is so usual for such companies to criticize the governments of states that this should not seem strange.

Every subordinate authority always looks with envy at its superior, and since it does not venture to dispute its power, it takes the liberty to disparage its conduct.

There is no mind so disciplined that it can stand even the slightest domination. This is what made one of the ancients say, with good reason, that since men are equal by nature, there are few who have any alternative but to endure the differences imposed by fortune, so that they criticize those who command them just to show that they are superior in merit.[191]

---

[191] A somewhat tortured reading of Aristotle, *Politics*, Bk. IV, Ch. 11.

FOURTH SECTION

On the officials of the finances

The financiers and the contractors as a group are very harmful to the state but nevertheless necessary.

This kind of officials is an evil that cannot be done without but that it is necessary to reduce to endurable proportions.

Their excessive number and the disorder that has crept up among them has reached the point that it cannot be endured, and it could not get any worse without ruining the state and without their floundering, giving grounds to confiscate their possessions simply with the knowledge of the excessive wealth that they have amassed in a short time and of the difference that will be proved between what they had when they entered into their post and what they will be found to possess.

Well do I know that such behavior may well be subject to great misunderstanding and that it could serve as a pretext for unjustified violence. Thus I raise this point only in passing so as to discuss a practice that is subject to a great deal of abuse. But I maintain that no one could justly complain if one acted with such circumspection as to punish only those who would have become too rich too quickly without touching the possessions of those who had enriched themselves by their thrift, which is one of the most innocent means that men have to get rich, or by donations coming from the pure favor of their master, which exempts them from any crime, or by pure compensation for their services, which is another that is not only irreproachable but as legitimate as can be since it is useful to individuals and good for the state, which will always be better served when those who serve it usefully are treated better.

It is absolutely necessary to remedy the disorder of the financiers. Otherwise they will finally cause the ruin of the kingdom, whose appearance is so transformed by their thefts that if their spread is not stopped, it would no longer be recognizable in a short time.

Gold and silver, in which they abound, give them the alliance of the best families in the kingdom, which become bastardized by this means and only produce motives as different from the generosity of their ancestors as they are different in their facial appearance. I can say, since I have seen it on many occasions, that their negligence or their malice has been extremely harmful to public affairs.

After having given a lot of thought about all the remedies to the evils that they have caused, I venture to say that there is no better one than to reduce them to the least possible number and commission respectable people who are fit for the offices to be with them on important occasions, rather than persons who think they are entitled to steal with impunity.

It would be easy in the midst of a profound peace to eliminate many of this kind of official and, by this means, deliver the state of those who perform no service while draining all of its substance in a short time.

Well do I know that it might be said that they are usually treated like leeches, who are often made with a grain of salt to give up all the blood that they have sucked, and, just as with sponges, one lets them soak because by squeezing them they give up all the liquid that they had previously absorbed. But this is a bad expedient in my opinion, and I feel that the contracts and the settlements that are sometimes made with the financiers are even worse than the evil since, when you come right down to it, this entitles them to steal again in the hope of another favor, and if one squeezes some money out of them in this manner, they recover not only the principal that they have given but also the interest at a much higher rate than the legal one, which leads me to conclude that aside from certain necessary officials, such as the treasurers of the treasury, a receiver general, or three Treasurers of France in each generality and as many selectmen[192] in the districts as cannot be dispensed with, it will be no small service to the state if, by reimbursing the individuals who have invested their money in good faith in order to advance themselves through such employments in the course of time, one eliminates all the rest. Without this remedy, whatever regulation one may make, it will be entirely impossible to conserve the money of the king, there being no cross to bear or punishment too great to keep the many officials of this kind from appropriating a part of what passes through their hands.

FIFTH SECTION

On the people

All politicians agree that if the people are too affluent, it would be impossible to contain them within the limits of their duty.

Their reasoning is that if they were not restrained by some necessity, since they have less knowledge than the other much more cultivated and better instructed orders of the state, they would not be likely to remain within the limits that are prescribed to them by reason and by the laws.

---

[192] I translate *élus*, officials chosen by intendants to collect the *taille* in their districts, as "selectmen."

Reason does not permit exempting them of all burdens because, in such a case, by losing the mark of their subjection, they would also lose the memory of their condition, and if they were free of all tributes, they would think that they were free of obedience.

It is necessary to consider them as mules accustomed to being burdened, who are more exhausted by rest than by work. But just as this work must be moderate and the burden on these animals must be proportionate to their force, so is it with the imposts in regard to the people. If they are not moderate, even if they are useful to the public, they would still be unjust.

Well do I know that when kings undertake public works, it true to say that the people earn from it through the payment of the *taille*. Likewise, it can be maintained that what kings take from the people returns to them and that they only lend it in order to get it back through the enjoyment of their peace and property, which cannot be preserved for them unless they contribute to the subsistence of the state.

I know, moreover, that some princes have lost their states and their subjects from not maintaining the forces necessary for their conservation from fear of burdening them and that some subjects have fallen under the servitude of their enemies from wanting too much liberty under their natural sovereign.

But there is a certain point which cannot be exceeded without injustice, since common sense teaches everyone that there must be a proportion between the load and the forces of those who support it.

This principle must be observed so religiously that just as a prince cannot be considered good if he draws more than is necessary from his subjects, the best are not always those who never raise only what is necessary.

Besides, just as when a man is wounded, the heart, which weakens him through the loss of the blood that he is shedding, draws help from the lower parts of the body only after most of the upper parts are exhausted, so also in the great necessities of the state, sovereigns must, as much as they can, make use of the wealth of the rich before bleeding the poor excessively.[193]

This is the best advice that Your Majesty can take, and it can be easily executed since in the future you can draw the principal sums for your state from your general farms, which concern the rich more than the poor, in that the latter spend less and contribute less to them.[194]

---

[193] Clearly Richelieu had not read William Harvey's *De motu cordis* (1628), which announced his discovery of the circulation of the blood, or René Descartes's *Discourse on Method* (1637), which popularized it.

[194] The *fermes générales*, or "general farms," was the section of the treasury that collected excise taxes.

Chapter V

Which considers the state in itself

FIRST SECTION

How important it is for each part
of the state to remain within its limits

After having spoken separately of the various orders out of which the state is composed, it only remains for me to say in general that just as an entity cannot subsist without the union of all its parts in their natural order and place, this great kingdom cannot flourish unless Your Majesty supports each of its parts in its order, with the Church holding the first, the nobility, the second, and the officials who march at the head of the people, the 3rd.

I say this boldly because it is as important as it is just to stop the spread of the schemes of certain officials who, whether because of their great wealth or the authority that comes from filling their great posts, are so full of themselves and presumptuous enough as to want to be in the 1st place instead of the 3rd, which is so contrary to reason and to the good of your service that it is absolutely necessary to stop the spread of such schemes, since otherwise France would no longer be what it has been and what it must be, but only a monstrous body, which could neither survive nor last as such.

Since it is very certain that the elements that have weight do not weigh anything when they are in their place, it is also a sure thing that none of the orders of your state will impose upon another when each one will be compelled to be in its natural place.[195]

And since neither fire nor air can hold a terrestrial body, because it is heavy and out of place, it is certain that neither the Church nor the nobility could endure the post of the officials if they were in their place.[196]

Since I am certain that Your Majesty will know how to retain everyone within his limits, I shall not elaborate further on this subject and shall proceed to two questions that I include in this chapter because they apply to each of the different orders of the state equally.

---

[195] Aristotle, *De caelo* IV. Part 3.
[196] More Aristotelian physics.

SECOND SECTION

Which examines if it is better to make the governorships triennial in this kingdom or to leave them perpetual as they have been up to now

Initially, everyone will feel that it is better to make them triennial. But when one has carefully compared the utility that might come from it with the drawbacks that are to be feared, perhaps it will be felt, as I have already noted, that even though the nomination to benefices is not as canonical as elections, still its use is so useful at this time for a great many reasons, and even if the elimination of the sale of offices may be desirable for various reasons, its use cannot help but be tolerated without falling into the many drawbacks discussed in their place. Also, one cannot make the governorships of provinces and strongholds triennial without exposing oneself to many more drawbacks that can be feared from the institution of perpetual governorships.

Well do I know that it can be said that whoever has the governorship for only 3 years would probably have no other thought than to leave it with a good reputation and act with such restraint that his administration would be preferred to that of his predecessor, and instead, if he is assured of it for life, his security of position gives him a lot of license.

But it is much more likely that whoever would not always be in a position would want to draw as much profit as quickly as possible during his lifetime and that it was to be feared, with the frivolity of our nation, that in order to avoid the end of their agreeable term of office, some sick minds would prefer to continue it by receiving as their masters those whom they should consider as their enemies.

If the practice of Spain, which often changes its governors, is put forward, I have already replied that there is nothing more dangerous than this example and add that just as there are fruits that are excellent in one country and poisonous in another, there are some institutions that are excellent in one state and pernicious in another.

It will be said, perhaps, to prevent the objections against using the procedure of Spain in this kingdom, that those who will come out of one position will not have any grounds for being dissatisfied since after their term of office they will be employed in others that might often be better. But such great difficulties will be found in the practice of such a procedure that it will be impossible to overcome them. Someone who will be proper to be governor of Picardy because he will be born in that province will not be good to be employed in Brittany, where he would have no connections and where the post that would be given to him would not give him the means to support himself.

Governorships in France are almost always so useless that if one does not give them to persons who want them more for the honor of it and for the convenience of the location than for any other consideration, few would be found who could support the expense, and there are not enough people in the provinces to make the changes that would be necessary if the employment were triennial.

Such movements are not only practicable but absolutely necessary for the great posts in Spain, such as the Viceroys of Naples, Sicily, and Sardinia, Governor of Milan, and other employments of similar importance, since they are so lucrative to those who possess them that they go from the abundance of one to the opulence of the other.

Places distant from the residence of their prince require a change of governors in posts as important as the ones I have just been discussing because a longer residence than three years could provide a means of forming enough connections to establish themselves permanently, seeing that the ambition of men is so great that as long as a mind is just a little bit unbridled, it is not difficult for it to think of changing its condition from that of subject to that of master.

But it is not the same in France, whose governorships are not so distant from the residence of the kings for such a drawback to be feared, nor the posts sufficiently powerful as to give enough authority to become their master.

Also, as long as Your Majesty and your successors reserve the right of changing the governors whenever they please on any grounds whatsoever and can always, if the sale of offices is abolished,[197] rightfully bestow them for free, I do not hesitate to say that it is better to remain on this point with the practice of France than to imitate that of Spain, which, however, is so politic and so reasonable in view of the extent of its dominions that even though it cannot usefully be practiced in this kingdom, it must, in my opinion, be utilized in the places that France will keep in its possession in Italy and in Lorraine.[198]

THIRD SECTION

Which condemns successions to offices

Successions to offices, which is the issue in this place, are accorded either against the wishes of the possessors or with their consent.

---

[197] Note that at this point in the writing, Richelieu is still thinking of abolishing the sale of offices entirely, which indicates that this chapter was written before Chapter IV, where he has thought better of it.

[198] This confirms the Succinct narration, where Richelieu is claiming to have given back some conquests by the peace, and note here that he is only intending to retain some strongholds in Italy and Lorraine.

No one denies that it is completely unjust to name a successor against the wishes of a living person, seeing as, by this means, his life is exposed to the guiles of whoever is to profit from his death, and the fear that might justly take over his mind is tantamount to a premature death.

This practice, which had previously spread all over the kingdom, is now prohibited. It is so dangerous that the Councils and various compacts of secular princes condemn it with good reason.

Even the consent of the possessors cannot justify this practice, whatever confidence they may have in those who are designated as their successors, seeing as they are often mistaken since it is impossible in a state to satisfy everyone by benefits. It is important to leave some hope to those for whom one cannot do more, which cannot be done if the posts, the offices, and the benefices are often assured to children, who would perhaps never venture at the height of their maturity to attain the honors and ranks that they have been given in the cradle.

Such favors, which greatly concern the state, seldom gratify individuals. Whoever sees his father or other relative in possession of something does not think he is getting anything but believes that the confirmation he is receiving is more of a hereditary right than an effect of the kindness of the prince.

Even though the good of the state requires that in promotions to posts the merit of the subjects who are raised to them be considered above all else, in successions more regard is given to services rendered than to those that might be rendered by the successor. On such occasions the favor of the ones often takes the place of the merit of the others, who have no other recommendation than their persistence.

Thusly, I conclude that the fewer of such favors that can be granted is most certainly the better and that it would be even more useful not to give any at all, because any special consideration that might be alleged, the consequence is dangerous in states where examples often have more force than reason.

If someone notes that in this section I condemn something that I have even practiced with my own dependents, I am certain that he will understand if he considers that while a disorder is spreading without any remedy, reason demands that this procedure be exploited, which I have tried to do by reserving posts that I have taken the care to institute to those whom I could most strictly oblige to follow my intentions and in my tracks. If, in the turmoil of a reign, troubled by various storms, I could have instituted the regulation that I propose, I would have observed it religiously.[199]

ᴮWhen the cardinal was put in charge of the sea, commerce was almost completely ruined, and the king did not have a single ship.ᴮ

---

[199] Richelieu is excusing himself for having placed his relatives, the Vignerots, the Maillés, and the La Meillerayes, in the most prestigious positions in the army and navy.

Chapter VI

Which indicates to the King what it is felt that he should consider in regard to his person

Since God is the principle of all things, the sovereign master of kings, and the one who makes their reigns happy, if Your Majesty's piety were not known to everybody, I would begin this chapter, which concerns your person, by indicating to you how, if you do not follow the will of your Creator and do not submit to His laws, you cannot expect to have your subjects observe yours and to see them obeying your orders.

But it would be superfluous to exhort Your Majesty to be pious. You are so brought to it by inclination and so confirmed in it by the habit of virtue that it is never to be feared that you will depart from it.

This is why, instead of indicating to you the advantages that religious principles have over the others, I will be satisfied with putting forward that the piety that is necessary to kings must be exempt from scruples. I say this, Sire, because the delicacy of your conscience often makes you fear to offend God while doing certain things that you could not abstain from doing without sinning.

Well do I know that deficiencies of this nature in a prince are much less dangerous for a state that those that incline him to presumption and disdain for what they must revere. But since they are categorized as faults, they must be corrected principally because it is most certainly true that many drawbacks can happen from them that are harmful to the state.

Considering this, I beg you to continue your struggle against your scruples by reminding yourself that you cannot be guilty before God if you follow, whenever delicate questions regarding your conscience should arise, the opinion of your council, confirmed by that of some sound theologians who are above suspicion on the fact in question.

Once this foundation is laid, since there is nothing more necessary for the good of your Majesty's affairs than the maintenance of your health, it is impossible for me not to return to such an important subject.

The long, careful, and diligent observations that I have made regarding everything that touches you embolden me to say that nothing is more required for such an important end than your own will, which, however, is the most powerful enemy that you can have on this subject in that it often takes no little pain to make princes want what is not only useful to them but entirely necessary.

The mind of Your Majesty so absolutely dominates your body that the least of your passions seizes your heart and disturbs all your bodily functions. This truth has been demonstrated to me so many times that I am so certain of it that I have never seen you getting sick in any other way.

God has graciously given Your Majesty the strength to act with firmness in dealing with your most important affairs. But as a counterweight to this great quality, He has permitted that you be sensitive to whatever strikes you on the smallest subjects, so that things that do not initially seem as if they could displease you arouse you initially in such a manner that it is impossible to relieve you as much as one would like on such occasions. Time, which gives the vapors that surprise the senses a chance to evaporate, has up to now been the only remedy to such evils in Your Majesty, who has never been seized by them without being immediately affected by some physical illness.

In this you are similar to those who are indifferent to being cut by a sword because of the greatness of their courage but cannot, by some natural aversion, endure being pricked for a bleeding.

It is impossible for all men to prevent by their reason the surprises they receive from their passions. I would not feel, however, that this was so with Your Majesty, who has many excellent qualities that others lack.

And thusly I believe that since the first effusions of your ardent youth have passed, the stamina of a more mature age will in the future allow you to protect yourself by your reasoning from an enemy all the more dangerous because it is inside you and that has been so bad for you, particularly the two or three times where it almost took your life.

As important as this is for your health, it is also for your reputation and for your glory, which cannot allow that what is nothing in reason be so much in your feelings, which must adhere to it in everything.

I cannot help reiterating in this regard a supplication that I have made many times to Your Majesty, pleading with you to apply your mind to the great things that are important to your state and disdain the little ones as being unworthy of your cares and your thoughts.

It will be useful and glorious for you above all to keep in mind the most important plans that the course of affairs will bring up and not to worry too much about the details of those that are not of this nature, for, on the contrary, this would do you a lot of harm, not only because such activities would keep you from better ones but also because, since tiny thorns are more prickly than bigger ones, it would be impossible for you to protect yourself from many annoyances unnecessary for your affairs and bad for your health.

The great disturbances that I have seen agitating your mind on various occasions oblige me to indicate to you in this place, as I have done in various situations, how even though certain cares are necessary in order to keep your affairs running smoothly, there are some that can produce no other effect than to alter the good intentions of whoever takes them badly and upsets your servants so much that they are less capable of doing what is desired of them.

The experience that twenty-five years of reigning and governing gives to Your Majesty does not permit you to ignore the fact that in great affairs one never entirely follows the orders that have been given. It also teaches you that you must sympathize with those to whom you commit the execution of your will if their labors do not succeed rather than impute to them the bad results for which they are not guilty. Only God can make His will infallible, and still His mercy is such that by letting men act in keeping with their weakness, He allows the difference between their doings and His intentions, which teaches kings to endure with reason and patience what their Creator only endures because of his mercy.[200]

Since Your Majesty is by nature delicate, sickly, moody, and impetuous, particularly, by this natural characteristic, when you are leading an army, I would be committing a crime if I did not beseech you to avoid war as much as possible in the future, which I do on this foundation: that the frivolity and infidelity of the French can only be overcome by the presence of their master, and Your Majesty cannot commit himself to a long-term plan or hope for its success without exposing yourself to your own loss.

You have demonstrated enough by your valor and strength under arms to think of nothing else in the future than of enjoying the peace that you have acquired for the kingdom by your past labors, keeping yourself ready to defend it against all those who would break the public trust by offending you again.

Since it is common enough for many men to act only when they are aroused by some passion that makes them react like incense, which only smells good when it is burning, I cannot help saying to Your Majesty that this characteristic, which is dangerous to all sorts of persons, is particularly so to kings, who must act more reasonably than anyone else.

And in fact, if passion is good for one time, this is only by chance, since by its nature it misleads as much as it blinds those it takes over, and just as

---

[200] This is the misleading dating hint that has so mystified the readers of the *Political Testament.* Since Louis became king on the assassination of Henry IV in 1610, twenty-five years after that was 1635, the very year that France declared war against Spain. These readers did not consider that the kings of France reached their majority in their thirteenth year. Thus Louis would have reached his on September 22, 1614. Twenty-five years after that began on September 22, 1639, which means that this passage was written between September 22, 1639, and September 21, 1640.

a blind man sometimes finds the right path, it is a marvel if he does not get lost, and even if he does not fall all over himself, he cannot avoid repeatedly stumbling unless he is extremely lucky. So many evils have happened to princes and their states when they have followed their feelings rather than their reason and when they have been guided by their passions instead of acting out of consideration for the public interest that it is impossible for me not to beseech Your Majesty to keep reflecting about this so as to be sure to keep doing just the contrary, as you have.

I beg you to go over just as frequently in your mind what I have indicated to you many times: that there is no prince as badly off as one who, if he is not able to do by himself the things he is obliged to do, is reluctant to have them done by someone else, and how being capable of letting oneself be served is not the least of the qualities of a great king since, without it, opportunities have slipped by that might have been taken, and in this manner, and for no good reason, chances to benefit the state are lost.

The late king your father, since he was extremely poor, paid his servants with good words and got them to do with his caresses things that his poverty did not permit him to do in any other ways.

Your Majesty, not having this characteristic, has a natural dryness that you draw from the queen your mother, as you have yourself told her many times in my presence, which keeps you from following on this matter in the tracks of the late king. I cannot help but remind you that your service requires you to benefit those who serve you and that at least it is reasonable that you take special care to say nothing that could alienate them.

Since I need to treat later of the generosity of princes, I will say no more about it in this place. But I will elaborate on the misfortunes that happen to those who speak too freely about their subjects.

The cuts of a sword are easy to heal. But it is not the same for those of a tongue, particularly those of kings, whose authority renders the cut almost without remedy if they do not remedy it themselves.

The heavier a rock, the harder it falls. Someone who would not care about being cut up by the weapons of the enemy of his master could not endure a scratch at his hand.

Just as a fly is not the prey of the eagle, the lion disdains the animals who are not as strong as he is. Just as a man who would attack a child would be blamed by everybody, I would also venture to say that great kings must never provoke with words individuals who are not proportionate to their greatness.

History is full of horrible things that have happened from the freedom with which the great have formerly insulted the small.

God has blessed Your Majesty with a kind nature, and thusly it would be reasonable for you to watch your words so that they do no harm.

I am sure that you would never fall deliberately into this drawback. But since it is difficult for you to control your emotions and knee-jerk reactions, I would not be your servant if I did not warn you that your reputation and your interests require that you be particularly careful about this, seeing as how such freedom of speech, while it would not harm your conscience, will not fail to disturb your affairs greatly.

Just as speaking well of one's enemies is a heroic virtue, a prince must not speak disparagingly of those who would sacrifice their lives a thousand times for him and for his service without committing a grave fault against the law of Christianity and against all good politics.

A king who has clean hands, a pure heart, and an innocent tongue has no little virtue, and whoever who, like Your Majesty, has the first two qualities in abundance can easily acquire the 3rd.

Since it befits the greatness of kings to be so restrained in their words that nothing leaves their mouth that could offend individuals, it also befits their prudence not to say anything detrimental about the principal companies of their state. But they must, moreover, speak so that they have every reason to believe that you hold them dear. The most important affairs of state so often oblige to upset them for the good of the public that prudence requires them to be satisfied about things that are not of this nature.

It is not enough for great princes never to open their mouth to speak badly of anyone, but reason requires that they refuse to listen to gossip and false reports; that they chase away and banish their authors as very dangerous plagues who often poison the hearts of princes and the minds of all those who approach them. If those who have free access to the ears of kings without meriting it are dangerous, those who possess their heart only because they are his favorites are all the more so since, to preserve such a treasure, it is necessary for art and malice to make up for their lack of virtue.[201]

I cannot help but say in this regard that I have always feared the power of such favors over Your Majesty more than the power of the greatest kings of the earth and that you need to protect yourself more from the guiles of a valet who wants to fool you than from all the factions that all great nobles in your state could form, even though they were aiming at the same end.

When I first came into office, those who had the honor of serving you previously firmly believed that there was no difference between complaining against them and convincing you of it. And on this foundation their principal

---

[201] With the dating of 1640, we can determine that Richelieu was already beginning at this time to worry about the influence of Henri Coiffier de Ruzé (1620–1642), the young Marquis de Cinq-Mars, whom he had himself introduced to Louis XIII. See notes 228, 229, and 230 below.

care was always to have their confidants at your side so as to protect themselves from what they feared.

Even though the experience that I have had with the firmness that Your Majesty has shown in my case obliges me to recognize that they had misjudged and that you have outgrown this weakness of your early youth, I will not omit to plead with you to confirm your treatment of me in such a way than no one can have any doubt about it.

Subsequently, I cannot help telling you that just as the ears of princes must be closed to calumnies, they must also be open to the truths useful to the state, and since their lips must be sealed so as not to say anything to harm anyone, they must also be free and bold to speak up when it is a question of the public interest.

I note these two points because I have often observed that it was no small thing for Your Majesty to be patient enough even to listen to what was most important and that, when the good of your affairs obliged you to let your will be known not only to the great nobles but also to the small ones and to persons of the middle class, you had no little reluctance to make up your mind when you suspected that they would not like it.

I admit that this fear bears witness to your kindness, but since I do not want to flatter you, I cannot help telling you that this is also the result of a weakness that may be tolerable in an individual but not in a great king, in view of its drawbacks.

I am not taking into account that such behavior would throw all the blame for the decisions on the council of Your Majesty because this would be a small price to pay for the good of your affairs. But it is to be considered that there are occasions when, however much authority a minister may have, it cannot be great enough to produce certain effects that require the voice of a sovereign and an absolute power.

Besides, once the great nobles become convinced that a king is ashamed of commanding absolutely, they will always try to obtain by pressure the contrary of what had been ordered with reason, and their audacity could finally reach the point where, once they realize that their prince is afraid to act like their master, they would get tired of acting like his subjects.

It is necessary to have a manly virtue and to do everything with reason without giving way to one's inclinations, which often bring princes to the brink, and if they follow them blindly, this may well bring about their fall. Personal dislikes, which they sometimes take without any grounds, are even worse if they are not tempered by reason, as is to be desired.

Regardless of the occasion, Your Majesty needs his prudence in order to restrain his leaning for these two passions, but toward the last more than the first because it is easier to be bad in keeping with one's dislikes, which only requires a king to command, than to be good by conquering one's inclination, which cannot be done without sacrificing something of oneself, which many persons have no little reluctance to do.

These two movements are contrary to the mentality of kings primarily if they do not think about them very often and they follow their instinct more often than their reasoning.

This leads them sometimes to take part in the disputes that usually occur between individuals in their courts, from which I have seen the great drawbacks that have resulted. Their dignity obliges them to sympathize with the one who is in the right, which is the only one they must espouse. In all sorts of situations they cannot do otherwise than to abandon the quality of judges and sovereign, join a party, and in some manner lower themselves to the condition of their subjects.

By this means, they expose their state to many cabals and factions that are subsequently formed. Those who need to defend themselves from the power of a king know too well that they cannot do it by force, so they have no other thought but to protect themselves by intrigues, guiles, and machinations, which often cause great troubles in states.

The sincerity of a man who makes his testament does not permit my pen to finish this section without making a confession that is as true as it is beneficial for the glory of Your Majesty, since it will prove to everybody that the law of God has always been a boundary capable of stopping the violence of any inclination or aversion that may have entered into your mind, which, since it is subject to the most minor deficiencies of men, has always, thanks to God, been exempt from the most notable imperfections of princes.

Chapter VII

Which points out the present state of the royal household and puts forward what seems to be necessary to set it right

The organization of the arts and all good discipline demands that one always begin his work with what is found to be easiest.

On this foundation, the first thing that an architect who wants to construct a great building does is to make a model of it, which is so perfect that it serves as a prototype for his great plan, and if he cannot succeed in this project, he abandons it, since common sense demonstrates that whoever cannot do a small thing is incapable of doing a big one.

Considering this, even the most limited minds know that just as the body of man is a miniature of the whole world, so also individual families are the true models of republics and states, and since everyone is absolutely certain that whoever cannot keep his own house in order is incapable of bringing much order to a state, reason demands that in order to attain the reform of this kingdom, one begin with that of the household of Your Majesty.

I confess, however, that I have never ventured to undertake it, because since the kindness of Your Majesty has always made you averse to giving orders that you considered of little importance when they involved certain individuals, one could not propose such a plan without openly going against your inclination and the interest of many people as, since they were continually at your side and very familiar with you, this could have deterred you from giving the orders that were most necessary for your state and kept you from setting your household straight.

But since a testament reveals many intentions that the testator had not ventured to divulge during his lifetime, this one will induce Your Majesty to reform his household, which has been disregarded both because, even though it seemed easier than that of the state, it was actually more difficult and because on certain occasions prudence obliges to endure a few losses in order to make many gains.

Just as everybody knows that there has never been a king who has brought the dignity of this state to such heights as Your Majesty, no one can deny that there never has been one who has let the brilliance of his household sink so low. The foreigners who have come to France in my time have often been astonished to see a state so uplifted and a household so debased.

In fact, it has gradually fallen to the point that someone has been in possession of the highest posts who during the reign of your predecessors would not have aspired to the middling ones, and everything from the kitchen up to the chambers has been in confusion.

Whereas during the time of the king your father the officials of the crown and all the great of the kingdom ordinarily ate at your tables, in your time they seem to be set only for valets or for simple light cavalrymen or men-at-arms. Even so, the service at them has been so bad that some have been so finicky as to disdain them instead of competing for them eagerly.

At your personal one, foreigners have often complained about being served by simple and dirty scullions instead of those of other kings, where they are served only by gentlemen.

Well do I know that this custom has not been introduced in your time. But it is not any more tolerable for being old if it is entirely distant from the dignity and the greatness of such a great prince.

Well do I also know that this practice has been endured up to the present on the pretext of the safety of the kings, saying that it is impossible for the officials to answer for their actions if they are not themselves the servants and if they do not see it served to Your Majesty.

But this reason seems of little importance to me, since there is no likelihood that a scullion should be more loyal to his master than a gentleman, who has various other occasions to betray him if he wanted to.

Eighty young gentlemen whom Your Majesty nourishes as pages either in your chambers or in his stables would be much better employed in this service than simply performing it for your 1st gentlemen or for your equerries who command them unless they want to pay for it themselves, and doubtless, since they are doing it with more dignity, they will not acquit themselves with less fidelity.

Cleanliness, which is fitting everywhere, is all the more requisite in the household of kings. The richness of the furnishings is all the more necessary there in that foreigners only conceive the greatness of princes by what appears on the outside. And still, even though Your Majesty has a number of beautiful and expensive ones, they are allowed to deteriorate in the places where they stand, and once you dispose of them, they have often been seen in a room where those who should profit from them have not wanted to use them.

Entry into your chambers has been permitted to everybody, not only to the detriment of your dignity but, moreover, in disregard of the safety of your person.

Ambassadors in their audiences have often found themselves surrounded by more footmen, pages, and other petty officials than by the great nobles of your state. And still, your dignity and the old custom of France demands that on such occasions Your Majesty be accompanied by princes, dukes, and peers, by officials of the crown, and by other great nobles of the state.

I know that different kingdoms have different customs. In Spain the greatest nobles do not see their king very often, and in England everything is so well organized that once the doors are thrown open, one only sees in his chambers those who have the right to enter by virtue of the dignity of their posts.

I know, moreover, that it is a privilege of those who wear your crown to be preceded by their train, but there must be this distinction: it must ordinarily consist of your nobility and, on the occasions when foreigners are received, by some of the many distinguished persons in your state, so as to show them off.

In a word, disorder is so common throughout the household of Your Majesty that there are no particular posts that are exempt.

Even though all great princes are careful to have a team of beautiful horses, commensurate with their greatness, Your Majesty has never had one in his great stable that you could ever have used, even though you spend more money on it than your predecessors ever did.

It would be easy for me to specify many other deficiencies no less remarkable than this one. But I shall not enter in detail into such a general disorder, both because this would be too difficult to do without stooping too low from the dignity of this work and because to prescribe the remedies, it suffices to identify the evil without having to make it public. I will do my duty if I propose to Your Majesty the true means to attain as much brilliance in your household as there now is baseness and disorder.

The first thing that is necessary to this end is for Your Majesty to want this reform seriously, since it is certain that in difficult affairs of this nature, the will of kings is like that of God, in which wanting and doing are the same thing.

The second is that it please you in the future to fill the first posts only with persons of high birth who have all the qualities required to acquit themselves worthily of their position. As great as an official may be, he will, if he is competent, dedicate himself to the most minute details of his post because he will consider them important, as indeed they are.

If, for example, the chief stewards do not take particular care to have the places where one eats cleaned every evening and morning as soon as the tables are cleared, they will fail in one of the most necessary duties of their post.

It is necessary to say as much of all the principal officials and primarily the first gentlemen of the chambers, who must be careful to keep the entire apartment of Your Majesty so clean and tidy that it will not be enough to have it cleaned and perfumed 5 or 6 times a day, because of the great flurry of people that cannot be avoided even when it will be most orderly.

Providing that each one is in his proper post, everything in your household will go as Your Majesty wishes, and on this point depends the regulation of all the rest. For whatever rule may be instituted, it will no doubt be useless if there are no people capable of having it enforced, and if they are, they will have the gumption to do what is reasonable for the dignity of their post and the service of their master.

The third consists of Your Majesty having himself served in the future by gentlemen in all the posts of your household, except for the most menial, which will contribute greatly to your dignity and make the nobility love you all the more since it will have more means to approach your person.

By this means Your Majesty can create four companies of his men-at-arms, the best in your kingdom, since it is certain that there are loads of gentlemen who will be thrilled to have the means of living in this status, as long as they get free of charge what is now sold to them at auction, since whoever gives the most is preferred to the others.[202]

In this case, someone will be delighted to have this position who would never think of taking it now that it is usurped by persons who do not merit it. And all will be happy to take it by the access that it will give them to the court, where chance and luck can make their fortune in a moment.

You will still get another advantage from this arrangement in that the fewer the commoners exempt from the *taille* because of their posts in your household there will be, the more people there will be to help carry the burden by which the people are now overwhelmed.

The fourth is that Your Majesty give the posts in your household free of charge in the future without permitting them to be sold for any consideration whatsoever.

Perhaps it might be said that it is unreasonable that those who have purchased the posts be deprived of the opportunity to sell them. But since it is impossible to create institutions very useful for the public without their causing some discomfort to individuals, this drawback is not great considering that since they had not purchased their posts with any assurance of selling them like offices under the *paulette*, no one can be blamed for dashing their hopes.

And even though some individuals may be injured by this change, the entire nobility and the greatest nobles will find notable advantage in it in that

---

[202] Once more, in this chapter, he is anticipating ending the sale of offices.

instead of being obliged, as in the past, to sell a notable part of their wealth in order to have the posts, which has often ruined some of the best families in the kingdom, they shall only hope to acquire them through their merit. This will keep them from losing their wealth and oblige them to acquire some virtue, which is all the more held in contempt in the present age, since the price of everything is only counted in money.

Besides, many means will be found to appease those who, for particular reasons, will be judged worthy of being exempted from the general rule, so that Your Majesty can procure some advantage for the public, while the individuals who might have some just complaint will not suffer any harm.

As it is impossible to doubt the utility of these proposals, the ease with which they can be executed is manifest since, as I have said above, it is only necessary for your firm and constant will to harvest the fruit and restore your household to its former brilliance.

Chapter VIII

Which treats of the council of the prince and is divided into seven sections, the first of which shows that the best princes need a good council

FIRST SECTION

It is no small matter between politicians as to whether a prince who thinks for himself is better than one who lacks enough self-confidence so that he leaves many things up to his council and does nothing without their advice.

Volumes could be brought forward on both sides. But in the particular case on which I am obliged to report here, I prefer a prince who follows the opinion of his council rather than his own, and I cannot help saying that just as a bad government is one that is headed by an incompetent prince who pays no attention to any advice, the best is one whose sovereign is perfectly capable of acting on his own but has the good sense not to do anything without seeking good advice, on the assumption that one person cannot see everything. Aside from this being perfectly rational, the truth obliges me to say that my own experience has confirmed it, and I cannot keep quiet about it without doing violence to myself.

A capable prince is a great treasure to a state. The right kind of council is no less. But both working together in concert is priceless, and the welfare of states depends on it.

It is certain that the most fortunate states are those with the wisest princes and councillors.

It is also certain that few princes can be found who can govern their states by themselves, and moreover, if there were many, they should still not do it.

The omnipotence, infinite wisdom, and Providence of God does not keep him from using secondary causes to do things that he could do by a mere act of will, and thusly kings, who have their limits, would be committing a serious error if they did not follow His example.

But since it is not in their power, as it is with God, to make up for the faults of their servants, they must be extremely careful to choose the best ones that they can.

Many qualities are required in a perfect councillor. They can, however, be reduced to four: competence, loyalty, courage, and dedication, which include many others.

SECOND SECTION

Which indicates the competence that councillors must have

The competence of councillors requires them not to be pedantic. There is nothing so dangerous for the state as those who want to govern kingdoms with maxims that they draw out of their books. They ruin them all too often by this means because the past has nothing to do with the present and because times, places, and persons make all the difference.

It only requires a good mind, solid judgment accompanied by prudence, a reasonable smattering of literature, general knowledge of history and the present condition of all the states in the world, and primarily of their own.

There are two principal things to consider in this regard:

The 1st is that geniuses do more harm than good in the government of a state. If they do not have a lot more to them than hot air, they are worthless for the state.[203]

There are some who are very imaginative, but they are so vacillating in their planning that they change their minds from one moment to the next and are so illogical that they do not even stick to their good ideas.

I can truthfully say, since I know it from experience, that the frivolity of such people is no less dangerous in the administration of public affairs than the malice of many others.

There is a lot to be feared from characters whose vivacity is accompanied by lack of judgment, and even if those who excel in their practical judgment are not that brilliant, they would not fail to be useful to the state.

The 2nd remark that must be made on this subject is that there is nothing more dangerous to a state than to put in great authority certain characters who are not too bright and still think that they do not need any help.

They can neither think for themselves nor follow good advice. Thus they make terrible mistakes.

Being presumptuous is one of the greatest vices that a man in public life can have, and if humility is required in statesmen, modesty is entirely necessary, since it is certain that the greater the genius, the less sociable and capable of governing he is, and these are qualities without which even those whom nature has made the brightest are unsuitable for government.

Since they lack modesty, geniuses are so taken with their own opinions that they condemn any others, even though they may be better, and their natural pride combined with their authority makes them unbearable. The ablest man in the world must often listen to the advice of those whom he considers inferior.

---

[203] Literally, "more lead than mercury."

Just as it is prudent for a minister of state to keep his mouth shut, he must be a good listener. Good advice is always good. Bad advice confirms the good.

In a word, a minister of state has to be modest, and if he is also kindhearted and judicious, he has all he needs on this point.

THIRD SECTION

Which indicates the integrity that councillors must have

It is one thing to be respectable before God, and it is something else to be so in the eyes of men.

Whoever observes the law of his Creator comes first of all, but in the second place, it is necessary to be honorable among men.

These different kinds of integrity are desirable in councillors of state, and it is certain that whoever has both of them is better, but this is often not the case. Someone might be extremely pious, but because he is lacking in the second kind, he might be less suited to public office than someone who has both but is not as pious as he should be.

However, since a lack of piety is the true source of all the imperfections of men, I say boldly that the two kinds of integrity of which I speak are equally required in a councillor of state, and he cannot have the second without the first.

In a word, the statesman must be loyal to God, to the state, to men, and to himself, which will be if, aside from the qualities mentioned above, he is devoted to the public and honest in his advice.

Integrity in a public minister does not imply a tender conscience. On the contrary, nothing is more dangerous in the government of the state, seeing as just like indifference can cause a lot of injustice and cruelty, scruples can produce a lot of omissions and leniency harmful to the public, and it is certain that those who are scared of their own shadows often lose their states along with themselves.

Just like the integrity of a councillor of state is not compatible with a certain strictness that accompanies injustices, it is not contrary to the severity that is necessary to use in many cases. On the contrary, it invites it, prescribes it, and often obliges to be pitiless.

It does not keep a man from taking care of his own affairs while doing those of the state, but it prohibits him from putting them ahead of the public interest, which must be dearer to him than his own life.

This integrity does not allow those in public life to be so kindhearted that it keeps them from refusing unjust claims. On the contrary, it demands that they grant those that are reasonable and resolutely reject those that are not.

I cannot skip this occasion without mentioning what Ferdinand, Duke of Florence, who lived in our time, used to say in this regard, namely, that he preferred a crooked man to one who is easily hoodwinked because, he would add, the crook only falls prey to his passions, which are not always obvious, whereas the easy touch is taken in by everyone who is pressuring him, which happens all the more often because he is known to be gullible.[204]

This integrity requires that all those who are employed in governing the state march in step, and since they are all working for the same end, they all speak in similar terms. Otherwise, there will be someone with the best intentions who will speak more openly in order to make a good impression. Aside from his not having the integrity required of a minister of state, he will tie the hands of those who know how to keep their mouths shut. There are some people who are good only for complaining about disorders instead of doing something about them.

These are not the people we are looking for. They only appear to be virtuous. They cannot be of any service. Their virtue is hardly any different from vice, which has no virtue at all.

The integrity of a councillor of state must be active. It refuses to complain and concentrates on doing something solid for the benefit of the public.

There are others who talk about nothing but the good of the state but are so ambitious at heart that they will stop at nothing to get what they want.

Others go further. Dissatisfied, they manage to combine the public interest with their own and, instead of putting the public ahead of the private, have the gall to do the contrary.

Such people are not only devoid of the integrity necessary for public affairs, but they are a plague on the state, boars in the biblical vineyard, who not only get drunk but trample all the grapes.[205]

Those who are vindictive from their birth prefer to follow their passions rather than reason and, instead of choosing men purely in consideration of their talents, do so only because they recognize them as affectionate to their person and attached to their interests, and cannot be felt to have the integrity required for the administration of states.

If a man is vindictive, giving him any authority is like putting a sword in the hands of a lunatic; if he is guided in his actions by his appetites and not by reason, the state will be served by hotheads instead of worthy people, which will expose it to all sorts of drawbacks.

A respectable man must only avenge his insults for reasons of state. Even then, it is necessary for him not to do it out of personal interests, and if he

---

[204] Ferdinand I (1549–1609), Grand Duke of Tuscany from 1587, the father of Marie de Medici.

[205] Psalm 80:13: "The boar out of the wood doth waste it [the vineyard] and the wild beast of the field doth devour it." Richelieu seems to be taking great liberties with this metaphor.

does, it may truly be said that instead of being bad with good intentions, he is being good with bad ones.

If the integrity of a councillor of state requires that he be impervious to all sorts of interests and passions, it also demands that the calumnies and obstructions that he may face must not deter him from doing his duty.

He must realize that his public service is seldom known by any private person and that he can hope for no other earthly reward than the personal satisfaction of a great soul.

He must realize, moreover, that the great men who govern states are similar to those who are condemned to suffer, except that the latter receive the punishment for their crimes and the others for their merit.

Moreover, he must realize that it is up to great souls to serve kings loyally and endure without relenting in their service to them the calumny that scoundrels and ignoramuses impute to respectable people.

He must even realize that the condition of those who are called to the administration of public affairs is to be greatly pitied, in that if they do well the maliciousness of the world often diminishes their glory by indicating that they could do better, even though this would be entirely impossible.

Finally, he must realize that ministers of state are obliged to imitate the stars, which, notwithstanding the barking of dogs, do not fail to light up the sky as they follow their course, which obliges to treat such injustice with such disdain that his integrity cannot be shaken nor deter him from acting resolutely in order to pursue his ends for the good of the state.[206]

FOURTH SECTION

Which indicates the courage and firmness that a councillor of state must have

Courage, of which it is now a question, does not require that a man be so bold as to disdain all kinds of perils. There is nothing that is more capable of ruining states, and far from a councillor of state having to act this way, on the contrary he must almost always move at a snail's pace and never undertake anything without due consideration.

Even farther from the courage required of a perfect councillor of state obliging him to think only of big things, which often happens with great souls who

---

[206] This interesting simile demonstrates that Richelieu is still accepting the astronomy of Ptolemy, which posited the motion of the stars and not of the earth, despite the theories of Copernicus, Galileo, and Kepler, which were then challenging those of Ptolemy. Almost equally interesting is the sloppy syntax of this paragraph, which makes it clear that Richelieu has been talking about himself.

have more courage than judgment, on the contrary it is entirely necessary that a councillor of state stoop to middling ones, even though they may initially seem beneath him, because great disorders often spring from little beginnings, and the most important institutions often have origins that seem insignificant.

But the courage in question requires that a man be exempt from weakness and fear, which render whoever is without these two deficiencies capable not only of making good decisions but also of executing them.

It requires a certain enthusiasm which makes one desire and pursue greatness with as much passion as wisdom.

It requires, moreover, a degree of firmness that makes a man withstand the greatest adversities of fortune.

It must give a minister of state an upstanding urge for glory without which the most capable and respectable people cannot distinguish themselves through any action advantageous to the public. It must give him the strength to resist envy, hatred, and all the calumnies and obstructions that ordinarily arise in the administration of public affairs.

Finally, he must exemplify in his person the desire of Aristotle, who asserts that whereas the weak use insincerity and ruses, whoever is strong has enough confidence in himself to feel contempt for both.[207]

It is necessary to remark in this regard that to be valiant and to be courageous are not the same thing.

Valor assumes a disposition to expose oneself willingly in every occasion to peril when it presents itself, while courage only requires enough resolution to disdain the peril in which one finds himself or to endure adversity when it occurs.

One can even go so far as to say that besides the above-mentioned disposition, valor also requires a body that renders a man fit to prove his valor by his brawn.

Well do I know that those who have spoken of the principal virtues of man in the past have been unaware of these distinctions. But if one considers them duly, since most people only conceive of a man as valiant if he comes out swinging to prove his worth, the first will be absolutely necessary and the second by no means superfluous.

However one defines valor, it is not necessary in a councillor of state. He does not need to expose himself to all perils or show his athletic skills. It is enough for him to have a heart stout enough that neither panic nor obstructions can deter him from his plans, and since they are in his mind and not in his hand, it is enough for his heart to sustain his head, even if he cannot act physically.

---

[207] *Nichomachean Ethics*, Bk IV: "To conceal one's feelings, i.e., to care less for truth than for what people will think, is a coward's part," whereas the proud man "speaks freely because he is contemptuous."

FIFTH SECTION

Which indicates the dedication that a councillor of state must have

Dedication does not require that a man should work continually on public affairs. On the contrary, nothing can make it more useless than this practice. The nature of affairs of state requires all the more relaxation, since they are so much more burdensome than any other and since the mind and body of men are so limited that continual work would have exhausted them in no time.

It permits all sorts of respectable diversions that do not divert those who take them from their primary attachments. But it requires that whoever is attached to public affairs concentrate on them and is attached to them in mind, thought, and affection. It requires that his greatest pleasure be the success of his affairs.

It requires that he keep looking around everywhere so as to foresee what can happen and find the means of preventing misfortunes by doing whatever reason suggests may be in the public interest.

Since it obliges never to lose a moment in certain affairs that may be ruined by the slightest delay, it also demands that one does not hurry in others where time is necessary in order to avoid making premature decisions.

One of the greatest evils in this kingdom is that everyone is more attached to things that are none of his business than to those he could not neglect without committing a crime.

A soldier complains about what his captain should do, the captain about the deficiencies of his field commander, the *mestre de camp* criticizes the general, the general puts all the blame on the conduct of the court, and none of them thinks of doing his own job properly.[208]

There are some people who are so inactive and have such weak characters that they can never do anything by themselves but merely react to things and are acted upon instead of acting.

Some are more fit for the cloister than for affairs of state, which require dedication and activity all together. Also, when they are handling them, they wreak as much havoc by their listless conduct as any good that someone who is dedicated could do.

Not much can be expected from such characters. One should neither thank them nor blame them for their services since, when you come right down to it, they are simply creatures of chance.

There is nothing more contrary to the dedication necessary for public affairs than the attachment that those who administer them may have to women. Well do I know that there are certain characters who are so superior

---

[208] The *mestre de camp* was a rank equivalent to colonel, the commander of a regiment.

and in control of themselves that even though they may be diverted in their duty to God by some of their unbridled affections, they are not diverted by that from their duty to the state. There are some who do not let the mistresses of their pleasure be the mistresses of their will and who attach themselves only to their duty.

But there are few of this nature, and it is necessary to admit that just as a woman has ruined the world, nothing is more disturbing to states than this sex. When it gets a hold of those who govern them, it often makes them move as it pleases, and consequently badly. The best thoughts of women are almost always bad in those who conduct themselves by their passions, which ordinarily replace reason in their minds, whereas reason is the only motive that must animate those who are employed in public affairs.[209] Whatever the force of a councillor, it is impossible for him to dedicate himself entirely to his post unless he is entirely free from all such attachments. With them he might well do his duty, but without them, he would do it much better.

However good his intentions, he must distribute his time so as to have enough to work by himself on the paperwork of his post and to give audiences to everybody. Reason demands that he treat everyone with courtesy and with as much civility as the class and the various statuses of the persons with whom he is dealing require.

This article will point out to posterity a token of my frankness, since it prescribes what it has not been possible for me to observe fully.

I have always been civil with those who have had to deal with me. The nature of affairs obliges one to refuse a lot of people, but it does not permit one to mistreat them in any way when one cannot satisfy them.

But my poor health has not allowed me to be available to everybody as I would have desired, which has made me so sad that I have sometimes thought of retiring.

However, I can truthfully say that I have managed my weakness in such a way that if I have not been able to please everybody, it has never kept me from performing my duty to the state.

Finally, the dedication of a perfect councillor of state and the combination of all these qualities must come together in his person.

Someone can be a respectable person, but if he has no talent for affairs of state, he would be completely useless in them and would occupy his posts without filling them.

Someone could be capable and have the integrity required, but if he could not stomach the discords that are impossible to avoid in governing a state, he would be harmful instead of useful.

---

[209] This is a classic expression of "exceptionalism." Notice the "*almost* always bad" and "*ordinarily* replace reason."

Someone could still be well intentioned, capable, and courageous; yet his laziness would be no less ruinous to the public if he did not dedicate himself to the functions of his position.

Someone could be conscientious, capable, courageous, and dedicated to his employment, but even though he may often be useful, if he is more interested in his own interests than in those of the state, he is no less to be greatly feared.

Competence and integrity give rise to such a perfect accord between the understanding and the will that whereas the understanding chooses the best objectives and the most proper means to achieve them, the will knows how to embrace them with so much enthusiasm that it does everything possible to attain the ends that the understanding has intended.

Integrity and courage give rise to the upstanding boldness to tell kings what they need to hear even if it is not always agreeable.

I say upstanding boldness, because if it is not restrained and always respectful, instead of being included as one of the perfections of councillors of state, it would be one of their vices.

It is necessary to speak to kings with silken words, since it is the duty of a loyal councillor to warn them privately and tactfully about their deficiencies. Discussing them publicly would be committing a great blunder.

Saying out loud what one should whisper in the ear may even be criminal if one exposes the imperfections of his prince just to show off rather than out of a sincere desire to correct them.

Courage and dedication give rise to such great firmness in the plans chosen by the understanding and embraced by the will that they are pursued diligently without the vacillations that often come from the frivolity of the French.

I have not spoken about the force and bodily health necessary to a minister of state because even though this is very desirable when it is combined with all the qualities of mind specified above, it is still not so indispensable that the councillors cannot perform their functions without it.

There are many employments in a state when it is absolutely required, because it is necessary to act not only with the mind but also with the body, going from place to place, which must often be done promptly. But whoever has his hand on the tiller of state and is only in charge of steering does not need this quality.

Just as the movement of the heavens needs only the intelligence that moves it, so also the force of the mind is sufficient for the governing of a state. Arms and legs are not necessary to move the world.[210]

Just as whoever is guiding a ship needs only to look at the compass with his eyes before giving orders to turn the helm wherever he thinks fit, in the

---

[210] Clearly, Richelieu is still living in a Ptolemaic universe.

government of the state, nothing is required but the operation of the mind, which sees and orders whatever it deems necessary.

If it is true that the heavens, which provide heat, are not themselves warm, it is clear that to move the physical world, the body is not required to act.[211]

I admit, however, that I have often wished to be out of government because of my health, which has been so bad that it has been almost impossible for me not to stretch it beyond endurance.

Finally, after having served Your Majesty for many years in the thorniest affairs of state, I can confirm from my own experience what reason teaches to everybody that it takes brains and not brawn to govern a state.

SIXTH SECTION

Which indicates how many councillors of state there must be and that one of them must have the superior authority

After having examined and recognized the qualities necessary to those who must be employed as minister of state, I cannot help but note that, just as many doctors sometimes cause the death of a patient instead of curing him, it will do the state more harm than good if there are many councillors. I add that it is fruitless to have more than four, and even then it is necessary to have only one who has the superior authority and who is like the prime mover who moves all the others with his own intelligence.

I have some reluctance about putting forward this proposition, because it will seem that I am being self-serving.

But considering that it would be easy to prove this by many authorities from Scripture, from fathers of the Church, and from politicians and that the particular confidence with which Your Majesty has always honored me while it has pleased him to involve me in the conduct of public affairs needs no other reason to defend it except for what was necessary in order to install me in it, that is to say, your will, which will pass in the eyes of posterity as sufficient reason for the authority that I have had in your councils, I find that I can speak on this subject without being suspect and that I must do it to prove by reason what the honor that I have always received from your goodness will authorize by example.

Natural envy, which is ordinarily common among equals, is too well known by everybody without needing a long discussion to point out the truth of the proposition I have put forward.

---

[211] Clearly, Richelieu is ignoring Galileo's discovery of sunspots.

I have had so many experiences in this matter that I would feel responsible toward God if the present testament did not state in precise terms that there is nothing more dangerous in a state than equal authorities in the administration of affairs.

What one undertakes is obstructed by another, and if the most respectable man is not the ablest, even if his proposals would be better, they will always be thwarted by the most intelligent.

Each one will have his supporters, who will form different parties in the state and will divide its forces instead of uniting them.

Just as the illnesses and the death of men come from a lack of harmony in the elements that make them up, it is certain that the conflict and disunion that is always found between equal powers will disturb the peace of the states that they govern and will produce various incidents that may finally ruin them.[212]

If it is true that monarchical government imitates that of God better than any other, if all politicians, spiritual and secular, teach that this kind of regime surpasses all those that have ever been put into practice, it can be said boldly that if the sovereign cannot or does not want to keep his eye continually on the compass, reason demands that he place someone in charge above all the others.

Just as various pilots never put all their hands on the helm at the same time, more than one is never necessary to steer the ship of state.

He may well receive advice from the others, he must even seek it sometimes, but it is up to him to evaluate it and turn his hand one way or the other, depending on what he feels to be best in order to avoid the storm and make his way.

It is just a matter of making the right decision on this occasion and not the wrong one.

There is nothing as easy as to find a prime mover who moves everything without being moved by any supreme authority except that of his master. But there is nothing as difficult as to find one who moves well without being moved by other considerations that may deflect his movement.

Every person will feel himself capable of this function, but no one can be a judge in his own cause. The judgment in anything of such importance must depend on those who have no interest that can blindfold their eyes.

Someone might not be capable of being moved by the bribery of the enemies of the state who might be by their guiles.

Someone will be capable of being moved by interests that may not be criminal but that, however, would still be very harmful to the state.

---

[212] A farfetched analogy because, according to classical medical doctrine, to which Richelieu is referring, the humors in a healthy person are presumed to act harmoniously.

There are often some who would die before violating their conscience, who would, however, not be useful to the public because they would not be capable of resisting the persistence or affection that they have for those whom they love.

Someone incapable of being moved by any interest whatsoever might be by fear, astonishment, or panic.

Well do I know that capacity, integrity, courage, and, in a word, the qualities that we have attributed to councillors of state can remedy such drawbacks. But, to be frank, since the minister whom we are discussing must be better than all the others, he must also have all these qualities preeminently, and consequently it is necessary to be extremely careful before making a choice.

The prince must determine by himself whom he wants to put in charge of such an important position, and his choice, if possible, must be accompanied by the approval of the public, for if he has it, he will have a better chance of being successful.[213]

Just as the most intelligent astronomers cannot make the slightest miscalculations without being wrong in their predictions, it is also true, thusly, that if the qualities of whoever must govern only appear good and his conduct will be bad or if he is a mediocrity, his governing will not be excellent.

It is easy to indicate the qualities that this principal minister must have, but it is difficult to find them all in one person.

However, it is true to say that the fortune or misfortune of states depends on this choice, which obliges sovereigns either to take this care upon themselves or to make sure that their decision will be approved in heaven and on earth.

SEVENTH SECTION

Which indicates what the King must be to his councillors

Thus, once Your Majesty has chosen his councillors, it is up to you to put them in such a state as to work for the greatness and happiness of your kingdom.

For this end, four principal things are required:

The 1st is that Your Majesty have confidence in them and that they know it, which is absolutely necessary because otherwise the best councillors could be suspect to other princes, and if the ministers were not sure of themselves, they would hold back on a great many occasions when their silence would be very harmful.

---

[213] The discussion that begins here suggests that at this time, late in 1640, Richelieu is not yet prepared to recommend that Louis XIII appoint Giulio Mazzarino, not yet a cardinal, as his successor.

It is an old saying that a physician who is liked by his patient and is liked back will profit all the more, and it is certain that there is no one who can work hard to cure a patient who he knew did not trust him.

The second is that he order them to speak freely to him and assure them that they can do it without peril.

This condition is absolutely necessary, not only for certain cold and timid characters who need to be encouraged but for those who, since they are not naturally timid, are all the more public spirited if they know that their boldness will not come back to haunt them.

The soldier who fires his musket under cover is much more secure than the one who does it in the open, and, indeed, there are few individuals who would want to endanger their life for the benefit of the public.

It is true enough that a respectable man must not consider his own interest when it is a question of the public one and that the highest level of fidelity that can be desired of a good servant is to do and say candidly to his master what he knows to be useful without fear of incurring either the hatred of those who have the most influence over him or displeasing him. But there are few with enough zeal to want to run such a risk.

The 3rd is that he treat them liberally and that they believe that their services will not remain without compensation, which is all the more necessary since there are few people who are completely virtuous and the true means of keeping a servant from thinking too much about his interests is to follow the advice of the emperor who recommended to his son to take good care of the affairs of those who took care of his own.[214]

No respectable man has ever thought of enriching himself at the expense of the public while serving it. As such a thought would be criminal, nothing is more shameful to a prince than to see those who have grown old in his service, loaded with age, merit, and poverty all together.

The 4th is that he authorize them and maintain them so openly that they be assured that they need not dread the guiles or fear the power of those who wish to ruin them.

The interest of the prince obliges him to do this since there is no man who can be of much service to the public without attracting the hatred and the envy of everybody, and there are few sufficiently virtuous to serve well if they expect to suffer from it.

There is no stronghold in the world that, as strong as it may be by itself, can protect itself from being captured in the long run if it does not defend its outskirts carefully.

---

[214] Charles I and V (1500–1558), King of Spain in 1516, Holy Roman Emperor in 1519, who abdicated in 1556, dividing his vast dominions between his son Philip and his brother Ferdinand.

It is the same of the greatest kings, who could not preserve their authority in its entirety if they are not particularly careful to sustain it in the least of their officials, near or far from their person, who are the first outworks to be attacked, whose capture emboldens an attack on those in the interior, even if they seem impenetrable and safe through their attachment to the person of the kings.

There are few persons who dare to attack openly those whom a king has chosen to serve him since there are none who do not recognize that their power cannot be equal to that of a sovereign, who has too much interest in protecting his servants so as not to lose them. But there are always some who try to ruin them by guiles and foul play difficult to discover.

On such occasions, it is all acted so smoothly that as inconspicuous as these plans may look, it is necessary to take them seriously, not in order to do anyone any harm but to prevent them out of prudence.

The guile of men is such that they disguise themselves in a hundred ways in order to achieve their ends. Someone speaks openly on the pretext that he cannot remain silent without committing a crime, but there are few of this kind. Someone feigns to be a friend of those whom he wants to ruin. Someone has someone else do the talking and steps in only to support the accusations that have been begun. Finally, there are so many ways of causing trouble of this kind that a prince cannot be too careful to protect himself from being surprised on such an important matter.

The moment one speaks secretly to him against the government of his state, on whatever pretext whatsoever, he can be sure that it is in order to subvert it.

Those who do this are like sick people whose fevers are all the worse because they are below the surface.

It is necessary to anticipate such evils and not to wait until they are fully known because often they can only be discovered once they have already happened and done their damage.

Those who engage in such schemes know too well the peril to which they expose themselves to begin them without the intention of completing them. On such occasions they go initially at a snail's pace and as the grass grows, but later the nature of such affairs requires them to step it up and to run from fear of being caught in the act.

They are like a rock thrown from the peak of a mountain. At first it moves slowly, and the farther down it goes, the heavier it gets, and the speed of its fall increases.[215]

And just as a greater force is necessary in order to stop it at its top speed than at the beginning, it is very difficult to stop a conspiracy that has not been stifled at its birth and is still growing.

---

[215] Richelieu's Aristotelian physics is no better than his classical medicine.

The more important a stronghold is, the harder the enemy tries to corrupt its governor. The more beautiful a woman is, the more the people who try to get into her good graces. Thus, the more useful a minister is to his master, the more influence he has over his mind and his favor, the more persons there are who envy him, who want his position, and who try to replace him.

Among the loyal governors the most esteemed not only resist any proposals that are made to them against their duty but refuse to listen to them and immediately shut the mouth of those who want to tempt them in such ways.

Among chaste women, those who will close their ears to the foul talk that is designed to tempt their purity are, by the judgment of all the wise, preferred to those who open them, even if they close their hearts.

Thus, among masters who have servants who have proven their fidelity on such different and important occasions that they cannot reasonably doubt of it, the ones who are the wisest shut the mouths of those who wish to speak badly of them.

Whatever virtue there is in resisting temptation, princes and husbands are felt to be too indulgent if they permit their governors and their wives to listen to something that they do not want them to entertain without committing a crime. And the masters must blame themselves if they lend an ear to what they are told against those whose fidelity is irreproachable. The primary reason for this is that just as to expose oneself boldly to peril at the right time is a valorous deed, doing it without rhyme or reason is a rash one. And this is why it has been said with great reason that whoever lends his ears to calumnies deserves to be fooled.

Perhaps someone will tell me that there is a great difference between the duty of a governor, of a woman, and of a prince in the matter that is indicated, that it is true that the governor and the woman would do much better not to listen because they cannot, in any case, consent to what they are told, but that it is not the same of a prince, who must keep his ears open, since he may be told some very important things and he will need to see to them.

To this I answer 1st that, speaking only of servants whose fidelity is irreproachable and whose conduct has been proven on a variety of such important occasions that it is unparalleled, the difference in the comparison put forward is so small that it must reasonably be held as insignificant, the rule in moral matters being not to count what is inconsequential.

I add in the 2nd place that even if there should be some drawback in shutting one's ears to what might be said against a servant of proven fidelity, it is so insignificant in respect to those that are inevitable that if one lends them against persons of this quality, I can say absolutely that the governor, the woman, or the prince should also have them on all of the occasions indicated above.

There are no grounds for presuming that whoever has been loyal all his life becomes disloyal all of a sudden without rhyme or reason primarily if all the interests of his fortune are attached to those of his master.

An evil that hardly ever happens must be presumed never to happen, primarily if in order to avoid it one exposes himself to many others that are inevitable and of much greater importance, which is the case in question, since it is certain that it is almost impossible that a prince can keep his most loyal servants if, on the pretext of not shutting his ears to the truth, he opens them to the malice of men, aside from it being patent that he will lose more advantages if he loses one of this quality than if, by failing to listen, he tolerates the minor deficiencies of someone who has proven faithful on the most important occasions.

If whoever knowingly opens the door to assassins who kill a man is guilty of his death, whoever accepts every kind of suspicions and calumnies against the fidelity of one of his servants without getting to the bottom of them is responsible before God for such behavior.

The best actions are taken badly by two sorts of characters, by the overly malicious who interpret everything badly through an excess of malice and by the overly suspicious who interpret everything badly out of weakness.

There is not a single man in this world, no matter how virtuous he may be, who passes for innocent in the eyes of a master who does not examine things for himself and lends his ears to calumnies.

Since there are only two ways to resist vice, either flight or combat, there are only two ways to resist calumnies: one is to reject them entirely without listening to them; the other is to examine them so carefully as to determine their truth or falsehood.

To avoid all drawbacks and to protect oneself from the guile that bad characters can use to ruin the most respectable people and not deprive oneself of the means to discover the bad conduct of those who serve badly, the prince must consider as calumny everything that someone simply wants to whisper in his ear and, on that occasion, refuse to hear it; and if someone wishes to maintain, in the presence of the accused, what he has put forward for or against him, then he can be heard, on the condition of being well rewarded if he says something of importance to the public that is found to be true and of being severely punished if his accusation is false and insignificant, even if it is true.

I have always beseeched Your Majesty to do likewise in my regard so as to give as much liberty to those who would want to censure my actions to do it since you would permit me, by this means, to defend them.

I can truthfully say that Your Majesty has never had any objection to my conduct except when you have not followed this advice, all the more acceptable since it can only be innocent.

Once the councillors of whom I have just been talking are securely in place, it is up to them to work as respectable people according to some general principles on which the good administration of states depends.

Even though many can be proposed that might seem useful, and since brevity is the soul of wit, since the sciences are much easier to understand the shorter they are, I shall reduce the principles that I have felt to be the most useful for the government of a state to nine, entirely necessary in my opinion. If some of them have various branches, this will not, however, augment their number any more than those of all the trees that we see multiply their trunks.

SECOND PART

Divided into ten chapters, the first nine of which are the nine general principles according to which a state cannot help but be well governed. The tenth is the conclusion of this work.

Chapter I

Which points out that the first foundation of the happiness of a state is the institution of the reign of God

The reign of God is the principle of all the governments of states, and, indeed, it is something so absolutely necessary that without this foundation no prince can reign well; nor can any state be happy and successful.

It would be easy to write entire volumes on such an important subject, on which the Scriptures, the fathers of the Church, and all sorts of histories furnish us with an infinite number of teachings, examples, and exhortations that add up to the same thing. But this is something so well known to everyone by his own reason, which tells him that he does not get his being from himself but that he is created by God and is consequently governed by Him, that there is no one who does not feel that nature has imprinted this truth in his heart in letters that cannot be erased.[216]

So many princes and so many states that have founded their conduct on the opposite principle have been lost, and so many have been showered with blessings for having submitted their authority to that from which it derived, for having sought their greatness only in that of their Creator, and for having cared more about His reign than about their own that I shall not elaborate on a truth so evident that it does not need any proof.

I shall only say, in a word, that just as it is impossible for the reign of a prince who allows the reign of disorder and vice in his state to be happy, God

---

[216] Lest one be tempted to jump to the conclusion here that Richelieu is inspired by Descartes's recent *Discourse on Method* (1637), we should recall that Saint Anselm (c.1033–1109) made the same point.

will not easily allow one who will take special care to establish His empire throughout his domains to be unfortunate.

Nothing is more useful for this holy institution than the good conduct of princes, which is a living law more compelling and effective than all those that they could enact in order to compel compliance with their good intentions.

If it is true that whatever crime a sovereign may commit, he sins more through his bad example than by the nature of his fault, it is no less indubitable that, whatever law he may enact, if he follows it himself, his example is not less useful to its observance than all the punishments of his ordinances as great as they may be.

The purity of a chaste prince will banish more impurity in his kingdom than all of the exertions he might make for this end.

The prudence and restraint of one who will not swear will do more to curtail the cursing and blasphemies that are too common in states than any strictness he might impose upon those who abandon themselves to such abominations.

This is not to say that it is not necessary to severely punish scandals, swearing, and blasphemy; on the contrary, one cannot be too exact, and no matter how saintly and exemplarily a prince or a magistrate may conduct his life, they will never be criticized for doing their duty if, while inducing by example, they constrain with the rigor of the laws.

There is no sovereign in the world who is not obliged, by this principle, to procure the conversion of those living under his rule who have strayed from the path of salvation. But since man is reasonable, in order to arrive at this good end, prudence does not permit him to try anything so risky that it might uproot the good wheat along with the chaff, so that it would be difficult to purge a state by any other way than that of mildness without shaking it up, or at least causing it great harm.

Since princes are obliged to establish the true religion of God, they must be very careful to banish its false appearances so harmful to the state, so that one may truthfully say that hypocrisy has always been used as a veil to cover the ugliness of the most pernicious undertakings.

Many persons, whose weakness is equivalent to malice, sometimes use this kind of ruses, all the more ordinary to women, the weakness of whose gender makes them more prone to devotion and more capable of such deceptions.

Chapter II

Which shows that reason must be the rule for the conduct of a state

The light of nature demonstrates to everyone that since man has been created with reason, he must not do anything without it, since otherwise he would go against his nature and consequently against its author. It also teaches that the greater the man, the more he must value this principle and the less he must squander his reason, which constitutes his being, because the advantages that he has over all other men constrain him to preserve what is natural to him and to the purpose for which his author intended him.[217]

From these two principles, it clearly follows that if man is supremely reasonable, he must make reason reign supreme, which not only requires that he do nothing without it but obliges him moreover to ensure that all those who are under his authority revere it and follow it religiously.

This consequence is the source of another, which teaches that just as it is necessary not to want anything that is not reasonable and just, it is necessary not to want anything than is not put into effect and whose orders are not followed with obedience, because otherwise reason would not reign supreme.

It is all the easier to practice this rule because love is the most powerful motive that obtains obedience, and it is impossible for subjects not to love their prince if they know that reason is the guide of all his actions.

Authority constrains obedience, but reason convinces it. It is much better to lead men by means that gradually gain their confidence than by those that, more often as not, only force them to act.

If it is true that reason must be the torch that lights the way for all the conduct of princes and their states, it is also true that since nothing in the world is less compatible with passion, which is so blinding that it may sometimes take a shadow for a body, a prince must above all avoid acting from such a principle, which would make him all the more hateful since it is directly contrary to the one that distinguishes men from animals. One often regrets what one has done out of passion and with haste, which is not the case with what one has done after careful consideration. One has to be firmly convinced of what one has resolved, since it is the only way to get oneself obeyed, and just as

---

[217] Right out of Thomas Aquinas's *Summa theologica* and *Summa contra gentiles*.

humility is the first foundation of Christian perfection, obedience is the most necessary for the maintenance of states.

There are many things that are perfectly easy to execute, but it is necessary to want them badly enough that after having ordered them to be done, one severely punishes those who do not obey.

Those that appear most difficult and almost impossible are only so because of the indifference with which they seem to be wanted and ordered. And it is true that subjects will always be religious in obeying when princes will be forceful and persevering in commanding, from which it follows that if states are disorganized, they are all the guiltier, and it is certainly their indifference and their weakness that causes it.

In a word, just as wanting firmly and doing what one wants are the same thing in a prince respected in his state, wanting feebly and not wanting amount to the same thing in the end.

The government of kingdoms requires a manly virtue and unshakable firmness, as opposed to the softness that exposes those who display it to the schemes of their enemies.

It is necessary to act vigorously in all things, seeing primarily as even if one does not succeed, one has at least avoided the shame of having failed.

Even if one did not succeed in doing his duty, the failure would be worthwhile, and, on the contrary, whatever success he might have had by going against his honor and conscience, he must be felt to be unfortunate, since it could not equal the discredit for how it had been procured.

In the past, most of the great plans of France have gone up in smoke because those who were to execute them stopped at the first difficulty they encountered, when, with good reason, they should nonetheless have persevered, and if it has turned out differently during the reign of Your Majesty, the perseverance with which it has constantly been pursued with good reason was the cause.

If at first one does not succeed in the execution of one's plan, one should try it again, and if it has to be postponed, reason demands one to bide one's time and try again.[218]

In a word, nothing must deter one from a good undertaking, except for some incident that makes it entirely impossible, and one must do everything possible to go forward with those that have been resolved upon with good reason.

This is what obliges me to speak here about secrecy and speed, which are more necessary than anything else for the success of one's affairs.

---

[218] We can now scratch Thomas H. Palmer's *Teacher's Manual* (1840): "Tis a lesson you should heed, Try, try, try again, If at first you don't succeed, Try, try, try again," and Frederick H. Maryat's (1792–1848) *Children of the New Forest* (1847). Also attributed to William Hickson, editor of the *Westminster Review* (1840–1852).

Aside from experience proving this, the reason is evident, seeing that surprise often removes the possibility of opposition, while dragging out the execution of a plan is tantamount to speaking about something and not doing it.

From which it comes that women, lazy and gossipy by nature, are so unsuitable to government that if one also considers that they are very subject to their passions, and consequently little susceptible to reason and justice, this principle alone excludes them from all public administration.

This is not to say that some may sometimes be found who are so exempt from these deficiencies that they could be admitted.

There are few general rules that are without exception. Even this century has brought us some who could not be sufficiently praised.[219] But it is true that ordinarily their softness renders them incapable of a manly virtue, necessary for administration, and that it is almost impossible for their governing to be exempt either from baseness or pettiness caused by the weakness of their sex or from injustice, cruelty, and the disorder of their passions, which replace their reason.

---

[219] Richelieu was not just talking through his skullcap. In a classic example of "exceptionalism," he had great admiration for Amalia Elizabeth (1602–1651), a Calvinist no less, who, in the interest of her own Landgravate of Hesse-Cassel, held firmly to her late husband's alliances with Catholic France and Lutheran Sweden during the Thirty Years' War.

Chapter III

Which shows that the public interest must be the only end of those who govern states or, at least, that it must be put above all others

The public interest must be the only end of the prince and of his councillors, or at least both are obliged to take it so seriously that they put it above all others.

It is impossible to conceive of the good that a prince and those who serve him in his affairs can do if they follow this principle religiously, and one cannot imagine the evil that can happen in a state when the private interest is put above the public and regulates it.

True philosophy, Christian law, and politics teach this truth so clearly that the councillors of a king should keep reminding him of such a necessary principle. Nor can the prince be too severe in punishing any of his councillors who are miserable enough not to practice it.

I cannot help but note in this regard that the prosperity that has always accompanied Spain in recent times has no other cause than the care of its council in putting the interests of the state above all others and that most of the misfortunes that have happened to France have been caused by the excessive attachment of many of those who have been employed in its administration to their own interests while harming those of the public.

The ones have always followed the public interest, which by its nature has inspired them to do what is best for the state, and the others by doing everything to suit themselves have often deterred them from their proper end.

Death or a change of ministers has never brought any transformation to the council of Spain, but it has not been the same in this kingdom, whose affairs have not only changed with the change of councillors but vacillated so much under the same ones that such behavior would have certainly ruined this monarchy if God in his mercy had not bailed this nation out.

If the variety of our interests and our natural inconstancy often carry us to the brink of disaster, we are so frivolous and incapable of standing firm even for our own good that our enemies do not have the time to react properly and to profit from our faults.

Since your council has changed its behavior of late, your affairs have also taken a turn to the great benefit of your kingdom, and if the example of the reign of Your Majesty is followed in the future, your neighbors will no longer have the advantages that they have had in the past. But if this kingdom partakes of their wisdom, it will doubtless have a share in their good fortune, since although being wise and fortunate is not always the same thing, the best thing one can do to avoid being unfortunate is to take the path of prudence and reason and not the unbridled one of most men and particularly of the French.

If those whom Your Majesty will trust with the care of your affairs have the capacity and integrity of which I have spoken above, you will only have to watch out for yourself concerning this matter, which should not be difficult for you, since the interest and the personal reputation of a prince only have the same end.

Princes are ordinarily willing enough to enforce the general laws of their states, because by doing this they have only reason and justice in mind, which is easy enough to do when there is no obstacle in their path, but when the opportunity arises to get some beneficial institutions under way, they do not always show the same firmness because this is when the interests of someone or other, piety and compassion, favor and pressures oppose his good intentions, and they often do not have enough will power to disdain these individual concerns. It is on such occasions that they must gather all their forces, keeping in mind that those whom God has chosen to govern others must do only what is best for the public and oblige it to follow all together.

Chapter IV

Which demonstrates how necessary foresight is in the governing of a state

Nothing is more necessary in the governing of a state than foresight, since by this means one can easily prevent many evils that can only be cured with great difficulty once they have happened.

Just as the doctor who knows how to prevent an illness is more appreciated than one who tries to cure them, ministers of state must often keep in mind and indicate to their masters what it is most important not to postpone, and the enemies of a state are evils that it is better to attack sooner than later.

Those who do differently will get into immense difficulties that will be very difficult to remedy subsequently. However, it is ordinary for the common people to prefer to shrug their shoulders and take it easy for a month rather than to take just a little time in order to protect themselves from many years of trouble.

Those who live from day to day live happily for themselves but not for those whom they lead.

Whoever thinks ahead does nothing in haste since he begins thinking early, and it is difficult to go astray if one has thought about it previously.

There are certain occasions when there is no time to deliberate at length because the situation does not permit it. But when it does, the best thing is to sleep on it and compensate for the delay by taking one's time.

There was a time in this kingdom when precautions were never taken, and even after something bad had happened, halfhearted measures were applied because it was impossible to do anything positive without offending someone or other.

Since the private interest was then put above the public, wounds were put up with instead of doing something about them, which has caused a great deal of evil in this kingdom.

For a few years now, thank God, we have turned things around, and so successfully that while reason induces us to continue, the excellent results oblige it imperatively.

It is necessary to sleep like the lion by keeping our eyes constantly open to foresee the least drawbacks that might happen and remember that just as consumption does not raise the pulse even though it is fatal, it also happens in states that evils that are barely noticeable when they originate often end up as the most dangerous.

Since it is necessary to take extraordinary care not to be surprised on such occasions, just as it has always been felt that states governed by people with wisdom were fortunate, it has also been believed that those governed by people with less wisdom were the less fortunate.

The abler a man is, the heavier is the load of governing.

Public service keeps the best minds so occupied in worrying about the future that they are never at peace except for any satisfaction they might draw from seeing people sleeping without fear under their watchful eye and happy in their misery.

Since it is necessary to try as much as possible not to be wrong in one's calculations about the success of one's undertakings, and since the intelligence of men has certain limits beyond which it cannot go, while only God can foresee the ultimate end of things, it suffices to know that one's projects are feasible before embarking on them.

God collaborates in general with all the actions of men, and it is up to them to use their liberty with prudence within the capacities that divine wisdom has given them.

But when it is a question of great undertakings that concern the leadership of men, once they have satisfied their obligation to make their plans well, and once they have exhausted all the resources of the human mind, men must put their trust in the grace of God, who sometimes inspires them to follow His eternal decrees and guides them to His own ends.[220]

---

[220] It is interesting that Richelieu here does not use the term "Providence," which he uses five times elsewhere in this work, but clearly here he is inspired by Augustine's *City of God* and the Augustinian conception of history, which he is adapting to his own view of the world.

Chapter V

Which shows that punishment and reward are two principles entirely necessary in the conduct of states

It is a common saying, all the truer since men have always said it, that punishment and reward are the two most important things in the conduct of a kingdom.

It is certain that even if one used no other principle in governing states than to be inflexible in punishing those who deserve it and religious in rewarding those who serve it well, that would not be a bad way of governing them, since there is no one who is not driven to his duty by fear or by hope.

I put punishment in front of reward because if it were necessary to deprive ourselves of one of the two, it would be better to dispense with the last than with the first.

Since one needs to be good out of self-respect, it is not strictly necessary to reward it. But since there is no crime that does not violate an obligation, there is none, consequently, that does not require any punishment for disobedience, and this obligation is so compelling that on many occasions, one cannot leave an offense unpunished without committing a new one.

I speak of things that injure the state with malicious intent and not of many others that happen by chance or misfortune, toward which princes can and must often be more lenient.

Even though pardoning, in such a case, is a laudable thing, not punishing a serious offense, which opens the door to license, is itself criminal.

Theologians as well as politicians are agreed that in certain situations when individuals would err not to pardon, those who are in charge of governing could not be excused if they were lenient.

Since experience teaches anyone who has been around that men easily lose the memory of their benefits and that the more they have, the more they want all together, it demonstrates to us that punishments are a better way of keeping everyone in line, seeing as they are harder to forget since they make a stronger impression on our senses than reason, which has no force at all on many minds.

To be severe with individuals who pride themselves on ignoring the rules is good for the public, and one could commit no worse crime against the public interest than to be lenient toward those who violate it.

Among the many swindles, factions, and machinations that have been concocted in this kingdom in my time, I have never seen that impunity has ever led any person who is naturally perverse to repent of his misconduct, most of them returning to their disgusting habits and getting better at them the 2nd time.

The leniency practiced up to the present in this kingdom has often reduced it to dire straits. Since crimes went unpunished, everyone turned his post into a craft and, instead of performing his duty, only tried to profit from it.

If the ancients felt that it was dangerous to live under a prince who is implacable in enforcing the law, they also noted that it was even worse to live in a state where impunity opens the door to licentiousness.[221]

A prince or magistrate who is afraid of sinning if he is too strict owes an accounting to God and deserves the criticism of wise men if he does not enforce the law.

I have often indicated to Your Majesty, and I beg you now to remember it carefully, because just as there are a great many princes who need to be deterred from severity in order to compensate for their inclination to cruelty, Your Majesty needs to be diverted from a false clemency that is even more dangerous than cruelty, since impunity breeds itself, and it can only be impeded by punishment.

The rod, which is the symbol of justice, can never rest. Well do I know that it must not be so accompanied by strictness that it is destitute of kindness. But this last quality is not found in leniency that authorizes disorders, which, as minor as they may be, are often so harmful to a state that they can cause its ruin.

If there is anyone in this kingdom so ill-advised as to condemn the severity necessary to states because it has not been practiced up to the present, it will only be necessary in order to open his eyes to demonstrate to him that the impunity that has been all too common up to the present is the only reason that there has never been any kind of law and order here and that the continuation of this disorder compels the recourse to extreme measures in order to stop it.

So many plots that have been concocted in the past against the kings have had no other source than their excessive leniency. Finally, anyone who knows our history cannot ignore this truth, which is all the less suspect because it comes from the mouth of one of our enemies.

When Cardinal Zapata, a very intelligent man, ran into Messers Barrault and Bautru in the antechamber of the king his master a quarter of an hour after the news had arrived in Madrid of the execution of the Duke de Montmorency, he asked them about the cause of the death of this duke. Bautru, in keeping with his fiery temperament, answered promptly in Spanish, "Sus falsas!"

---

[221] The ancients here appear to be Aristotle and Polybius, who theorized (anacyclosis) that monarchy degenerated into tyranny, aristocracy into oligarchy, and democracy into mob rule. Richelieu, however, stretches their point in favor of tyranny versus mob rule.

"No! [Zapata replied] because of the clemency of the previous kings,"[222] by which he meant that the faults that the king's predecessors had committed by their excessive leniency were a bigger cause of the punishment of the duke.

When it is a matter of crimes against the state, one must close the door to pity, disdain the complaints of the persons concerned and the mumblings of the ignorant populace, which sometimes criticizes what is best for it and often entirely necessary. Christians must forget the offenses that they receive themselves, but magistrates are obliged not to forget those that concern the public. In fact, leaving them unpunished is more like committing them all over again.

There are many people whose ignorance is so gross that they feel that it is enough to remedy an evil by prohibiting it again. But far from this being the case, I can truthfully say that new laws are not so much remedies to the disorders of states as they are admissions of the illness and living proofs of the weakness of the government, seeing as if the old laws had been well enforced, there would be no need either to renew them or to make any new ones in order to stop disorders that would never have started in the first place.

Ordinances and laws are entirely useless if they are not followed by being enforced, which is so absolutely necessary that even though in the course of ordinary affairs justice requires a complete proof, it is not the same for what concerns the state, because in such a case appearances in an emergency must sometimes be taken at face value, inasmuch as the plots and swindles that are devised against the public safety are usually so secretive that they are impossible to verify until it is too late.

It is sometimes necessary, on such occasions, to begin by enforcing them, whereas in all other cases it is necessary to have the legal proof by witnesses or by documentary evidence.

These maxims seem dangerous, and in fact they are not entirely exempt from peril. But they would only be so if they are utilized as anything but extreme remedies for evils that can only be verified by speculation. They can only be stopped by humane measures like exile or imprisonment of the suspects.

The perspicacity of a judicious person who is more knowledgeable than a superficial one about the course of affairs at present and is almost as certain about their course in the future will keep this practice from having bad consequences, and the worst that can happen is that the misfortune will only harm individuals, whose lives are preserved in this manner, and which is still valuable, seeing as their interest is not comparable to that of the public.[223]

However, it is necessary on such an occasion to be very careful not to open, by this means, the door to tyranny, which can undoubtedly be done, as I said above, by only using humane remedies in questionable cases.

---

[222] Antonio Zapata (1550–1638?), cardinal in 1603, Antoine de Jaubert (1577–1655), Count de Barrault, Guillaume de Bautrou (1588–1665), Count de Serrant.
[223] The manuscripts all say *à la veue*, which I read and translate as "whose life."

Punishments are so necessary in what concerns the public interest that it is not even possible to be lenient by equating a present evil with a good past, that is to say, leaving a disservice unpunished because the guilty party has previously served well.

This is nevertheless what has frequently been practiced in this kingdom up to the present, where not only minor offenses have been forgiven in consideration of great services but the most serious crimes nullified for insignificant services, which is entirely unbearable.

Good and evil are so diametrically opposed that they must not be compared with one another. They are two enemies between which there is no compromise. If someone deserves to be rewarded and someone else to be punished, both must be treated as they deserve.

Even if one could let noteworthy deeds remain unrewarded and dastardly crimes go unpunished, reason of state would not permit it. Crime and punishment concern the future more than the past. It is absolutely necessary for a prince to be severe in order to deter what might occur if he were known to be too lenient so that those who are most useful to the public can continue their good work and so that everybody can follow their example.

It would be wonderful if one could pardon a crime without having any grounds to fear its bad consequences and if the state did not need to pay a person for his services and still expect him to serve it in the future.

Since great souls take as much pleasure in doing good as they regret to do harm, I leave this discussion of crimes and punishments so as to finish this chapter on a good note with benefits and rewards, on which I cannot help but note that there is a great difference between favors granted as gratitude for services and those that have no other foundation than the pure favor of kings, since the ones must be greatly reduced whereas the others must have no limits other than those of the services that have been rendered to the public.

The good of the state absolutely requires that their princes be generous, and it has occurred to me that even though not being generous may be deplorable in men who are not naturally beneficent, I have always felt that such a deplorable deficiency in all sorts of persons is a dangerous imperfection in sovereigns, who have been created more than anyone else in the image of their Creator, who is naturally generous to everybody, so that they cannot fail to imitate Him on this point without offending Him.

The reason is that He wants sovereigns to take pleasure in following His example and to distribute their benefits graciously. Otherwise, they would be more like misers who cook up the food so badly when they are obliged to hold a celebration that none of his guests would want to eat it even if it were given away.

I would elaborate on this subject if I had not already talked about it in a previous chapter, indicating how important it is for princes to be good to their councillors who serve them loyally.

Chapter VI

Which points out that constantly negotiating is of no little help in foreign affairs

States receive so many advantages from continual negotiations when they are conducted prudently, and one has to see it in order to believe it.

I admit that I did not realize this truth until five or six years after I had entered into office, but I am so certain of it now that I venture to say boldly that even if one does not derive any immediate results or expect any future ones from it, constantly negotiating, either openly or secretly, is totally necessary for the good of the state.

I can truly say that in my time I have seen the affairs of France and Christendom turn entirely around after having put this principle into practice for the first time in this kingdom, under the king's authority.

There are some seeds that sprout quicker than others. There are some that are no sooner planted than they germinate into the sky and others that remain there for a long time before producing the same effect.

Whoever is constantly negotiating will ultimately find the right moment to achieve his end, and even if it does not come, there was no harm in trying, and by his negotiations he will be keeping up on what is going on in the world, which is of no small importance.

Negotiations are mild medicines that can never hurt you. It is necessary to act far and wide, and above all in Rome.

One of the three things that Antonio Perez advised the late king was to be powerful in that court, and not without reason, since all the ambassadors who are there from all the princes of Christendom find that those whose masters carry the most weight are the most influential. And indeed this opinion is not to be sneezed at since it is certain that there is no one in the world who needs to be more realistic than the Pope, and there is no place where power is more respected than in his court, where the respect that is shown to the ambassadors of princes rises and falls depending on how well or badly the affairs of their masters are going, and where it often happens that ministers get different receptions on the same day if a courier who arrived in the evening is carrying different news from the one who arrived in the morning.[224]

---

[224] Antonio Perez (1540–1611) was a trusted advisor of Philip II of Spain who fell into disgrace, ultimately escaping to France and dying there.

States are like human bodies. A good complexion leads a doctor to think that there is nothing rotting inside, and just as the good color comes from the good condition of the vital parts, the best thing that a prince can do to be influential in Rome is to be in good shape at home, and it is almost impossible to be highly reputed in that town, which, unfortunately for the public interest, has long been the key and the center of the world.

It is just plain common sense to look out for one's neighbors because they are in the best position to disturb you. They are also in a position to be useful, since the approaches to a stronghold are its first line of defense.

Mediocrities cannot see beyond the ends of their noses. But those who have been better endowed by God have learned from their doctors that what they catch from the farthest distances is nothing in comparison to how sick their own body can make them.

It is necessary to act everywhere and, what is more, to be aware of the bent of your counterparts.

Different nations move at different speeds. Some jump to conclusions; others crawl at a snail's pace.

Republics are of this last kind. They move slowly, and usually one does not get anything out of them on the first try, but it is necessary to be satisfied to go step-by-step.

And for this reason, prudence obliges those who negotiate with them to give them time and to pressure them only as much as their character permits.

It is to be noted that even though good reasons are excellent for great and powerful geniuses, stupid ones are better for the bent of mediocrities.

Everyone sees things according to his competence. With men of intelligence and great courage, everything seems easy. Those who do not possess these qualities ordinarily find difficulty in everything.

Since such persons are incapable of getting the point, they tend to waste their time debating the wrong issues.

It is necessary to treat each person according to the bent of his mind and depending on the circumstances. Far from defending one's rights vigorously without coming to a break being a way to provoke a war, it is more like a way of stifling a dispute at its birth.

On other occasions, instead of reacting violently to certain impudent statements of our counterparts, it is necessary to endure them prudently and skillfully all together and to take advantage of what they say for one's own ends.

There are people who are so presumptuous that they feel they should always act arrogantly on every occasion, since they believe that what they cannot achieve by reason, they can achieve by force. They are ashamed of themselves if they do not use threats, but aside from this being unreasonable, it never works.

Just as idiots are not good at negotiating, some characters are so tricky that they are not any better. They are like those who break the point of a needle while trying to sharpen it.

In order to succeed it is necessary to have people who are between these two extremes, and the most flexible use their wits to keep themselves from being fooled while being very careful not to fool their counterparts.

No one trusts a person who seems to be insincere, and whoever gives the impression of being honest has the advantage over him.

Since the same words often have two meanings, one that depends on the integrity of men and the other on their duplicity, it is very easy to twist them around as one wishes, and it is totally necessary to employ persons in negotiations who know how to weigh their words and who know how to write well.

The most important negotiations must not be interrupted for a minute. It is necessary to stick to them relentlessly so that they are only broken off for good reason and not because of lassitude, indifference, distraction, and changes of opinion.

One must not be discouraged by failure because it sometimes happens that what is undertaken for the best reasons turns out badly.

One cannot win all the time. And it is a great blessing when great things turn out well and only small ones turn out badly.

It would be wonderful if negotiations were so easy that they could always be successful and never turn out badly.

If someone says that this often happens, I grant that this may be so, but instead of imputing the failure to the remedy, I propose that he should impute it to those who have not known how to use it.[225]

Even if something does not always work, sometimes it does, which can be very useful to states, just like any port in a storm.

Even though the marriages that are often contracted between the crowns do not always produce the desired effect, they must not be neglected and are often one of the most important parts of the negotiations.

They are always good for keeping states on good terms with each other for a while, and that is sometimes good enough.

In order to get the best results, one has to begin with families of equally high rank so that their illustrious bloodlines are not blemished.

Besides, marriages are sometimes useful for extinguishing animosities between great states, and even though they do not always work out, what they have done for the house of Austria points out that they are not to be neglected.[226]

---

[225] Richelieu appears to be referring here to the two that stuck in his craw in the *Succinct narration*: the treaty with Spain and the Treaty of Regensburg. See notes 7 and 41 above.

[226] By its marital alliances with the heiress of the Duke of Burgundy (who was himself descended from the French royal family) and by the marriage of the eldest son of this marriage with the heiress of the Spanish monarchy, the house of Austria had ended up with the

In matters of state, it is necessary to take advantage of whatever may be useful, and nothing must be disdained.

Leagues are of this kind. Their result is often uncertain, and still they must not be dismissed, true as it is that I would never advise a great prince to enter into a league with a plan that is difficult to execute, unless he feels strong enough to succeed even if his colleagues should abandon him.

I say this for two reasons. The first is the weakness of unions, which are never too sure between sovereigns. The second is that petty princes are often as quick in involving great kings as they are lazy in supporting them, even going so far sometimes as to be the first to pull out.

Even though there is a saying that might makes right, it is nevertheless true that when two powers of unequal strength make an alliance, the more powerful runs a greater risk of being abandoned than the weaker. The reason is obvious. The reputation of a great prince is so important to him that nothing could compensate him for breaking his word. A middling sovereign is more likely to accept a good offer, since he would probably put his interest above his honor, while his ally would not even prevent it and would rather be abandoned than break his word.

Kings must be careful what treaties they make, but once they make them, they must observe them religiously.

Well do I know that a lot of politicians do not think so. But without considering in this place what Christianity has to say about such maxims, I maintain that since losing one's honor is worse than losing one's life, a great prince must prefer to sacrifice his person and the interests of his state before breaking his word, which he cannot violate without losing his reputation, which is his greatest asset.

The importance of this point makes me note that it is entirely necessary to be scrupulous in the choice of ambassadors and other negotiators and that one cannot be too severe in punishing those who exceed their powers, since this compromises the reputation of princes and the interests of their states all together.

The weakness of certain characters or the eagerness of others, who are neither weak nor malicious, to get something done is often so extraordinary that unless they are restrained by the fear of disgrace, they will always prefer to conclude bad treaties than not to conclude any.

I have seen this so often that I must end this chapter by saying that whoever fails to be strict on such an occasion is failing do what is necessary for the subsistence of a state.[227]

---

intercontinental empire against which Richelieu was then contending. Its motto was "Let others make war, you happy Austria marry!"

[227] Richelieu seems to still be fuming about the behavior of his diplomats in signing the Treaties of Monzòn and Regensburg, although he was more responsible than they were for their instructions. See notes 7, 41, and 225 above.

Chapter VII

Which demonstrates that one of the greatest advantages that a state can have is to place everyone in the employment for which he is proper

So many states have been ruined by the incompetence of those who are employed in the principal posts that a prince and his councillors cannot be too careful to make sure that everyone is placed only in functions for which he is proper.

Since even the most farsighted minds sometimes think too well of themselves and there are few men who are modest enough to be rational, the favorites of princes always think they are worthy of all sorts of employments, and they do everything they possibly can to obtain them.

However, it is true that someone who may able to serve the public in certain functions can ruin it in others.

I have seen such peculiar drawbacks from the bad choices that have been made in my time that I cannot help railing about them so that this does not happen again.

If doctors will not allow a new experiment to be tried on important persons, it is easy to see how dangerous it is to put inexperienced persons in the principal posts of a state, thereby allowing apprentices to practice where masters are necessary.

Nothing would be more capable of ruining a state than raising all sorts of havoc with such behavior.

A bad choice of ambassador to negotiate an important treaty can by his incompetence cause a great deal of harm.

A general who is incapable of such employment is capable of risking the fortunes of his master and the welfare of his state.

The governor of an important stronghold who is completely lacking in what it takes to defend it could do enough damage in a moment to ruin an entire kingdom for a whole century.

On the contrary, I venture to say that if all those who were in public employment were worthy of it, not only would states avoid a great many incidents which would disturb their peace, but they would be deliriously happy.

Well do I know that it is very difficult to find subjects with the requisite qualifications for the loads that they are designed to bear, but they must at least possess the principal ones, and when one can find the best of the lot in such a dismal age, it is no small pleasure to have done so.

If the mask under which most men hide their faces and the guiles that they ordinarily use in order to hide their deficiencies disguise them to the point that their malice is only discovered once they are in the big posts, it is necessary to act promptly in order to repair the damage. And if some degree of incompetence may charitably be tolerated, the interest of the state can never be sacrificed to the interest of individuals.

It is in this place that it is necessary to indicate to kings how answerable they are to God when they distribute the most important employments and posts out of pure favor, which cannot be done with mediocrities without harming their states.

It is on this occasion that it is necessary to demonstrate to them without condemning their personal likes and dislikes, which are perfectly natural, that this does not excuse princes who let themselves go to the point of distributing posts that are useful to whomever they like while harming the state.

The public cannot reasonably complain about those who are fortunate enough to receive such favors from a prince even if they are not worthy of them, unless they are excessive. But it is a bad omen when someone who is most valued for his merit is not the most valued by his prince, and states are never in such bad shape as when his inclinations for some individual prevail over the services of those who are the most useful to the public. In such a case, neither being well considered by the sovereign, nor his affection, nor the hope of reward arouses any virtue. One becomes indifferent, jealous, and frustrated. Everyone neglects his duty because no one thinks it is worth doing.[228]

A prince who wants to be loved by his subjects must fill the principal posts and highest dignities in his state with persons of such high repute that everybody can tell why he made this choice.

Such people must be sought for everywhere in the state and not just in the crowd that spends more time in mobbing the antechambers of kings and their favorites than in serving the state.

If favor plays no part in the selections and they are only based on merit, not only will the state be well served but princes will avoid a great deal of ingratitude, since those who are the least appreciative of the benefits that they receive deserve them the least, and the same qualities that make men worthy of their benefits are those that make them capable of appreciating what they are getting.

---

[228] Cinq-Mars, again! In some ways, the fear of this fop almost trumps the fear of going to hell as a running subtext of this entire work. See also notes 229 and 230 below.

Many begin with the best of intentions. But they are carried away by their character to be quick to forget their obligations because they are thinking only of themselves, and just like the fire that turns everything into flames, they only consider the public interest as something to burn, while ignoring both their benefactors and their country. Favor can be harmless enough now and then. But a kingdom is in bad shape when the throne of this false goddess is raised higher than reason.

Merit must always carry the most weight, and when justice is on one side, favor becomes injustice.

Favorites are all the more dangerous because those who are raised by fortune rarely utilize their reason, and since it not always favorable to their plans, it is usually powerless to stop the damage that they are doing to the state.

To be frank, I know of nothing more capable of ruining the most flourishing kingdom in the world than the appetite of such people or the wiles of a woman, when a prince is infatuated.

I assert this all the more boldly in that there is no other remedy to this kind of evil except pure chance, which, like a bad doctor, allows its patients to die without lifting a finger.

Thus, just as the most shining light will not help a blind man even get a glimpse of his way, there is no reason that can open the eyes of a prince who has put on the blindfold of favoritism and passion.

Whoever has his eyes covered can only make the right choice by pure chance, and thusly, since the security of the state requires that this always be done with reason, it also requires that princes not be possessed by persons who keep them from seeing what is put before their eyes.

When the hearts of princes are captured in such ways, it is almost impossible to get anything done, because the guiles of those who are masters of their affections blacken the purest actions and make the most noteworthy services pass as offenses.

Many princes have been lost for having preferred their personal affections to the public interest.

Some of their misfortunes have happened to them because of their unbridled passions for women.

Some have fallen into similar drawbacks by a simple but blind passion for their servants and have ruined themselves in trying to make their fortune.

There are others who may be cold by nature, but they have no less become so infatuated with some individuals that they have been the cause of their loss.

This proposition may seem strange, perhaps, but it is perfectly understandable if one considers that such drawbacks are the illnesses of a disturbed mind, so that just as fevers are caused by the deficiency of humors, infatuations have more to do with the weakness of the donor than with the merits of the recipient.

Such illnesses ordinarily cure themselves in that they are short and sweet. But, just like any fever, if they continue, they may be very difficult to cure or even lead to the death of the patient.[229]

The wisest princes have avoided all these kinds of illnesses by controlling their affections and letting reason be their guide.

Many have recovered after having learned, at their expense, that if they had not done so, they would inevitably have been lost.

To return to the point of this chapter, which was to demonstrate how important it is to determine who is most proper for employments. I shall finish by saying that, since the interest of men is what ordinarily interferes with their duties, when it is a question of the highest employments, clergymen are most often preferable to others, not because they are less devoted to their own interest but because they have fewer close relations, since they have neither wives nor children.

---

[229] Cf. notes 201 and 228 above, as well as note 230 below. Richelieu seems to be getting ever more desperate about Cinq-Mars.

Chapter VIII

Which treats of the damage that flatterers, gossips, and intriguers ordinarily cause in states and indicates how important it is to keep them away from kings and remove them from their court

There is no plague more capable of ruining a state than flatterers, gossips, and certain characters who have no other plan than to raise trouble at its court.

They are so industrious in spreading their poison in various lethal doses that it is difficult to protect oneself against them without being extremely careful.

Since they have neither the class nor the merit to participate in affairs or in the public interest, they are only interested in disturbing it. Thus, since they think they can gain a great deal by confusion, they do everything that they can to disrupt law and order by guiles and gossip, which makes them entirely hopeless in a well-disciplined state, which can only be founded on the very qualities they lack.

Aside from the fact that whoever is not in on an affair ordinarily tries to ruin it, such people will stop at nothing in order to do so, and thusly princes must take every precaution against their malice, which is often very hard to do.

There are some completely lacking in courage and wit who still have enough to feign great firmness and profound wisdom and who show off by criticizing everything, even though it may have been the best thing to do under the circumstances.

There is nothing so easy as to find plausible reasons for condemning something that could not have been done any better without making a terrible mistake.

Others who do not have a clue disapprove by their gestures, by shaking their heads, and by their frowns what they are in no position to judge.

To be perfectly frank, when it is a question of such people, it is not enough for princes to turn a deaf ear to them, but they must be banished both from their councils and from their court all together, because aside from the fact that they may be smooth talkers, even if they are not convincing, the princes will retain some impression that will return the next time they hear the same argument. And indeed, their lack of dedication to affairs often makes them judge by the number of witnesses rather than by the weight of the accusation.

I can hardly recount how many misfortunes these bad characters have brought about during the reign of Your Majesty, and I am so concerned for the good of the state that I am compelled to say that it is necessary to be pitiless toward such people and to get them out of the way quickly to prevent any more occurrences like those that have occurred in my time.

As unbending as a prince may be, he cannot afford to keep bad characters around him who might catch him unawares, as can happen in a moment to the healthiest of men.

It is necessary to kick out these public pests and never bring them back unless they have entirely disposed of their venom, which hardly ever happens. The desirability of peace requires the continuation of their separation rather than the charity of their recall.

I put forward this proposal boldly because I have never seen any characters who are lovers of factions and have been brought up in the intrigues of the court shed the bad habits in their nature except by their loss of power, which, when you come right down to it, does not even change them, since their desire to cause trouble remains even after they have no more power.[230]

Well do I know that some of these bad characters may sincerely reform. But since experience has taught me that for one who truly repents, one hundred return to their wretched habits, I have boldly decided that it is better to be severe toward an individual who is worthy of forgiveness than to expose the state to harm for being too lenient, either to those who only pay lip service to their faults or to those whose frivolity is likely to get them into even worse trouble.

It should hardly be surprising that angels are never bad because they are in a constant state of grace, but that characters bent on this kind of malice should behave when they can be bad, that would be a miracle that only God can perform. And it is certain that a man of great integrity would have much more trouble in this corrupt age than one who is almost as corrupt as it is.

It is sometimes felt to be part of the kindness of kings to tolerate things that seem of little importance in their beginnings, and I, myself, say that they could not be too careful to extinguish the smallest intrigues in their council and in their court at their birth.

Great conflagrations ordinarily start with small sparks. Whoever snuffs one out never knows what fire he has prevented, but if he allows another one to

---

[230] In this chapter Richelieu seems to be warning Louis XIII about Cinq-Mars even more frantically than in the previous one. Yet the cardinal is not daring to do this to his face. However, once he obtained evidence that the marquis had authorized a treaty with Spain to arrest Richelieu and force the king to make peace, he did confront Louis with the proof. Cinq-Mars was arrested in Narbonne on June 13, 1642, and executed in Lyon on September 12.

burn just to see, even though the same causes do not always produce the same effects, it might be too late to do anything about it. Whether it is true or false,

^BRemora^B

as the naturalists tell us, that a small fish can stop a ship from sailing even though it cannot steer it, it is easy to see that it is necessary to be extremely careful to purge whoever wants to stop the course of affairs even though he can never advance them.[231]

On such occasions, it is not enough to keep away the great nobles because of their power. It is also necessary to do the same with the small because of their malice. All are equally dangerous, and if there is any difference between them, the little people, since they are more obscure, are more to be feared.

Just as the bad air, about which I have already spoken, locked up in a chest often infests a house, from where the contagion of the plague subsequently spreads to an entire city, so backroom intrigues often fill the courts of princes with factions that disturb the body politic, and I can truthfully say that I have never seen disturbances in this kingdom that have had any other beginning. I repeat one more time that it is more important than it seems to stifle the first sparks of such discords when they appear and even to prevent them by sending away those who have no other desire than to light them up.

The peace of the state is much too important not to resort to this remedy without being responsible to God.

I have sometimes seen the court in peace time so full of factions for not having followed this good advice that it has almost overthrown the government.

Since this knowledge, which is what history has taught Your Majesty about similar perils in which many, and particularly the latest, of your predecessors have found themselves, has caused you to have recourse to this remedy, I have seen France enjoying such a perfect peace at home while fighting a war abroad that no one would never have guessed that she had the greatest powers on her hands.[232]

Maybe it will be said that the factions and troubles that I have just mentioned have happened more through the industry of women than the malice of flatterers.

But, on the contrary, far from this case contradicting what I have put forward, it confirms it powerfully since, in speaking of flatterers and other similar characters, I do not mean to exclude women, who are more dangerous than men and whose attractions are more capable of overthrowing councils, courts, and states than the most fiendish types imaginable.

---

[231] The naturalist in question is Pliny the Younger. See his *Historia naturalis*, Bk. IX, Ch. 41 and Bk. XXXII, Ch. 1. The name of the fish was inserted and underlined by Cherré in B[11] and appears in all subsequent copies that we have.

[232] Richelieu seems to have forgotten about the nu-pied peasant revolt in Normandy in 1639.

It is true that while the queens Catherine and Marie de Medici participated in the running of the state, various women got involved in affairs under their shadow, and some were so ingenious and attractive that they caused unimaginable evils since their charms captivated the best men in the kingdom and the most unfortunate. They achieved their ends, since they gratified their own passions while often discrediting whomever they did not like, just because they were useful to the state.[233]

I could elaborate on this subject, but I shall hold my tongue for various reasons, since I cannot condemn flattery and engage in it at the same time, except to say that favorites, of whom I have spoken in the preceding chapter, are the epitome of all of those whose malice I have just examined.

In conclusion, it only remains for me to say that it is impossible to protect a state from all the misfortunes that these kinds of characters can cause without sending them away from the court, since no one can keep a snake in his bosom without getting bitten.

---

[233] A reference to Catherine de Medici's "flying squadron," a group of about eighty beautiful and intelligent women used by her to seduce and spy upon important personages in her court.

Chapter IX

Which treats of the power of a prince

FIRST SECTION

Which shows that a prince must be powerful in order to be esteemed by his subjects and by foreigners

Since power is one of the things that is most necessary for the greatness of kings and the success of their government, those who have the principal conduct of a state have a particular obligation to do everything possible in order to make their master so well respected that he may be considered powerful by everybody.

Just as kindness is the object of love, power is the cause of fear. It is certain that of all the principles capable of animating a state, fear, which is founded on esteem and respect, has the most force because it affects everyone most of all.

If this principle is extremely efficacious with regard to the interior of a state, it is no less of its exterior, since both subjects and foreigners view the power of the state in the same light and avoid offending a prince who they realize is able to hurt them at his will.

I have noted in passing that the foundation of the power I am talking about must be esteem and respect. I add now that it is so necessary that if it draws its origin from any other principle, it is very dangerous in that instead of causing a reasonable fear, it brings hatred to princes, and they are never as bad off as when they are despised by the public.

Power, which makes princes esteemed and feared, is of many different species. It is a tree with many branches, which spring from the same roots:

The prince must be powerful by his reputation.

By a reasonable number of soldiers in a well-equipped standing army.

By enough revenue for sustaining his ordinary expenses and by enough money in his coffers for those that often come up when they are least expected. Finally, by being loved by his subjects, as we will clearly prove.

SECOND SECTION

Which points out that a king must be powerful by his reputation and proposes what is necessary to him for this end

A reputation is all the more necessary to a prince because whoever is held in high repute can do more with his name alone than those held in low esteem can do with their armies.

They are obliged to cherish it more than their own life, and they must prefer to risk everything they have than to allow it to be tarnished in any way, since it is certain that the first crack in the reputation of a prince, as tiny as it may be, is the first step to his ruin.

Considering this, I say boldly that princes must never feel that they can profit from anything if it blemishes their honor in any small way. They are blind or deaf to their own interests if they do such a thing. In fact, history teaches us that in each and every instance, princes with a good reputation have always accomplished more than those who have been deficient in this quality, even though they may have surpassed them in strength, wealth, and any other kind of power. Just as they cannot be too jealous of it, their councillors cannot be too careful to exploit their good personal qualities.

Those who will formulate their conduct on the rules and principles contained in the present testament will doubtless acquire a reputation that will carry no little weight in the minds of their subjects and their neighbors, particularly since, if they are faithful to God, they will be with themselves, that is to say, true to their word and loyal in their promises, conditions so absolutely necessary to the reputation of a prince that whoever is without them will not be esteemed by anybody, just as it is impossible for him who possesses them not to be revered and trusted by everybody.

I could recount many examples of this truth, but since I do not want this work to be a collection of extracts from other books, easy enough for anyone to make, I am satisfied with not putting forward anything that is not so obvious that any sensible person will find the proof in his own reasoning.

THIRD SECTION

Which clearly proves that a prince must have powerful forces on his frontiers

One would have to be lacking in common sense not to realize how important it is for great states to have their frontiers well furbished and fortified.

This is all the more necessary for this kingdom, where, even if the frivolity of our nation would render it incapable of making great conquests, its valor will render it invincible in defense if it has some great strongholds so well fortified and so well provisioned that it could demonstrate its courage without being exposed to allowing a great many discomforts, which are the only enemies it has to fear.

A well-fortified frontier is capable either of making the enemies lose any desire they may have to conspire against the state or, at least, to make them think twice before venturing to resort to force.

Our nation is so excitable that it needs to be protected against any terror that might result from an unforeseen attack if it did not know that the border of this kingdom has ramparts so strong that no sneak attack is powerful enough to overrun them and that it would take a lot of time to take them over.

Since the latest method of some of the enemies of this state is to prefer to starve the strongholds that they besiege rather than to capture them by brute force and to ruin the countryside with cavalry instead of advancing on foot with large bodies of infantry, as they previously did, it is clear not only that the frontier strongholds are useful to stymie such efforts but that they are a godsend to states. It is impossible for the enemy to make much progress if they leave cities behind them to cut their communications and their convoys all together.

This consideration obliges me to indicate that it is not enough to fortify strongholds for as long as they can resist an attack by brute force, but it is also necessary that they be furnished at least with everything needed for more than a year, which is enough time to ruin an enemy army or to be allowed to raise the siege conveniently.

Well do I know that it is impossible for the greatest kings to provision too many citadels thusly. But this is not the case with large cities where the population produces huge quantities of things, whose governor could not manage to find a way to collect enough provisions, and where it is easy to oblige the inhabitants to store up enough victuals for a year, which could also suffice for six more months, if, as reason demands, the useless mouths are expelled.[234]

Far from claiming that such a system should dispense sovereigns from having public storehouses, I feel, on the contrary, that they could not have too many and that they should establish such good regulations for their conservation that the governors, who are responsible for their maintenance, would not be able to misuse them or to use them for their own profit.

---

[234] This analysis by Richelieu provides an amazing insight into the relative resources of rich cities in comparison to monarchs in the seventeenth century. It is in this manner that the rich cities of the Dutch Republic were able to fight the Spanish monarchy to a standstill and that the city of London was about to stand up to the English monarchy, but Richelieu is too self-confident to see danger for his own monarchy coming from the same source.

I cannot positively specify the number of cannons, powder, balls, and other munitions that have to be in each stronghold, because it has to be different, depending on their size. But I insist that the victuals are no less necessary than the weapons and that no stronghold under siege could have enough if it were lacking in what is absolutely necessary for its defense, since experience has demonstrated that those who do the most shooting ordinarily also do the most killing. When a stronghold is besieged, it is almost better to save the bread than the powder.

[B]Just to make sure, I shall note in this place that stores of saltpeter, sulfur, and coal are better than ground powder because it spoils easily over time, and an explosion is to be feared.[B]

Since the ancients have noted very appropriately that the true strength of strongholds lies in their men, I can only say subsequently that fortifications are useless if the governor and the officers who command in a stronghold do not have the courage to match their walls and ramparts and if the garrison is not sufficient for the size of the stronghold and the locations to be defended.

Experience has pointed out to us on various occasions that the smallest shacks have often been impregnable because of the firmness and courage of those who defend them and that the best citadels are not worth much when those inside them do not have the courage to do so.

Considering this, princes could not be too careful to choose carefully those to whom they entrust their frontiers, because the security and tranquility of the state depend primarily on their fidelity, their vigilance, their courage, and their experience, and the deficiency of one of these qualities costs states a great deal if not everything.

FOURTH SECTION

Which treats of the force of the army that a state must have on land

Because of its length, this section has various subdivisions that will be marked in the margins.[235]

The most powerful state in the world can never rest easily if it is not able to protect itself at any time from an unexpected invasion or a surprise attack.

For this purpose, it is necessary that a great kingdom like this one should always maintain a body of men-at-arms sufficient to prevent the plans that hatred or envy might formulate against its prosperity and greatness while it might seem to be resting easily, or at least to stifle them at their birth.

---

[235] The titles of these subdivisions appear neither in our Text A nor in our Text B¹, but they do appear in all the remaining Texts B, so they must have been intended as Text A and as Text B was being developed. I have inserted them in the margin enclosed by the marker [B], exactly like those that identify the other additions in Text B.

Might is most often right in matters of state, and the weak are almost always wrong in most everybody's eyes.

Just as a soldier who is not always carrying his sword invariably runs into trouble, a kingdom that is not always on its guard and able to protect itself from a surprise attack has a great deal to fear.

The public interest obliges those who govern states to protect them not only from misfortune but also from the fear of it.

ᴮThe power of princes is the only thing that can produce this effect, and thusly it remains to see what forces must be maintained in this kingdomᴮ

Since reason demands for there to be a geometric proportion between what sustains and what is sustained, it is certain that it is necessary to have more than token forces in order to sustain such a great kingdom as this one.

For such an important end, there can and must be two kinds of soldiers for the preservation of this state: some must be enrolled so as to be ready whenever needed and others to be constantly in service and ready immediately.

ᴮNumber of soldiers who must be maintained in this kingdomᴮ

In order to keep the frontier towns well furbished and be able to resist any surprise attack, it is necessary to maintain a body of at least 4,000 horse and 40,000 infantrymen constantly in service, and if it is not too expensive to the state, a thousand gentlemen for the cavalry and five thousand for the infantry, ready to be raised whenever the occasion requires it.

Perhaps it will be said that the defense of the state does not require such great preparations.

But, far from this institution being a burden to France, I say that it is necessary in order to wage a long war if the good of the state will demand it, and the nobility and the people will get relief and advantages out of it.

ᴮWar is sometimes necessaryᴮ

In the opinion of the most sensible, war is sometimes a necessary evil and at other times absolutely necessary and desirable.

States need certain periods of time in order to purge their ill humors to recover what belongs to them, to avenge an insult that would otherwise bring on another, to protect their allies from being oppressed, to humble the pride of a conqueror, to prevent imminent threats if they cannot be avoided, and, finally, in a variety of other instances.

I maintain, and it is true, that any successful war is a just one, because if it were not, even though it turned out well in the eyes of the world, it would be necessary to answer for it before the tribunal of God.

Considering this, the first thing to do when compelled to take up arms is carefully to examine the justice of doing it with theologians of competence and integrity.

If this is the case, one must think only of the means of waging the war effectively, not the least of which is to choose one's time.

The difference between whoever flies off the handle and whoever is reasonable is that the first runs the risk of doing harm to himself in order to hurt his enemy, whereas the last hides his feelings until he can to hurt his enemy without hurting himself.

The first acts in haste, following his natural instincts, and the last acts like a rational human being.

In order to wage war well, it is not enough to find the right time or to have a good number of men, an abundance of money, victuals, and military supplies; what is most important is that the men be well trained and properly disciplined for their intended roles and that the money for victuals and supplies is spent properly.

It is easy to talk in generalities, but it is difficult to put them into practice; however, if this is neglected, the war could only be won by chance or by a miracle, which no wise people can expect.

There is no nation in the world as unsuitable for war as ours. Its frivolity and impatience in whatever it does are the two principles that, to my great regret, only go to prove this proposition.

Even though Caesar said that the Franks know two things, the art of war and the art of talking, I admit that I have not as yet been able to understand on what foundation he attributes this first quality to them, seeing as how the two qualities necessary in war, patience and endurance, are only rarely found in them.[236]

If this condition accompanied their valor, the universe would not be big enough to hold their conquests. But since the great courage that God has given them renders them suitable to defeat whoever opposes them with strength, their frivolity and laziness render them incapable of surmounting the feeblest delaying tactics of their enemy.

From which it comes that they are not suited to conquests that require time or to preserving those they could make in an instant.

They are not only frivolous and impatient and unaccustomed to work, but, aside from that, they are accused of constantly complaining and of being unpatriotic, and this accusation is so well founded, because there are more of them who fail in their obligation to their birth than in all the nations of the world.

There are a few who bear arms against their natural prince, and there is no war against France where there are no Frenchmen, and when they do fight

---

[236] In point of fact, Caesar, in his *Gallic Wars*, Book IV, accuses them of being credulous and irresponsible.

for their country, they show such little interest in its cause that they make no effort to overcome their natural deficiencies on its behalf.

They dash off for two hundred leagues looking for a battle, and they will not wait eight days for one. They get bored even before getting to work.

They do not fear peril, but they do not want it to cause them any discomfort. They cannot bear its slightest inconveniences. They do not have the stamina to defer their pleasure for a moment. They even get bored in the midst of their prosperity.

At the beginning of their undertakings, their enthusiasm is no less extraordinary, and, in fact, they are more than men for a moment, but in a short time this passes so that they become no better than average, and in the long run they get disgusted and so flabby that they are worse than women.

They always have the courage to fight provided one wants them to come to blows right away. But they will not wait, even though their honor, the reputation of their nation, and the service of their master oblige them to do it.

They know neither how to draw the fruits of victory nor how to resist the fortune of a victorious enemy. They are blinded more than anyone else by prosperity and go to pieces in adversity and under stress. Finally, they are subject to so many deficiencies that it is not without reason that some perspicacious minds have been astonished at how this monarchy could have lasted for as long as it has, seeing as how, even though she has always found children who have been faithful to her, she has never been attacked without the enemies having found vipers in her midst who have done everything they could to eat the entrails of their mother.

Well do I know that in exchange for these imperfections, the French have many good qualities. They are valiant, courteous, and humane; their hearts are far from being cruel and so bereft of any rancor that they easily forgive and forget. But even though these qualities are the gems of civil life and the essence of Christianity, it still remains that since they are devoid of stamina, patience, and discipline, they are delicious meats, readily served and easily eaten.

I am well aware that the prudence of God, which is admirable in everything, is particularly so in having wanted to balance the bad qualities of each nation by other advantages to make up for them.

If the French nation is frivolous and impatient, its valor and impetuosity often let them do in a single try what it takes others a long time to accomplish.

If their restlessness keeps them from hanging around in the armies, the goodness of God has made this kingdom so abundant in men that there are always enough who are frivolous enough to want to join up whenever the others want to go off.[237]

---

[237] A few folios down, Richelieu will forget what he has written here.

If their lack of patriotism sometimes makes them take up arms against their king, their inconstancy and the vacillation to which they are subject makes it so difficult to rely on them that they do more harm to themselves than they can do to their country.

It is certain that the Spanish surpass us in steadfastness, in firmness, in zeal, and in loyalty toward their king, but on the other hand, this kingdom is barren, almost desert in certain places, and it has so few men that without this firmness, it would often be left to itself.

Besides, if among the French, some individuals take sides against their master, the Spanish sometimes decide to mutiny in entire units of their armies.

If the Emperor has the advantage of dominating a nation that is the breeding ground of soldiers, he also has the disadvantage that it is constantly changing sides and religions, that it is extraordinarily given to drinking and much more unbridled than ours when on campaign.

In a word, every nation has its deficiencies, and the most prudent are those who try to acquire artificially what nature has not given them.

It is easier to add stamina, patience, and discipline to the courage, valor, and courtesy of the French than to give to the more phlegmatic nations the fire that they have not been born with.

The French can do anything provided that their commanders are able to teach them what to do.

Their courage, which leads them to go looking for war to the four corners of the world, proves this point, since they get along with the Spanish in their armies, with the Swedes in their country, with the Croats among their troops, and with the Dutch in their provinces.

They submit to their discipline, which clearly shows that if we put up with their natural deficiencies at home, it is because we do not know what to do about them.

It is not as much their fault if they are so undisciplined in this kingdom as that of their commanders, who are ordinarily satisfied with issuing impressive orders without bothering to have them obeyed.

There is nothing so easy as to issue the right rules, and even though it may be difficult to put them into practice, it is not impossible.

It is necessary, if possible, to explain oneself by reason and subsequently to be absolutely pitiless in punishing those who violate it.

If one, two, or three punishments do not stop the disobedience, it will eventually prevail, and I venture to answer Your Majesty that if you find some competent leaders worthy of command, you will find some obedient subjects, and it is certain that the widespread opinion that the French are absolutely incapable of any kind of discipline is only founded on the incompetence of the commanders, who do not know how to find the means necessary to achieve their ends.

The siege of La Rochelle, when an army of 25,000 men lived like monks under arms, the trip to Pinerolo, where they did the same, clearly prove what I say.

But it is necessary for the commander to have no superior and that he be taken as such, since it is certain that if it was seen that he did not have enough firmness to be inflexible in enforcing his rules, no one would think himself obliged to follow them, or at least some would want to take the chance of violating them, thinking that they could do it with impunity. But if a commander gets less tired of punishing than the delinquents of disobeying, his resolution will stop the spread of our outrageous frivolity. Without such a remedy, there is no hope of restraining a nation as bursting with impetuosity as ours.

The punishments of Marillac and Montmorency returned the great nobles of this kingdom to their duty in a moment, and I venture to assure that doing this to ᴮtenᴮ officers and ᴮfiftyᴮ soldiers will maintain entire armies in their discipline and able to do everything that is wanted of them.

Thus, by not failing to punish all those who fail to do their duty, one will punish less, seeing as how not many will flippantly want to expose themselves to their ruin when they know it will be inevitable, and through a few deaths, one will save many a life and maintain order at the same time.

The deficiencies of this nation have never appeared larger than in the reign of Your Majesty, who, as noteworthy as you are for your great success and extreme prudence, will also go down in history for all the treachery you have had to put up with and for all the frivolities committed against your service.

After having searched many times for the reasons for the one and the other, I do not hesitate to say that the rage for treachery comes from the weakness of Your Majesty's minor years, during which people got so accustomed to every kind of license that they believed that they could continue it with the same impunity during your reign. ᴮMany reasons for these deficiencies may be noted.ᴮ

The first is that since there are too many schools, too many monks, too many officials of justice and of finance, and a lot fewer soldiers than before, the number of those who desert from the army is more alarming because there are not so many to replace those who abandon their duty.[238]

The second is that in the past, military men made more money than they do now, while the financiers and contractors fatten up on all of France, to the great disgust of those who are compelled to expose their lives almost in vain.

---

[238] Richelieu forgets here what he has stated twenty paragraphs previously about always being able to fill the ranks of his army and now deplores the shortage of recruits for the army by attempting to explain the reasons for it. He also seems to have forgotten a transition from the previous paragraph that Cherré had to supply in his Bᴵᴵ.

The third is that the commanders of today are less careful about military discipline and less strict about punishing deserters than our fathers were.

The fourth is that the long spell during which the French did not have any foreign wars or any powerful enemies to fight had almost made them forget how to do it and incapable of undergoing its fatigues, even though it is necessary to withstand a lot of them when one has to deal with such crafty and powerful enemies.

I add to these considerations that the health of Your Majesty has not always permitted you to be at the head of your armies and that the French are so demanding that they do not feel comfortable about risking their life unless their master reassures them by his presence.

Only the enemies of this state can wage war successfully with mere lieutenants. The stamina of their nation gives them this advantage. But France is less suitable than any other to do the same because the enthusiasm that gives them the courage and the desire to fight also gives them the impatience that can only be controlled by the presence of their king.

If it has sometimes happened that a great undertaking has succeeded under some lieutenants, it will undoubtedly be found that those who have had this success have been persons of great authority, whether because of the confidence of their master and by their personal merit or that the wars were so short that it was not necessary to overcome the disposition of the French.

It causes me no little pain in this place to be obliged to demonstrate to Your Majesty the deficiencies that you have frequently noticed in your nobility. However, they are so well known that it is impossible to hide them. And my affection for it makes it necessary to examine them so as to excuse them and look for a good remedy. It has not done too badly at certain times during the reign of Your Majesty. But I can undoubtedly demonstrate the reason why.

There is no one who does not easily understand that there is a huge difference between persons who make it to the top on their own and the numbskulls who remain at the bottom.

The cream of the nobility who willingly go to war are the persons who rise, and they are admired by everybody, while those who go only out of necessity because of the laws of the kingdom are, if not the dregs, at least the wine at the bottom of the barrel that smells of wood and is so worthless that it can hardly be used for the valets.

There is no community that does not have many more worse members than good ones, and, thusly, since a little chaff is able to spoil a heap of wheat, it is no wonder if, when the nobility meets, the majority corrupts the minority, easy as it is for the cowards and those who are indifferent to the public interest to spoil the good by a contagion almost inevitable on such occasions. And just as the best wine becomes worthless if it is mixed with the dregs, the service of the best nobility is not only useless but harmful when it is joined by the dregs.

BCall to arms made in 1635B
Since this discussion gives me occasion to discuss the call to arms and the second call to arms, I cannot avoid saying that it is an assembly of the nobility without anyone in authority, an assembly conducted without any rules or discipline, whose duration is so unpredictable that the frivolity, cowardice, malice, and disgust of three or four persons is capable of dissolving it in a moment, an assembly that ruins many more of the places it passes through than the regular troops who are in the pay of Your Majesty and who pay for a part of what they receive there, whereas it does not pay for anything at all.[239]

It never stands guard in an army, with the result that it does nothing, and everyone else gets disgusted. If it does not fight as soon as it arrives, just as it has been quick to come, it is ready to return, and it is constantly threatening to do so. In withdrawing, it corrupts a lot of people by its bad example, but its most malicious troopers do their best to cover their infamy by hinting that they did not leave without reason, so that it weakens and flusters the armies at the same time.

Your Majesty knows these truths better than I do, since you have seen them with your very eyes. Without emphasizing the deficiencies of an order whose perfections I would rather indicate, my conscience obliges me to say boldly that one must never have recourse to such help, which does the state more harm than good.

But, so that this kingdom is not deprived of the services of the nobility, which has always been its primary nerve and which is obliged to serve it in time of war because of the fiefs that are given to it on this condition and the privileges that it enjoys over the people in time of peace, it is necessary to tax all the fiefs in each bailiwick according to its revenue and to form regular companies with the returns in which those who prefer to serve in person than to pay the assessment of their fief will be received, provided they commit themselves to fulfill the terms of their obligation.[240]

Prudence demands that men be used according to their bent, that nature is supplemented by art, and for this reason, it is necessary to use the body of the nobility if some use is to be made of them.[241]

---

[239] I translate *ban* and *arrière-ban* as "call to arms" and "second call to arms." These refer to two stages of calling out the nobility to aid in defending the country.

[240] See also First Part, Chapter III, First Section. One wonders what complications would arise in a noble family whose patriarch was too old to serve, whose son or sons were infirm or who had no male children of military age, whose late grandparent had served, or who had a male son or sons serving in a diplomatic post.

[241] I guess that would cover the diplomats.

Next, I am further obliged to note that it is almost impossible to undertake great wars successfully only with the French.[242]

Foreigners are absolutely necessary to maintain   ᴮForeigners necessaryᴮ
the units of the armies, and if the French cavalry
is good for fighting, it cannot do without the foreign one to stand guard and endure the fatigues of an army.

Our nation, bursting and enthusiastic for combat, is not as vigilant in being on guard or suitable for formulating plans or enterprises that cannot easily be executed.

Half of the Roman armies were always composed of foreigners, and we have experienced the danger of doing otherwise. It is necessary to compensate for the deficiency of our nation by the good qualities of those who can assist us while still correcting our imperfections as much as possible.

Now, since we are lacking in well-disciplined soldiers, firm and reliable in their duty, we are even more lacking in leaders with the necessary qualities, and it is not enough to remedy one of these deficiencies; it is also necessary to see to both.

There are few in the world, but more in France than anywhere else, who do not go wild in prosperity and do not go to pieces in adversity and in the face of obstructions.

It is nevertheless necessary for there to be people in the administration of states and in command of armies who are exempt from these deficiencies. Otherwise, one would be at risk of never drawing any advantage from the favorable opportunities that God could send us and losing a great deal with the 1ˢᵗ misfortune that would happen to us. Even though it is the head that guides the rest of the body and judgment is the most essential part of a commander, it is nevertheless true that in a general I prefer more courage to more brains.

This proposition may seem astonishing, perhaps, because it is contrary to what many have thought on this subject, but its reason is evident.

Since those who are courageous are not daunted by peril, they retain the intelligence that God has given them, and their judgment serves them very well on such occasions, whereas those who do not have much courage get flustered easily. They get so disturbed that however ingenious they may be, they get so frightened that they lose their head. I do not think there is much difference between putting a thief in charge of the finances and giving command of an army to someone with less courage.

Since the avarice and acquisitiveness of the first does not always make him take every opportunity to augment the wealth of his master, the desire of the second to save his life and limb, which may well be imaginary in many cases,

---

[242] This and the next few articles are a direct rebuttal of Machiavelli's *The Prince*, Chapters XII and XIII.

is liable to lose many advantages for the armies, so that just as the 1st is liable to make mistakes out of desire to fill his purse, the latter is just as liable to do it out of desire to save his life.

Among courageous people, there are some who are valiant by nature and others who are so only by reason. The first are much better as soldiers than as captains, because their valor is ordinarily accompanied by brutality, but the second are good as leaders. However, it is still desirable that their reasonable valor not be lacking along with the natural one, because otherwise it is to be feared that the foresight of the many drawbacks that as often as not never happen might deter the one who acts more rationally from undertaking what might succeed for others who are less intellectual and bolder.

A lack of judgment contributes a great deal to the valor of certain persons who run great risks because they do not realize the peril to which they are exposing themselves.

Judgment is of no little value for others in order to feign to be rash on certain occasions that appear more dangerous than they actually are in the mind of those to whom God has given a superior intelligence.

Just as valor without judgment is not good in a general, if he is eminently farsighted and judicious, he needs sincerity, which keeps him from presenting his guile as courage. Since men often disguise themselves in various fashions, it is difficult to distinguish what comes from the head from what comes from the heart.

There are some people naturally so valiant that they almost stay that way to their grave. Others, who are not of this sort, make an effort in their youth to appear as such so as to acquire some reputation, under the cover of which they can pass their life without infamy.

These last have no sooner attained their end than the signs of their valor disappear because they have their payment, and guile and not their natural inclination was the source of their courage.

It is necessary to be careful not to choose a commander of this nature by remembering that guile is as dangerous to commanders as judgment and courage is necessary to them.

These two qualities must march in lock step, along with many others.

Great enterprises are no child's play. If the truth be said, they require maturity in those who undertake them. But it is also true that just as the maturity of judgment that advances with age is useful in order to formulate a plan, the fire of youth is no less necessary to execute it, and it is certain that fortune often smiles on the young and turns its back on the old.[243]

It is necessary to note in this regard that there is a great difference between being inexperienced, young, and old.

---

[243] Cf. Machiavelli's *The Prince*, Chapter XXV.

It is difficult to be good and inexperienced all together. To be excellent, it is necessary to be young in years, but not in years of service, and even though the old are ordinarily the wisest, they are not the best for the mission, since they are often lacking in the fire of youth required on that occasion.

To conclude, intelligence, courage, and good fortune are three qualities so necessary in a leader that even though it is hard to find many who have them all together, it does not make sense to expect much from those who are entirely lacking in one of them.

But if one is fortunate enough to find someone with all these qualifications, it would be very easy to remedy the deficiencies of those under his command.

One of those that does the most harm is, as I have noted, that the frivolity of our nation, which renders it almost incapable of standing still for a long time, results in an army that is no sooner put into service than it loses half its strength. I have sometimes felt that the best expedient that might be found for supporting the soldiers is to return to the institution of legions, as *B*Remedies to supply the armies and to wage war effectively*B* was formerly practiced in this kingdom, along with some special organization entirely necessary in order to be sure of them. But trial and error has made me drop this idea, reason clearly demonstrating that what is delegated to the cares of many is all the less sure because the buck is always passed to somebody else and decisions that are made by common consent are rarely reached through reason alone because, even though there are many perfectly good people, the number of malicious fools is greater.[244]

Everyone knows that there is no money so badly spent as by local communities. *B*This truth is clearly proved by the poor administration of the tolls of the towns and the workshops of the churches*B*

Other than that, I can truthfully say that when emergencies have compelled us to have recourse to troops sent by princes commanded and paid by their officers, which I have seen twice during this last war, they have cost twice as much and created as much if not more disorder as those that were at the same time raised by individuals at our expense.

These considerations have clearly pointed out to me that in order to entrust the provinces with the raising and maintenance of soldiers, sovereigns must take them over, and they can do it if they use the right means for this end *B*in the following order:[245]

---

[244] The legions were established by Francis I by an ordinance of July 24, 1534, to be raised by individuals and/or groups or provinces in imitation of the ancient Roman army of citizen soldiers. They were ill trained and proved extremely unreliable, not unlike the citizen army that Machiavelli had attempted to raise in Florence a few years previously.
[245] This begins the first long addition in Text B, which continues to p. 176.

All the soldiers must be on a list. The list to be drawn up must carry their name, place of birth, parents, and occupation, so that if they should absent themselves, they can more easily be found.

The local registrar will be responsible for the number to be raised in his jurisdiction and the judges obliged to arrest and punish according to the ordinances all those who return from the armies without the benefit of a leave under penalty of the judges being deprived of their posts if it is proved that they have been derelict in their duty.

For the enlistment of the soldiers, each one must be obliged to serve three years without leave, unless he is obviously sick, also on the condition that at the expiration of this period, it cannot be refused to them if they ask for it.

This condition seems all the more necessary because a Frenchman who believes he is being held against his will would rather die a thousand deaths and ordinarily thinks of nothing but escaping, whereas if he is free to leave, it is very likely that he will remain in the army voluntarily, since it is natural for men to prefer what is forbidden to what is permitted to them.

Every soldier who will have obtained his leave will be required to register it in the registry of the jurisdiction where he has been raised.

Commanders and officers of one regiment cannot for any reason whatsoever enlist soldiers from any other under penalty of being deprived of their rank and even of their nobility if they are gentlemen.

And any soldier who has abandoned his captain without leave will without delay be sent to the galleys the moment he is arrested, without any excuse.

No leave will be considered valid unless it is signed by the commandant of the regiment or, in his absence, by another commander of the unit and sealed with the seal of the regiment.[246]

Each regiment will have its judge, a commissioner, a comptroller, and a paymaster, who will all be obliged to accompany the regiment under the penalty not only of dismissal but of exemplary punishment.

If there is some disorder that the judge does not punish according to military law, he will himself be punished when the complaint for this disorder comes to the attention of Your Majesty or of your generals.

If the regiment is not up to its full strength and if the commissioner and the comptroller do not report it, they will be personally responsible and will be severely punished.

If there is no pay through the fault of the paymaster either by misappropriation of funds or just by delaying tactics, he will be subject to four times the amount and exemplary punishment.

---

[246] I translate *mestre de camp*, a rank later changed to colonel, as "commandant of the regiment."

The said officials will only be employed by commission, since experience has demonstrated that nothing corrupts the officials of the king, particularly when it comes to war, more than giving these posts the title of offices, which, when you come right down to it, is nothing else but a license to steal.

The commanders of the troops will be obliged to line them up for inspection whenever the commissioners will require it.

So that those who will have such commissions can acquit themselves faithfully, the commissioner will receive two hundred livres a month, the comptroller one hundred fifty livres, the judge one hundred livres, the registrar fifty livres, and each of his archers thirty livres.

Now, because there is no way to get anywhere in disciplining the soldiers and the petty officers if one did not prescribe the rules that must be observed by the principal commanders, the commandant of the regiment, captains, sergeant majors, lieutenants, and ensigns cannot leave their posts without leave from their generals and commanders of the troops or of Your Majesty, and in case any of them violate this rule, they must be cashiered, deprived of their nobility and their rank if they are nobles, or merely cashiered from their posts if they are not, without excluding greater punishments.

Your Majesty will impose, if you please, upon yourself never to give anyone leave during a war without legitimate reason, unless the troops are in garrison.

If, with this beneficent regulation that cannot be felt to be too harsh even by those who have to endure it, a particular care is taken of the soldiers, if they are fed during the entire year, given six payments, and a suit of clothing, if the military missions begun in 1639 to keep them from falling ill are continued, along with the hospitals that were also set up that same year, which follow the army everywhere, and if the life of those who have been crippled in the service of the king is secure in the commandery of Saint Louis established for this end, I venture to predict that the infantry of this kingdom will be well disciplined in the future.[247]

The same will be true of the cavalry, if it is raised with the same regulations which I need not repeat, Cavalry and every trooper is obliged to have two horses to ride, one for his baggage, and no more than that, if they are made to observe strictly the ordinances that oblige them never to go unarmed, and if they are put in garrison in closed spaces during the peace in order to avoid the disorders from which it is impossible to protect the people when the soldiers live in the countryside.

It has behaved so badly in these last wars that if it were to remain in its present state, it would be worthless.

---

[247] Another useful dating reference. This section was written after 1639.

The real cause of its decline is the great number that have had to be raised in recent times in order to oppose that of the enemy, who puts just about anybody on a horse.

As a result, it has been impossible to make it up, as in the past, with skilled and courageous nobles, but only with old soldiers and with youth of all classes who have never shown their mettle.

If our cavalry had imitated the foreigners who enlisted all sorts of people in their cavalry and had learned how to endure fatigue as well as theirs, even though it would have lost a part of its old valor that made it famous, we might have found occasion to console ourselves, but since the frivolous delicacy of almost all of the classes of our nation has brought it back to its first deficiencies, it has lost its best qualities without acquiring any new ones.

Even though doctors feel that the cure of an illness is easy to find when its true cause is known, I admit that even knowing the original source of the one in question, its cure is no less difficult.

If the cavalry is reduced only to the nobility, it would not have sufficient numbers to oppose that of the enemy, and if all sorts of people are admitted, it is impossible to have it as history indicates the French one to have been.

In my opinion, the only expedient that can be taken in this crisis is to exhort the captains to enlist in their companies as many nobles as they can and to order that none will be paid on payday unless half are gentlemen.

To oblige all those of this class who are over 20 years old to carry arms, declaring that they will never be eligible for any posts or dignities unless they have served for at least three years in the troops of Your Majesty.

To prohibit all the officers in the cavalry to enlist in their companies any soldier who is not a gentleman unless he is over 25 years old and who has not served in the infantry for at least three years.

Finally, rigorously enforce the old military orders that require that all troopers who abandon their leader in a battle be decimated on the simple knowledge of their defection.

If this regulation is religiously observed, I have no doubt that the French cavalry will regain its original reputation and Your Majesty, with his well-disciplined infantry and cavalry, can feel strong enough at any time to protect your subjects and intimidate your enemies.

It only remains to see if the state will be able to support the expense of such a large body of soldiers as I have projected. This will be examined later.[248]

However, even though there are grounds to hope that by means of such a useful regulation as the one that I propose the armies will subsist in the

---

[248] The project was never inserted, although it was later referred to as amounting to 12 million livres. See p. 199.

future as desired, or at least better than in the past, I will not fail to make six remarks all the more necessary for a great war, since prudence requires that in important affairs one should never run short of expedients.

The first is that if one wants to have fifty thousand men, in fact it is necessary to raise one hundred thousand, on the assumption that a regiment that should have two thousand men will only have one thousand.

Remarks for supplying the armies and waging war effectively

The second is that it is often necessary to reinforce the armies with new levies, without which, even though they are strong on paper, they will actually be very weak.

The third is that such reinforcements can better be made through frequent recruiting by old units, which are necessary to retain even when they are extremely weak because, in any case, in order to reorganize the regiments in an emergency, soldiers prefer to be enlisted by the officers.

The fourth is that when the troops are assembled, it is better to pay them on the basis of their present strength than to create new units, because it is impossible to do this without losing excellent and veteran soldiers.

Well do I know that one could order the remaining soldiers to transfer to other regiments, but it is entirely impossible to put this into practice since the affection that every soldier has for his captain gives him grounds, or at least an excuse, for leaving.

Well do I also know that in reorganizing the regiments, one might imitate the Spanish, who transfer the officers as well as the soldiers.

The fifth is that it is absolutely impossible in wars that require extraordinary efforts to pay the troops as regularly as can be done in one that a state can afford, but in such a case two expedients can be tried.

The first consists of having enough provisions so that the soldiers do not lack bread.

The second is to satisfy the leaders, who would then find it in their interest to take care of their subordinates, whereas if the soldiers are badly treated, they will think of deserting if they would not have thought of it already.

However, I do not want to forget to note that, ideally, it is necessary to make three payments during a campaign, aside from five months of pay during winter quarters.

Now, since nothing is more important for the subsistence of the soldiers and for the success of all the plans that may be undertaken that the victuals never be lacking, I add as a sixth remark that this care is one of the principal ones to have and that economy and discipline are the principal parts of being a general.

Armies hardly ever fight more than once a year, but it is necessary that they make it through every day in good order, which cannot be done without good management and extraordinary discipline.

In history, more armies have perished for lack of bread and discipline than from any effort of arms by their enemies, and I can vouch for the fact that all the unsuccessful enterprises of my time have only failed because of this deficiency.

Those who have no experience ordinarily feel that they have done enough when they have raised armies and have provided for their pay, but whatever payment is made to them, if they are not in a position to live comfortably, their money is useless and cannot keep them from perishing.

I cannot help saying in this regard that it is necessary not to trust the word of a simple supplier who contracts to furnish the bread for an army.

The life of such people is not enough to repay the damage that their negligence can cause.

The care for victuals must be committed to persons of quality, known for their vigilance, fidelity, and competence, because the subsistence of the armies and often enough that of the state depends on it.

Nobody is too good to be employed in such posts.

One wagon drawn by four horses must carry seven or eight septiers[249] of wheat over any ground, which will come to 1,500 pounds, each septier weighing 240 in bread. It must carry 1,000 rations that must weigh 1,500 pounds. Thus 15 good wagons will carry 15 days of bread for one thousand men and three weeks of biscuit. And thusly 225 wagons must carry 15 days of bread and 30 of biscuit for an army of 15,000 men

So as not to miscalculate about raising an army, it is necessary to have enough victuals so that each regiment of one thousand men has fifteen wagons in order to follow it with fifteen-day supply of bread, which is just about what is necessary for an important undertaking. Still, it is necessary to have one or two hundred rations above the estimate. Otherwise one would run short.

It is necessary not to forget to bring some mills and ovens, because even though they are not ordinarily used, it is always necessary to have some to use in certain places where it would be impossible to subsist otherwise and where a delay of four days is of great benefit to the enemy.

Since the most minor details are important to consider in the greatest plans, a general must take particular care of his equipment. He must realize that carts are more mobile than wagons, that they turn more easily in narrow places, but that, on the other hand, they are more subject to overturning and that one accident is capable of blocking an entire column for a long time. Thus, it is up to him to consider where he is going so as to use one or the other most appropriately. Moreover, he must realize that there are two ways of transporting bread, either in chests that are heavy and very cumbersome or in carts covered with wicker on their sides and with waxed foil on the top, which is much more convenient.[B]

---

[249] About four bushels.

Subsequent to ᴮthese six remarksᴮ, it only remains for me to give some advice to our commanders:

The first is always to be the first on campaign, since it is difficult for an army, as powerful as it may be, to make much progress if it finds another one in service ready to face it, and it is often easy for the first one in the field to be sure of success.

The second to choose to be the attacker, if this is not rash, rather than to be defender, because the attacker tends to intimidate the defender. The impatient and frivolous nature of the French is also unsuitable to defense, just as their first bursts of fire give them qualities that are good for attacking.

I speak from long experience, and I am sure that any experienced commander will agree with me.

FIFTH SECTION

Which treats of sea power

The force of arms requires the king not only to be strong on land but also to be powerful on the sea.

When Antonio Perez was received in France by the late king your father, this great king, in order to ease his misery, provided him with a handsome salary, and since this unfortunate foreigner wanted to express his appreciation and emphasize his gratitude, he gave him three pieces of advice in three words, "Rome, Council, and Sea," which are of no little importance.

The opinion of this old Spaniard, who was wise in affairs of state, must be considered not simply on the authority of its author but also on its own merit.

We have already spoken about the care that must be taken to be provided with a good council and to be respected in Rome. It remains to indicate why it is in the interest of the king to be powerful at sea.

The sea is the one legacy that all sovereigns claim as their own; yet it is the one on which their rights are least clear.

The empire over this element has never been assured to anybody. It has been subject to various changes depending on the unpredictability of its nature, so subject to the winds that it belongs to whoever humors it the most, and its power is so unbridled that it is in a position to do violence to anyone who would challenge its dominion.

In a word, the true titles to this dominion are force and not reason. It is necessary to be powerful to lay claim to this legacy.[250]

---

[250] In this statement Richelieu consciously takes issue with the theories of Hugo Grotius (1583–1645), the already famous author of *Mare liberum* (1609) and *De jure belli ac pacis*

To act with order and method on this point, it is necessary to consider the Ocean[251] and the Mediterranean separately and to distinguish between the sailing ships useful on these two seas and the galleys whose use is good only in the one that nature seems to have purposely placed between land so as to expose it to fewer tempests and provide it with more shelter. A great state must never take the chance of being insulted without being able to take its revenge.

And thusly, since England is located where it is, if France did not have enough ships, she could undertake whatever she wanted to harm her without any fear of retaliation.

She could impede our fishing, disturb our commerce, and pay our merchants whatever duties she wanted by blocking the mouths of our great rivers.[252]

She could fall with impunity upon our islands and even upon our coasts. Finally, since the location of this proud nation gives her no cause to fear the greatest powers on earth if they are powerless at sea, her old spite against this kingdom would give her occasion to take everything away from us if we were too weak to respond.

The insolence that she displayed to the Duke de Sully in the time of the late king obliges us to be ready not to allow anything like it anymore.

This duke, chosen by Henry the Great for an extraordinary embassy to England, embarked in Calais on a vessel flying the French flag from its mainmast. It was no sooner in the channel than it met a skiff that was coming to meet it. Its commander ordered the French ship to lower its flag. This duke, believing that his status protected him from such an affront, bravely refused. But this refusal, having been followed by three cannon balls that hit the ship, struck the heart of the good Frenchman. He was compelled by force to do what was forbidden to him by reason. He never got any apology from the English captain, except that just as it was his duty to honor his status as ambassador, he was also obliged to have the flag of his master receive the honor that was due to him as sovereign of the sea. If the words of King James were more civil, they had no other effect, however, than to oblige the duke to make the best of his own prudence, feigning to have recovered even though his pain was growing and his wound was incurable.

It was necessary for the king your father to dissimulate on this occasion, but he was resolved to defend his rights by force in the future. I imagine this great prince as planning on this occasion to do what Your Majesty must do now.

(1625). Between 1634 and 1644 this exiled Dutchman was the Swedish ambassador in Paris, and Richelieu was in constant contact with him.

[251] By "Ocean" Richelieu is referring to the Atlantic.

[252] This is the way all the manuscripts read. Obviously, Richelieu meant to say "make our merchants pay."

Reason demands resorting to an expedient that does not involve any other crowns, while maintaining good relations between all the princes of Christendom.

Among the many that may be proposed, those that follow are in my opinion the most practical.

It could be agreed that when the French ships meet the English on the coasts of England, they be the first to salute and lower their flags, and when English ships meet the French, they pay them the same honors, on the condition that when the English and French fleets might meet beyond the shores of the two kingdoms, each would go its way without any ceremony other than to identify each other through some pinnaces, which would only get within cannon shot. It could also be decided that regardless of the coasts of France and England, the fleet with the most warships would be saluted by the weaker one, either by lowering its flag or by not lowering it.

Whatever expedient is resorted to on this subject, provided that it is equal on both sides, if Your Majesty is strong at sea, it will be fair. I do not know if what is reasonable will seem as such to the English, who are so blind about this matter that they know no other justice than force.

Since the importance of the Indies to the Spanish, who take pride in being our present enemies, obliges them to be strong on the Ocean Sea, we cannot afford to be weak there, but reason demands that we be ready to oppose any other plans against us that they may have and to obstruct their enterprises.

If Your Majesty is powerful at sea, Spain will justly fear to see its fleets, which are the only source of its subsistence, attacked, its coasts, which extend over 600 leagues, raided, her great number of weak maritime strongholds surprised. This fear, I say, will oblige it to be so powerful at sea and to keep its garrisons so strong that most of the revenue from the Indies will be exhausted by the expenses of preserving the whole. And if the remainder will suffice to defend its states, we will at least have the advantage that it will no longer have the means to disturb those of its neighbors, as it has done up to the present. If Your Majesty had been as weak as your predecessors, you would not have burned to a crisp all the forces that Spain could gather on the Ocean in 1638.[253]

This conceited and haughty nation would not have been compelled to allow the humbling of its pride, in the eyes of not only all Italy but all Christendom, at seeing the Islands of Sainte-Marguerite and Saint-Honorat, which it had only taken over by surprise, torn from its hands by brute force at the same moment and with the same result to the shame of this insolent nation and the glory and reputation of yours.[254]

---

[253] The Battle of Guetaria (see note 111 above) on August 22, 1638, however, was part of the disaster of Fuentarabia.

[254] Not quite at the same moment. See notes 105, 106, and 107 above.

Finally, you would not have gained that famous battle of galleys on the coast of Genova, which has terrorized your enemies, augmented the admiration of your allies, and drawn the neutrals entirely to your side. Since Your Majesty has allies who are so distant from this kingdom that you can only communicate with them by sea, if they see France without the means of helping them in time of need, it would be easy for the envious to sow as much discord between minds as there is between states, whereas if you have a strong navy, in spite of the distances, they will remain tightly united by their feelings of affection to this state.[255]

It seems as if nature had wanted to offer the empire of the sea to France because of the advantageous location of its two coasts, equally provided with excellent ports on the Ocean and in the Mediterranean.

Brittany alone has the most beautiful of the entire Ocean, and Provence, which has only twenty-eight miles of seacoast, has many bigger and safer ones than Spain and Italy all together.

The distance between the states that form the body of the Spanish monarchy renders the communication between them so inconvenient that the only means Spain has to keep them connected is the maintenance of a great number of ships in the Ocean and of galleys in the Mediterranean, whose continual crossing reunites its members after a fashion to their leader by bringing everything necessary to their subsistence back and forth, as well as orders for undertakings, the leaders to command, the soldiers to execute them, and money, which is not only the sinew of war but also the grease of peace, from which it follows that if the freedom of these movements is impeded, these states, which could not subsist by themselves, could not avoid the confusion, the weakness, and the devastation that God brings upon a divided kingdom.

Now, since the west coast[256] of this kingdom separates Spain from all of its possessions in Italy, it seems as if the Providence of God, which wants to keep things balanced, has wanted the location of France to separate the states of Spain in order to weaken them by dividing them.

If Your Majesty always keeps forty well-armed and well-provisioned ships in his ports ready to put to sea whenever the occasion will present itself, you will have the wherewithal to protect yourself from any insult and to be feared in the Ocean by those who up to the present have disdained your forces.

Just as sailing ships are necessary for this end in the Ocean Sea, the galleys and light ships that can be rowed at great speed through the more frequent calms in the Mediterranean are just as good in the sea of the East.

With 30 galleys, Your Majesty will not only equal the power of Spain, which can, with the assistance of its allies, add fifty more. But yours will get

---

[255] See note 253 above.
[256] Richelieu means the "east" coast.

even greater by dint of the union, which doubles the power of the forces that it unites, since your galleys can remain in a body either at Marseilles or at Toulon, and they will always be able to oppose the junction of those of Spain and Italy, separated by the location of your kingdom so that they cannot combine without passing by the ports and harbors of Provence or without anchoring sometimes because of the tempests that interrupt them in mid-passage, which such light ships cannot endure without great risk in this difficult passage.

The Gulf of Lyon is the most difficult crossing of all in the seas of the East. The unpredictability and perversity of the prevailing winds make it difficult to find a safe passage no matter what the season.[257]

All squalls are very dangerous, and since our coasts are not very favorable to those who pass by them, they rarely make the crossing without peril.

The real reason for the risk of this passage comes from the perversity of the winds, caused by the irregularity of the coastlines.

The more mountainous and higher a coastline is, the windier it is when the heat of the land meets the cold and humidity of the water or of the snow that covers it.

From this it comes that the coasts of Provence, which are of this nature, are always drenched in rain or snow and are always difficult to approach.

Now, since these winds are contrary to the approach, they are also not strong enough to bring them back from where they came, because there are other winds from the land that ordinarily drive them away, from which it happens that by the perversity of the winds of our coasts and those of Spain or Italy, the ships are driven into the gulf, where more often than not they run into a squall and their loss is inevitable.

To get from Spain to Italy, the ships and the galleys always leave the Cape of Creus or the Gulf or Rosas. They ordinarily wait for the west wind or the mistral to get to the coast of Genova successfully or to Monaco, which is their first approach. Even though they leave in good weather, they are never halfway through the gulf before it changes.[258]

If the winds are southwesterly or at noon and southwesterly, they must necessarily wait on the coasts of Provence, and if they pass during the sirocco or the east wind, it is impossible for the galleys and ships that are near our land to finish their voyage to Italy or to return to Spain, and in a squall, it is a miracle if they do not run ashore on the lines or other beaches of our coasts. On the other hand, the ships that go to Italy or to Spain ordinarily leave from Monaco, which is the last port of Italy.

To make a good voyage, they wait for the mistral or a tramontane or the Greek and tramontane. But they are never halfway through the gulf without the

---

[257] It is located along the southern coast of France.
[258] Seems to be the same as Cadaqués or Cabo de Creus on the coast of Catalonia.

weather changing and without peril all together, because a violent sirocco or a tempest at dusk with our ports not open to them makes their loss inevitable.

Thus if France is strong in galleys and galleons all together, they cannot make any crossing safely, since it is certain that they could not manage to get through during winter without floundering either on our coasts or in Barbary if the winds are all blowing North.

And even though the Greek or the tramontane takes them toward Majorca or Minorca, the mistral and the tramontane carries them to Corsica and Sardinia. Most often the most violent tempests cut them to pieces before they find refuge in these islands, which are on their side. And if, to protect themselves from this peril, they decide to await a favorable wind so as to skirt our lands, they still will not make it once out of twenty crossings, with the weather against them as we watch. And even though they might have a favorable wind at their disposal, so that they would have nothing to fear from the sea, we can always put out to sea at the first sign of their passage and obstruct them all the more easily since we can always return safely whenever we wish in case the weather changes for the worse because of the proximity of our ports, which they do not dare to approach.

30 galleys will give this advantage to Your Majesty, and if to this fleet you add 10 galleons, which are veritable citadels of the sea because of their size and are fearsome to the much lighter galleys in a good wind while they have nothing to fear from them even in the greatest calm because they have cannons as good as those of their antagonists, they can do them a great deal of damage if they get too close. If the King of Spain were to augment by half as much his forces on this sea, which he cannot do without a great expense, he would not be able to repair the damage that we could do to him because of the union of our forces and the division of his own.

There is nothing that such a fleet cannot undertake. It can go and attack the armadas of Spain in their ports when they assemble there, since our experience has shown us in the recapture of the Islands of Saint-Marguerite and Saint-Honorat that if one uses them boldly, the floating fortresses prevail over the best on the land.

By this means, Your Majesty will preserve the liberty of the princes of Italy, who have up to the present been like slaves to the King of Spain. You will encourage those who have wanted to shake off the yoke of this tyranny, which they only endure because they cannot free themselves from it, and arouse the affection of those who are French at heart.

When the late king your father charged M. Dalincourt with reproaching the Grand Duke Ferdinand, who, in spite of the alliance he had contracted with him after the marriage of the queen your mother, did not fail to make a connection with Spain, the grand duke, after having patiently heard what was said to him, made a short reply that is worth a thousand words and that must be carefully considered by Your Majesty and his successors. "If the king," this prince said, "had had 40 galleys in Marseilles, I would not have done what I did."[259]

If the door into Italy that Pinerolo gives to Your Majesty is properly defended, and if you open another one by the sea, time and the firmness of your councillors, whose change is to be feared given the frivolity of our nation, will change the sentiments of a great many Italians, or, to put it in other words, they will show their true colors.

Italy is considered the heart of the world and, to be frank, the most important part of the entire Spanish empire. It is the place where they fear the most to be attacked and disturbed and the place where it is easiest to get the upper hand on them as long as it is done right. And consequently, even though one had no intention of harming them, it is at least necessary, when they would like to undertake something against France, to be able to strike back so close to their heart that they will not have the chance to rear back and execute their malicious plans against her. This force will not only keep Spain in check, but it will be such that the Grand Seigneur and his subjects, who only measure the power of distant kings by their navies, will be more careful than they have been up to the present to maintain their treaties with them.

Algiers, Tunis, and the entire Barbary coast will respect and fear your power, whereas up to the present they have disdained it outrageously. In this case, either these barbarians are sufficiently reasonable or wise to live at peace with the subjects of Your Majesty, or they will be compelled to do by force what they will not stoop to doing by reason, and instead of thinking, as we do at present, that we are not at war while enduring all of its miseries, we shall find calm and security through a war that is most advantageous against people whose natural treachery is so great that one cannot protect oneself against it except by force.

It remains for me to see to what the expense amounts for the maintenance of the number of ships projected above. Great as it may be, it must be felt to be small in comparison with the advantages that we shall receive from it. Still, it can be done so carefully that it can be sustained for two million five hundred thousand livres, as the lists that will be inserted at the end of this work will prove.[260]

---

[259] Charles de Neufville-Villeroy (1566–1642), Marquis d'Alincourt (Liancourt), who had negotiated with Ferdinand I the marriage of his daughter, Marie de Medici, to Henry IV in 1600.

[260] These lists were never inserted.

SIXTH SECTION

Which treats of commerce as depending on sea power and specifies which is the most convenient

There is a tried-and-true saying that just as states often expand by war, they usually get rich by commerce.

The opulence of the Dutch, who, when you come right down to it, are only a handful of people relegated to a corner of the earth where there is nothing but water and plateaus, is an example of the utility of commerce that cannot be denied.

Navigation has made them so famous and so powerful all over the world that after having taken over the commerce of the East Indies from the Portuguese, who had been there a long time, they are causing no little trouble for the Spanish in the West Indies by occupying most of Brazil. As in England, the majority of the underprivileged earn their living by their trading all over the world, by the manufacture of cloth, and by the selling of the lead, the tin, and the coal that their country produces. It is only the Kingdom of China, which is not open to anyone, where this nation has not established a station for its trade.[261]

The city of Genova, which has nothing but cliffs to its name, exploits its trade so well that it can be considered the richest in Italy without contradiction, and Spain would have difficulty in conserving a part of her dominions without the help that she gets from the Indies. Only France, because she has more than she needs for herself, has neglected it up to the present, even though she could carry it out just as conveniently as its neighbors and rid herself by this means of the assistance that they only give her at her own expense.

Fishing on the Ocean Sea is the easiest and the most useful kind of commerce that can be carried out in this kingdom. It is all the more necessary since there is no country in the world as populous as France, and the number of those who have strayed from the path of salvation is very small in comparison to the Catholics, who, as members of the Roman Church, abstain for one-third of the year from the use of meat and do not make any use at all of the dispensations used in Spain to eat meat under false pretenses.

This commerce is all the easier in that we have a great number of sailors who up to the present have gone to seek employment with our enemies since they do not find it in their country, and we would not merely reap the haul of cod and herring but would be able to occupy our sailors instead of being compelled to fortify our enemies while weakening ourselves by taking to

---

[261] On the Dutch in Brazil, see note 264 below.

Spain and to other foreign countries what they have only brought to us up to the present by means of our own in their service.

France is so fertile in grains and so abundant in wine and so full of flax and hemp in order to make the sails and rigging necessary to navigation that Spain, England, and all our neighbors need to have recourse to her. And provided that we knew how to help ourselves with the advantages that nature has given us, we could extract money from those who would want these necessities, and they would not load us with their useless commodities.

The cloth of Spain. England, and Holland is only necessary for luxury. We can make it as well as they do by getting the wool from Spain. We can do it even more cheaply with our grains and textiles if we want to gain at both ends in the exchange.

Since our fathers did very well without the cloth of Berry, we can do just as well at present with the cloth with a seal and from the miller, which is now made in France, without resorting to foreign ones, whose use will be abolished just as the cloth of Châlons and Chartres has abolished that of Milan. BThe cloth with a seal is made in Rouen, and the cloth from the miller is made in Romorantin.B

In fact, the cloth with a seal is so well received in the East that the Turks prefer it to any other except the one made in Venice with wool from Spain, and the cities of Marseilles and Lyon have always sold a lot of it up to the present.

France is sufficiently industrious, if she wants, to do without the best products of its neighbors. At present, such beautiful silk cloth is made in Tours that it is bought in Italy, Spain, and other foreign countries. The uniform taffeta made there is also sold widely throughout France so that there is no need to go looking for it elsewhere. Our red, violet, and yellow velvet is now more beautiful than the Genovese. We are almost the only place where silk serge is made. Our black is as beautiful as the English. Our modest gold textiles are more beautiful and cheaper than the Italian ones.

It would thus be very easy for us to deprive ourselves of a commerce that can only serve to foment our indolence and nourish our luxury while firmly embracing one that can augment our abundance and occupy our sailors so that our neighbors do not make use of their work at our expense.

Aside from those specified above, which are best in the Ocean Sea, there are many others that can be done.

That of the Canadian fur trade is all the more useful since it is not carried on with money but in exchange for commodities that only depend on the skill of workers, such as sacks, scissors, knives, penknives, needles, billhooks and axes, watches, buckles for hats, needle points, and all sorts of other supplies.

That of the coast of Guinea in Africa, where the Portuguese have long been in occupation of a station named Castel de Mino, which the Dutch from the

East India Company took away from them 2 or 3 years ago, is of a similar nature in that they only carry hardware, canvas, and cheap cloth there and bring out gold dust that the Blacks give in exchange.[262]

The merchants of Rouen have previously traded in textiles and cloth in the Kingdom of Fez in Morocco, by means of which they brought out a great quantity of gold.

If the subjects of the king had enough ships, they could engage in all of the trade with the North that the Flemish and Dutch have taken over all the more easily because all of the North is in dire need of wine, vinegar, brandy, chestnuts, prunes, and nuts, which we have more of than can be consumed in the kingdom, and we can bring back wood, skins, pitch, and tar, things that are not only useful to us but necessary to our neighbors, who could not get them without our goods if they do not want to lose the cargo of their ships on the way.

I will not go into the East Indian trade because the disposition of the French is so impatient that it insists on instant gratification, so long voyages are not for them.

However, since a large quantity of silks and carpets come from Persia, many curiosities from China, and all sorts of diamonds from different places in this part of the world, this trade can be very useful and must not be neglected.

To get things started it would be necessary to have 2 or 3 ships in the East, commanded by prudent and wise persons of quality with the necessary credentials and powers to negotiate with all the princes and make alliances with all the surrounding peoples, just as the Portuguese, the English, and the Flemish have done.

This plan would be even more infallible since those who have established themselves in this nation are now despised, either because they have misled it or because they have subjugated it by force.[263]

As to the West, there is little trading to be done, since Drake, Thomas Cavendish, Sperberg, L'Hermite, Le Maire, and the late Count Maurice, who sent 12 500-ton ships with the intention of trading either amicably or by force, found it impossible to establish anything there peacefully or by force, so that there is little to be hoped there unless one goes to the length of trying to take over in a major war in the places that the King of Spain is now occupying.[264]

---

[262] Helpful dating hint. The Dutch drove the Portuguese from this station in August 1637. Two years from August 1637 is August 1639. Three years is August 1640.

[263] He is apparently still referring to Persia, which had been contending with the Portuguese for control of the Strait of Hormuz, not unlike how it is presently contending with the United States of America.

[264] Francis Drake (c. 1540–1596), legendary English freebooter and circumnavigator of the globe, Jacques L'Hermite (c. 1581–1624), Dutch freebooter and circumnavigator of the globe, Jacob Le Maire (c.1585–1616), Dutch explorer and circumnavigator of the globe,

The small islands of Saint-Christopher and others situated on the outskirts of the Indies can bring in some tobacco and furs and other things of little importance.[265]

It remains to see what can be done in the Mediterranean:

[B]Commerce of the Mediterranean Sea[B266]

[B]Mémoire on the various kinds of trade in the Levant

Napoli in Romagna[267]

The French carry both goods and money there and bring back silks, leather goods, woolens, waxes, and cheeses, a part of which are distributed and sold in Italy.

Satalia[268]

The French only carry money there and bring back cotton goods, waxes, and all sorts of leather goods.

Smyrna[269]

The French carry much more in goods than in money there since they sell a lot of goods there for Chios, the Archipelago, and Constantinople. The goods carried there are paper, hats, Paris and Languedoc cloth, brazilwood, cochineal, spices, satins manufactured in Lyon, and sometimes Persian silk and rhubarbs that the Persians bring there, cotton spun into wool, waxes, putty, and rag carpets are brought back. Close to Smyrna, there is a new port named Scala Nova. Sometimes our ships load wheat and vegetables there.

Thomas Cavendish (1560–1592), English freebooter and circumnavigator of the globe, and Joris van Spilbergen (1568–1620), Dutch captain who circumnavigated the globe. Richelieu is confusing the late great Maurice of Nassau (1567–1625), who never sent a fleet to Brazil, with his cousin John Maurice of Nassau (1604–1679), whom the Dutch West India Company sent to Brazil in 1636 as its governor. The large fleet sent there by the West India Company in 1630 only managed to get a tiny foothold, and it was John Maurice who extended the Dutch holdings about which Richelieu expresses such admiration in a previous paragraph.

[265] These islands were first colonized by English and French Huguenots early in the seventeenth century, and they were shared by both monarchies between that time and 1713, when the English acquired them by the Peace of Utrecht.

[266] This *mémoire* combines information from the Archives of the Ministry of Foreign Affairs, Correspondance Politique *Turquie* 3, fols.780–782 (1628), with material from another currently in the same archives, Mémoires et Documents *France* 834, fols. 209–221 (1639).

[267] Napoli is todays Nafplio, ancient seaport in the Peloponnese and part of the Ottoman Empire at the time that Richelieu was writing his *Political Testament.*

[268] Satalia is today's Antalya, a resort town in southwestern Turkey roughly across from the island of Cyprus.

[269] Smyrna is today's Izmir. Scala Nova is today's Kusadasi.

Constantinople[270]

The French carry a lot of the same goods there that are brought to Smyrna, except for gold, silver, and silk textiles, which sell widely. They bring back leather goods and woolens for lack of anything else, and since they often have nothing else to buy with their money, they send it for use in Smyrna or by letters of credit to Aleppo, where there is always something to carry back to Christendom.

Island of Cyprus

Where there are various ports, money is carried, some cloth, and hats. Cotton spun into wool, silk textiles manufactured in the said island, and some chloroquine drugs are brought back.

Alexandretta and the Port of Aleppo[271]

A great quantity of goods and money is carried from France. The goods are just the same as are carried to Smyrna, and a whole lot of silk and drugs, all sorts of cotton textiles, galls, red, yellow, and blue leather goods, called Levantine, cotton canvas, and sometimes goods from the Indies that are brought there by way of Persia are brought back. Before the English and the Dutch went to the Indies, all the silks, drugs, and other Persian goods came to Aleppo, from where they were carried to Marseilles and sold throughout France, England, Holland, and Germany, and now the English and Dutch have this commerce and provide France with the goods not only of Persia but even of the lands of the Great Turk that they send through Persia to be loaded in Goa. The goods that are brought from the Levant are sold in Sicily, Naples, Genova, Livorno, Majorca, and throughout Spain, Flanders, and Germany.

Seyda, the Port of Tripoli, Beirut, and Saint-Jean-d'Acre[272]

Some few goods are carried from France, and almost everything in money and a lot of silks, spun cotton, ashes for the making of soap, drugs that come from Damascus are brought back, rice is sometimes loaded, and when the wheat harvest is good, they let it be loaded on our ships.

Alexandria, the Egyptian ports, and great Cairo

The French carry some goods there from France, such as cloth, knives, paper, brazil-wood, cochineal, but more money than goods, natron,[273] drugs of various sorts, and most of the goods that are sold in Italy or Spain are brought back. Formerly the spices

---

[270] Constantinople is, of course, today's Istanbul.

[271] Alexandretta is today's Iskenderun. The gall that Richelieu is referring to seems to be the Aleppo gall, used in tanning.

[272] Seyda is today's As-Suwayda, or Sweida, in southern Syria, close to the border with Jordan. Tripoli refers to today's Tripoli, a seaport in northern Lebanon. Beirut is still Beirut in today's Lebanon. Saint-Jean d'Acre is today's Acre in Israel.

[273] Today's bicarbonate of soda.

that were brought from the Red Sea to Alexandria were brought to Marseilles, and now that the English and the Dutch go to the Indies, it is necessary for us to resort to them.

Tunis

Some wine, honey, tartar, cloth, paper, and other goods are carried there from Marseilles, and rarely money; and leather goods and waxes are bought back.

Algiers and nearby ports

The same goods that are carried to Tunis are brought there sometimes, and waxes and leather goods are brought back.[B]

I admit that for a long time I have been mistaken about the trade that the people of Provence carry on in the East.

I felt along with many others that it was harmful to the state on the prevailing notion that it exhausted the money of the kingdom only to bring worthless goods into it, but after having studied this trade thoroughly, I have changed my mind for such good reasons that whoever hears them will certainly agree. It is certain that we cannot do without a part of the goods that we get from the East, the silk, the cotton, the wax, the leather, the rhubarb, and many other drugs that are necessary to us.

It is also certain that if we do not go after them, foreigners will bring them to us and deprive us of all the profit that we can make for ourselves. And it is also very certain that we carry much less money to the East than products we manufacture in France, our hemp, our textiles, and our lumber for shipbuilding being in greater demand there than money.

Everyone who knows anything about the trade of the East certainly knows that the money that is carried there is not from France but from Spain, which we then get through our trade in the East, amazing as this may be. They know that the city of Marseilles has gotten rich from trading with the East, that the silk and the spun cotton, which are the principal products that are imported into France from the East, are exported to foreign countries at a profit of 10% and that this trade supports a great number of craftsmen and sailors who are useful in peace time and necessary in war.

Finally, the import and export duties that the king receives from this commerce are considerable, and thusly one would have to be blind not to realize that his trade is not only advantageous but entirely necessary.

Whatever can be said about the commerce of these two seas, the French will never become enthusiastic about it if one does not point out to them how easy and useful it is.

One of the best ways of making them do what is for their own good is if it pleases Your Majesty to sell them some of his ships inexpensively every year on the condition that they will use them for trade and not sell them outside the kingdom. This means will curb their impatience, since they cannot wait until a ship is finished before they want to use it, and it will be all the more effective for our purposes, since it will give them a chance to reap before they sow.

Aside from its profitability for individuals, this procedure will give the state a great advantage in that in 5 or 6 years the merchants will have so many ships and will be so prosperous that they will be in a position to assist the kingdom in case of need, as is practiced in England, where the king uses those of his subjects in case of war, without which he would not be as powerful at sea as he is.[274]

Besides, the number of ships that Your Majesty wishes to maintain will not diminish because every year the shipyards that you have decided to reestablish will produce as many as you want.

There is no state in Europe as proper for shipbuilding as this kingdom, abundant in iron, hemp, and workers that our neighbors ordinarily appropriate for lack of employment in this state. The Loire and Garonne Rivers are so convenient for shipyards that nature might have had this in mind when it formed them. The low cost of victuals for the craftsmen and the convenience of the various tributaries that can bring in whatever is necessary justify this proposal.

If, after doing this, Your Majesty decides to accord the same kind of privileges to the merchants who engage in this trade that they only secure now from various offices, which are only good for keeping them idle and their wives flattered, you will reestablish commerce to such a point that one and all will gain a great advantage.

Finally, if, aside from these two great advantages, care is particularly taken to keep the coasts of this kingdom free from pirates, which can be done easily, France will quickly add to its natural abundance what commerce brings to the most infertile countries.

To secure the Ocean, only six well-armed coastguard ships of 200 tons and six well-armed pinnaces are needed, provided that this number of ships be always at sea.

And to patrol the seas of the East, it will suffice to dispatch every year around the month of April a squadron of six galleys that go by the way of Corsica and Sardinia and follow the Barbary coast up to the straits and return by the same route when the season requires it, in which case 5 or 6 well-equipped ships will take their place and serve in their stead during the winter.[275]

---

[274] Richelieu is not anticipating that such a fleet might turn against the king, as it did during the English civil war, which was on the horizon.

[275] It would appear as if Richelieu considers North Africa to be a part of the Levant, or East. It is true that most of it is east of France.

SEVENTH SECTION

Which points out that gold and silver are one of the principal and most necessary powers of the state, puts forward the means to make this kingdom plentiful in each, points out what its revenue is at present and what it can be in the future by relieving the people from three-quarters of the load that overwhelms them now

It has always been said that the finances are the sinews of the state, and it is true that they are like the place of Archimedes, who can move the world if he is standing on it firmly enough. A needy prince could not undertake any glorious action, since poverty breeds contempt, and he would not be up to it without being exposed to the envy of his enemies.

Gold and silver are the tyrants of the word, and even though their reign and their empire are not unjust in themselves and their dominion is sometimes so reasonable that it must be endured, it is sometimes so unbridled that it is impossible not to find it unbearable.

It is necessary, as I have already noted, for there to be some proportion between what a prince gets from his subjects and what they can give him, not only without ruining themselves but without great discomfort.

Just as it is necessary not to exceed the means of those who give, it is also necessary not to demand more than the needs of the state require.

It is only for pedants and true enemies of the state to say that a prince must extract nothing from his subjects and that his only treasures must be in the hearts of those who are subject to his dominion. But it is only for flatterers and real plagues upon the court to whisper in the ears of princes that they can demand as much as they please and that on this point their will is their rule of thumb. There is nothing as easy as to find plausible reasons in favor of a levy, even when it is not fair, and nothing is easier than to produce appearances in order to condemn those that are most necessary.

It is necessary to be entirely dispassionate in order to decide what is reasonable on such an occasion. There is no little difficulty in finding just the right amount.

If the expenses absolutely necessary for the subsistence of the state are assured, the less one needs to levy on the people the better.

In order not to be compelled to make these great levies, it is necessary to be economical, and there is no better means of moderating expenses than to banish all extravagance and condemn everything connected with it.

France would be oh so rich and its people oh so prosperous if she did not suffer, unlike other states, from the waste of its public money.

She loses more, in my opinion, than other competing kingdoms spend on themselves.

[B]A Venetian ambassador once told me something very interesting in this regard in speaking of the opulence of France. He told me that to make her thrive, he only wished for her to know how to spend wisely as much as she wasted foolishly and that his republic knew how not to waste a single farthing needlessly and without much management.[B]

If one could control the appetite of the French, I would feel that the best means to manage the purse of the king would be to resort to this expedient. But since it is impossible to set limits on the covetousness of minds as unbridled as ours, the only means to restrain them is to treat them like doctors do when they constrain their hungry patients to fast.

For this purpose, it is necessary to begin the reform of the finances by eliminating the principal ways by which one can illicitly withdraw money from the king's coffers.

Among others, none is so dangerous as that of the requisitions, whose abuse has come to the point that not remedying it is tantamount to losing the state.[276]

Though it is useful to use them on some occasions and it is even necessary on others, nevertheless, their great drawbacks and abuses so far outweigh their utility that it is absolutely necessary to abolish them.

Millions will be saved by this means, and a thousand hidden transactions will be remedied, which are impossible to uncover as long as the secret ways of spending the public treasures are in use.

[B]Money in coffers[B277]   Well do I know that it will be said that certain foreign expenditures must by their nature be secret and are very fruitful to the state, which would be deprived of them if the recipients of these favors will think that their name could be known.

But, the thievery under this pretext is so bad that, after having thought this over, it is better to close the door to any occasional utility that might be drawn from them than to leave it open to the perpetual abuses that ruin the state.

However, so as not to lose the advantage of making some advantageous secret expense, one million in gold might be reserved for requisitions on the condition that copies be signed by the king and by the participants.

If it is put forward that requisitions are necessary in order to pay the usual commissions, I say that this is one of the reasons that they must be stopped.

We have lived during the last century without requisitions; we will live for even more. If by banning their use, we also banish that of contractors in time of peace, far from being something good that causes something bad, it will be something good that will cause another good.

---

[276] I translate *comptants* as "requisitions." These were orders for payment issued by the king to the treasury on the basis of his absolute power over it without any oversight by the *Chambre des Comptes*, the court that had jurisdiction over official public finances.

[277] This marginal note is clearly misplaced.

Perhaps it will be asked why, since I knew that the use of requisitions was so bad, I have not had it curtailed in my own time.

The great Henry knew how bad it was and that it was introduced during the reign of his predecessor, but he could not stop the disturbances, the internal strife, the foreign wars, and consequently the great expenses, and extraordinary contracts that it was necessary to make did not permit him to think about doing anything about such a good idea.

Ruining the Huguenot party, humbling the pride of the great nobles, waging a great war against extremely powerful enemies in order to attain a lasting peace that will finally preserve the tranquility in the future has only paved the way for the ends that I propose.[278]

Since the subject of the requisitions gives occasion to speak about the extraordinary contracts, it is impossible for me not to say that far from the great augmentations in revenue that can be made in this way being advantageous to the state, they are on the contrary harmful and impoverish it rather than enrich it.

Perhaps this proposal might initially be taken as a paradox, but it is impossible to examine it carefully without agreeing with it.

Any augmentation in the revenues of the king can only be made by the taxes that are put on all sorts of commodities, and thusly it is clear that if one increases the receipts in this manner, one also increases the expense since it is necessary to buy at a higher price what was previously cheaper. If meat is more expensive, if the price of linen and of everything else augments, the soldier will be harder put to feed and maintain himself, so that it will be necessary to pay him more, and the salary of all the craftsmen will be greater than it was previously, which will make the augmentation in expenditures very close to the increase in receipts, causing the individual to lose much more than the prince will gain.

For example, the poor gentleman whose wealth consists only of a patch of land will not augment his revenue by such a tax, since the fruits of the land almost always remain at the same price primarily in his regard, and if they grow in the course of time, the rise in price will decrease the sale, so that at the end of the year, the poor noble will find an augmentation not in his revenue but in his expenses, since the new imposts will have made everything necessary for the maintenance of his family more expensive, which he can still manage to support without leaving his home, but no longer send his children to the army to serve his king and country in keeping with their birthright.

Besides, if it is true, and it is very certain, that the sale of what is on the market among subjects diminishes in proportion to the augmentation in taxes,

---

[278] Richelieu here is hearkening back to what he claims in the Succinct narration that he promised Louis XIII in 1624.

it may well be that such augmentations will reduce the duties received by the kingdom instead of augmenting them.

If, on the other hand, it is a question of the commodities that are exported from the kingdom, it is clear that the foreigners who are currently attracted to grab our goods at a moderate price will procure them elsewhere if they can do so to their advantage, which will leave France rich in the fruits of the land but poor in gold and silver. And instead, if the taxes are moderated, the great quantity of goods that will be bought up by foreigners will compensate for the loss that might be caused by the lowering of the imposts.

There is more! Raising taxes is capable of reducing a great number of the king's subjects to indolence, since it is certain that the majority of poor people and craftsmen employed in manufacturing would prefer to remain idle with their hands in their pockets than to squander all their life in unrewarding and useless work if the excess of the imposts keeps them from selling the fruits of the land and of their handiworks, thereby keeping them from making a living with the sweat of their brows.

To resume the thread of my discussion, after having condemned the abuse of requisitions and pointed out that their augmentation is sometimes not only useless but often harmful, I say that there must be a geometrical proportion between the imposts and the necessities of the state; that is to say, one must only tax what is totally necessary for the subsistence of the kingdom in its greatness and its glory. These last words mean a great deal, since they point out that not only can one impose upon the people what is required to keep the kingdom in whatever condition it may be, but one can also draw from it what may be necessary to maintain its brilliance and reputation.

However, it is necessary to be careful not to stretch these last conditions to the point that on this pretext the will of the prince is the only rule for his levies.

Reason alone has to be it! And if the prince exceeds its limits by drawing more from his subjects than he must, even though in this case they must obey him, he will be responsible to God, who will hold him to a strict accounting.

Besides, there is no political reason for anyone to augment the burdens on the people without getting anything out of it except for the curses of the public, which carry with them all sorts of drawbacks since it is certain that a prince who draws more than he must from his subjects does nothing else by exhausting their purse than to exhaust their love and their fidelity, which is even more necessary for the subsistence of his state and the safety of his person than the reserves of gold and silver that he can keep in his coffers.

Well do I know that in a great state, it is always necessary to keep some money in reserve in order to provide for emergencies. But these savings must be in proportion to the wealth of the state and to the quantity of gold and silver minted in the kingdom. And if it is not done at this rate, the wealth of the prince would be tantamount to his poverty, since his subjects would no longer have the funds either to maintain their commerce or to pay the duties that they rightfully owe to their sovereign.

As necessary as it is to be careful to accumulate enough money to provide for the necessities of the state and to be scrupulous in conserving it when obligations do not oblige one to spend it, it is necessary to be generous in employing it when the good of the public requires it and to do it in time and appropriately.

Otherwise the delay in such occasions is often costly to the state and loses time that can never be regained.

Princes have often been seen who in order to save their money have lost both it and their states, and it is certain that those who are cheap often spend more than those who are not because they do it too late. It takes no lack of judgment to realize when to do it, and whoever is good at accumulating without being good at spending can cause unimaginable evils.

Now, because general maxims are always useless if one does not apply them to specific subjects, it remains to see:

What the revenue of the kingdom can be.
What its expenses can be.
How much money it is necessary to keep in reserve in the coffers and how far the people can and must be relieved.[279]

The revenue of the kingdom can be considered in two fashions—either what it can be in time of peace without changing the nature of the money that is presently drawn from receipts and from the general farms or making any other augmentation besides what can come from reducing to 6.25% the old bonds that might be retained and the salaries of certain officials, who would be more willing to endure the elimination of their post with reimbursement—or what it could be by making certain changes considered so reasonable and useful to the state by those whom I have seen managing the finances that in their judgment they have nothing more to fear from them than its novelty.

---

[279] Richelieu has drawn the discussion that follows mainly from the longer version of a document in the Archives Nationales, Series *K* 891, n⁰ 2, titled "Mémoire de la valleur des finances du roy en l annee 1640 extrait sur l'estat donné a Mr le Cardinal de Richelieu," which includes two subsections with even more revealing titles, one being "Projet pour augmenter le revenue de sa ma^té & descharger son peuple," the other being "Projet de despense apres la paix."

[B]Bonds issued on the city at 8.33%

Salt	1,231,411 *livres*
Aides	851,000
General receipts	474,584

All these bonds have been constituted between the years 1551 and 1558.

Since the reign of the late king, no bonds were issued, not even in the one of Henry III.

There are 23 generalities, 24 officials in each office, which makes 552 in all, each one of which receives one thousand *écus*, a third of which comes to 552,000 livres.[B]

On the first footing the treasury can count on receiving 25,150,000 *livres* a year according to the following list:

From the *taille*	17,350,000 *livres*
From all the *gabelles*	5,250,000
From the *aides*	2,450,000
From the reduction of the bonds to 6.25%	1,000,000
From the reduction of the wages of the Treasurers of France by two-thirds of what they received, which they will voluntarily endure, provided that they are assured of being delivered from the new taxes by which they are constantly overwhelmed	550,000
From the Incidental Investments	2,000,000
From the tax farm of Bordeaux	1,800,000
From the three livres from each barrel of wine entering Paris	850,000
From the 30 old and new pennies and 10 pennies of wine	504,000
From the tax farm of 45 pennies instead of tariffs	504,000
From the 9 livres 18 pennies per ton of Picardy	154,000
From the tax farm of Brouage	254,000
From the contract for the forests of Languedoc, spices and drugs of Marseilles, and 2% of Arles	480,000
From the surtaxes of Lyon	60,000
From the Five Great Tax Farms	2,400,000
From the new imposts of Normandy	250,000
From those of the Loire River	225,000
From the tax farm on iron	80,000
From the ordinary sale of wood from the domains	550,000[280]

---

[280] In all Text B's first and second footings, the entry "From the ordinary sale of wood from the domains" is divided into two entries: "From the ordinary sale of wood" and "From the domains," each at 550,000 livres.

On the second, by entirely relieving the people from 17 million *livres*, which now come into the coffers of the king from the levying of the *taille*, the receipts can rise up to 50 millions, as the following list clearly shows:

From an impost to place on salt, whether on the flats or otherwise, in all the provinces of the kingdom can bring into the king after all expenses 25,000,000 *livres*

From the penny per pound of all the goods and commodities in the kingdom	12,000,000
From the *aides*	400,000
From the reduction through the repurchasing of bonds constituted by the city of Paris	5,000,000
From the Incidental Investments	2,000,000
From the tax farm of Bordeaux	1,800,000
From the three *livres* from each barrel of wine entering Paris, new impost	750,000
From the old 30 pennies and new 10 pennies for each barrel of wine entering Paris	580,000
For the tax farm of 45 pennies instead of the tariffs and tolls	530,000
BFrom the 9 *livres* per ton of Picardy	174,000B
From the tax farm of Brouage	254,000
From the arrangement for the forests of Languedoc, spices and drugs of Marseilles, and 2% of Arles	380,000
From the surtaxes of Lyon	60,000
From the five great farms	2,400,000
From the new imposts of Normandy	150,000
From those of the Loire river	225,000
From the tax farms on iron	80,000
From the ordinary sale of wood from the domains	550,000

Total 50,483,000 *livres*[281]

Well do I know that if this institution is well understood, it will be found fair and reasonable by anyone who has any experience and competence in the conduct of the state.

Of all the superintendents of finances whom I have ever met in my time, the most experienced ones in matters of finance believed the tax on salt to be worth as much as the Indies to the King of Spain, and they considered it to be the fundamental secret for the relief of the people as well as for the reform and opulence of states.

---

[281] This total is incorrect, no matter how one adds it up.

And in fact, it would take a complete fool not to imagine how delighted the people would be if they could buy as much salt as they pleased as if it were wheat.

It is certain that eliminating a large number of the officials who are established for the salt tax and that being delivered from the litigation and trickery to which they sometimes resort, either in the course of their duty or often maliciously in order to compel the people to buy the salt, would bring them immense relief.

It is certain, moreover, that one could very justly recompense the provinces that have up to the present enjoyed an exemption from the salt tax by reducing their *taille*, so that if in the future it would be more expensive to buy than it was in the past, the lowering of the *taille* would be equivalent to the augmentation in the price of salt, which they would have to buy, although they could buy it freely.

It is just as certain, even though one may say that the lowering of the *taille* only touches the people and the rise in the price of salt, which has up to the present been sold in the provinces exempt from the tax, would affect the clergy, the nobility, and anyone else who is exempt, everyone would benefit from the lowering of the *tailles*; property values would rise since the farmers who exploit them would have to pay lower taxes.[282]

Finally, it is certain that even though there are great difficulties in instituting this, they can still be overcome.

If, after having considered instituting this for salt, one examines doing it for the penny per pound, it will be found all the more fair in that it is instituted in various provinces and has already been decided on twice in the council of state under the great king Francis and in the assembly of notables of Rouen under the great Henry of immortal memory.[283]

However, because the people and their communities are naturally so suspicious and so distrustful of everything that they are even fearful of what is best for them, they are usually shocked by great changes, so instead of proposing such an arrangement, I venture to avoid it, and I do it all the more boldly because such innovations must never be undertaken unless they are absolutely necessary.

---

[282] By "sold" Richelieu means "sold outright" without a sales tax. By "farmers" he is not referring to tillers of the soil but to tax collectors who contract in order to collect taxes.

[283] The *sol pour livre*, which I translate as "penny per pound," was an old surtax on specific commodities that dated back to the Hundred Years' War. In 1596, however, Henry IV, in the face of a financial crisis and in lieu an Estates-General, called together an Assembly of Notables, which supported him by imposing such a surtax on all commodities except wheat for the entire kingdom and was to be paid by all. The assembly voted the tax for only three years, but it was periodically either renewed or amended.

Now, since France is far from being at this point with its subjects, I feel, on the contrary, that it is much easier to calm the people down and make the state rich without resorting to such expedients, and even though there are no great difficulties about them that could not be overcome, there are undoubtedly enough of them that are much greater, so some management as will enrich the kingdom without resorting to such changes must be found.

To verify this proposition, it is only necessary to examine the expense that would suffice in time of peace and see how much profit the treasury can draw from the tranquility.

The safety and the greatness of this kingdom cannot endure expenses for war lower than the 12 millions carried in the above project. It is necessary to expect them to come to some 12 millions.

The expense for the ordinary garrisons, which comes to 3 millions every year, could be eliminated both because most of the military men who would then be included in the list would become parts of the garrison in the strongholds and because most of the 12 millions only leave the coffers of the king to enter into the purses of individual governors, who ordinarily only maintain ten men when they should have one hundred.

But since it is difficult for there not to be some special stronghold of such importance that the governors cannot be refused a garrison that they can choose for themselves and in which they have all the better confidence, it is necessary, in my opinion, to be satisfied with cutting ⅔ of this expense and reduce it to 1 million.[284]

The expense for the navies of the West and East can be no less than 2 millions as it appears in the particular lists that have been prepared	2,600,000 *livres*
That for the artillery will come to	600,000 *livres*
That for the households of the king, of the queen, and for Monsieur to	3,600,000
Pensions for the Swiss who cannot honorably be excused are of	400,000
Buildings will cost	300,000
Ambassadors	250,000
Fortifications	600,000

One could entirely eliminate all the pensions that cost the king 4 millions every year. But since it is impossible to pass from one extreme to another without pausing, and since it is not possible in France to resist even the most ridiculous pressures, I think that it is necessary to be satisfied with reducing

---

[284] This is clearly an error, since two-thirds of 12 million is 8 million.

pensions by half, which is all the more necessary since it is advantageous to the public for the idleness of the court not to be rewarded and for it to be entirely devoted to the dangers of war. Thusly the pensions and payments will be expended in the future only up to 2,000,000.

King's ordinances	50,000 *livres*
Patented payment orders	400,000
Unexpected expenses and voyages	2,000,000
Intangibles	150,000
King's cash on hand	300,000

All these expenses will only come to 25 millions, which, being subtracted from the 35 millions in receipts, leaves 10, which will be employed from the very first year for lowering the *tailles*.

The true means of establishing good order and relieving the people is to lessen one and the other of these burdens. By reducing those of the state, one can lower the *tailles*, and there is no other way, and thusly this is the principal goal that one must have in the regulation of this kingdom.

BOf the 44 millions, which is what all the various kinds of levies that are drawn from the people by virtue of the assessment of the *taille* come to, there are 26 millions that are employed in the payment of the burdens constituted on the *taille*, which consist of wages and taxations of offices or of duties that have been mortgaged to them.

Even though the tax farm of the aides produces 4 millions every year, only 400,000 come to the treasury; the bonds, wages, taxations, and duties mortgaged to the said aides consume the rest, which is more than 3½ millions.

Even though nearly 19 millions are collected from the gabelle, only some 5,500,000 livres come to the treasury because the rest, which comes to nearly 13 millions, is employed for the payment of the bonds issued on the said gabelles, or on the wages, taxations, and duties of the officials of the salt stations, or the wages of the *parlement* of Paris, the *Chambre des Comptes*, the Cour des Aides, the Grand Conseil, or the secretaries of the king.

Even though all the other tax farms of the state produce 12 millions, only 6 come to the king, because it is necessary to deduct more than two millions, diverted to the payment of some bonds, wages of officials, taxations, and alienated rights.B

To take the right measures in such an important affair, it is necessary to realize that even though all the levies that are made in this kingdom come to close to 80 millions, more than 45 are in overhead, so it can be said that the overhead is now the ruin of the kingdom. I venture to say that with better management, this will be turned into its comfort and opulence.

Many will undoubtedly consider it desirable for the state to be relieved of all these loads. But since it is impossible to support a great body without various expenses absolutely necessary for its maintenance, as the weight of all these burdens together cannot be endured by the state, suppressing them entirely cannot reasonably be desired.

One might propose three means of reducing the said burdens:

The first is the claim that individuals have made excessive use of the king's money for the funds that they have disbursed in order to acquire the bonds, the offices, and the rights that they enjoy.

I know that it would not be very difficult to dispossess certain individuals of their bonds and their rights, that a good audit of the money they have collected, aside from the interest permitted by the ordinances, would undoubtedly also find the reimbursement for the price of their investment. But if the fairness of this expedient could not be denied, reason would not advise it, because the practice would eliminate any means to find any money in the future for the needs of the state, no matter what commitment one was willing to make.

It is important to emphasize in this regard that something that may be perfectly just may not fail to be politically unreasonable, and it is very necessary to be on one's guard against expedients that may not violate reason but would still violate the public trust.

If someone says that the public interest must be preferred to individual ones, this I admit, but I beg him to consider in discussing this point not only that interests of a different nature must be balanced against each other but that the public ones have to be weighed against the future, and it lasts longer than the present, which passes in an instant.

Future interests must be preferred to present ones, and with good reason, contrary to the habit of irrational men, who prefer what they can see up close because their reason can reach no farther than their senses. If, as I feel, it is entirely necessary that one keep the faith with the public on this point, the state will be much better served than it would be if one eliminated a part of its burdens without replacing them because it would retain control over the purses of individuals at any time and would still increase its revenue.

The second means of reducing the burdens on the kingdom consists of reimbursing them at the rate of the amount presently paid by individuals. But since this would be difficult to verify, seeing as how in order to facilitate the sale of what the necessities of the state had compelled to alienate, it was given at 25% and 6.25%, this measure, fair in itself, cannot be put into practice without giving vent to a lot of complaints, as ill founded as they may be.

The third means of reducing the burdens on the state consists of reimbursing those that are not necessary at the same price as they sell on the market.

By reimbursing the owners of offices, of bonds, and of duties that would be eliminated, the owners will not suffer any harm, and the king will only make use of what was most advantageous for individuals who can free themselves from the burden of their debts, when they have the means of paying them at the same price as they are ordinarily sold.

This measure, which is the only one that can and must be put into practice, can produce its effect in various fashions, either in the long run through the simple savings from the repossession of the burdens or in one year through the huge sum of ready money that might be necessary in case of an emergency.

Since the natural impatience of our nation gives us no grounds to expect that we can persevere in the same resolution for fifteen or twenty years, the first way, which requires that long a time, is not acceptable.

The huge sum that would be necessary in order to reimburse the burdens on the state all at once makes the second way just as ridiculous and impossible. Thus the third is the only practical one.

To use it fairly so that no one can complain, it is necessary to consider the burdens that would be eliminated at three different rates, depending on the various markets where they are sold.

[B]Most of the bonds constituted on the *taille* since 1612 are still at present in the hands of individuals, their heirs, or those to whom they have transferred them, and they have acquired them at such a cheap price that they are expecting their reimbursement to be much less advantageous than if they were reimbursed at the current price.[B]

The last bonds constituted on the *taille*, which ordinarily sell at 20%, must not be considered or reimbursed according to their present value by reimbursing them entirely in seven and a half years.

The other bonds constituted on the *taille* since the death of the late king, which are paid in the local districts or out of the general fund, must be reimbursed at the rate of 16.66% because this is the price at which they are sold, at which they can only be reimbursed in eight and a half years.

The officials in the districts, with their wages, taxes of office, and other rights granted to them, must be reimbursed at the rate of 12.5%, which is the ordinary price of such posts.

[B]The new bonds constituted on the *aides* are only issued at 14.51%, and they are for 2 millions. The new bonds for the *gabelles* sell at 16.08%, and they are for 5 million two hundred sixty thousand *livres*.[B]

The same reason obliges the same rate to be set for the obligations constituted on the *aides*, the *gabelles*, the five great tax farms, on the tax farm of Languedoc and Provence, on the customs of Lyon, on the convoy of Bordeaux, the customs of Bayonne, the tax farm of Brouage, and levies of other natures that are laid on the kingdom, and such reimbursement can only be made in twelve years.

Well do I know that bonds of this nature are sold every day at less than 12.5%. But I propose that they be reimbursed at this rate for the satisfaction of individuals, since I feel that in an affair of such importance, if there has to be any loss, it is better for it to fall on the king than on them.

Once the rate of all the reimbursements has been fairly established, it is necessary to consider that there are certain burdens that are so necessary in this kingdom or mortgaged at such a high price that they are not to be included among those whose reimbursement I now propose.

These are the salaries of the *parlements* and other sovereign courts, of the presidial courts and royal judges, of the secretaries of the king, of the Treasurers of France, and of the receivers general.

It is not that I do not feel that is it necessary never to eliminate these kinds of offices. Perish the thought! But in order to proceed methodically in the reduction of posts in the kingdom, reason demands that one begin by reimbursing those that are at the lowest price and are most discomforting to the public.

Considering this, I prefer the elimination above all of the bonds established on the *tailles* and for the posts of many selectmen, since bonds of this kind because of their price and the posts of selectmen because their number, which is excessive, adds up to four million,[285] and these officials are the true source of the people's poverty.

ᴮThis same consideration is the only one that keeps me from speaking now about the elimination of many useless offices in the judiciary, which sell for much more than they are worth. It would be poor management to repurchase them in our present financial straits merely in order to reduce their number. The means to attain this end will be to make a good regulation on the *paulette* by which the price of the offices will decrease so that the king can then reimburse the possessors and eliminate them all together.ᴮ

I do not include here the old bonds that were created in the time of your predecessors and are paid in the city hall of Paris, both because the actual amount paid by the purchasers is greater than all the others and because it is good that the interest of individuals be, in some fashion, intertwined with that of their sovereign, but because they have finally passed on to various religious orders, hospitals, and communities to whose subsistence they are necessary, and since they have at various times been shared by families, it seems as if they have taken root there, and they cannot be uprooted without disturbing the whole institution.

---

[285] He means "from paying the *taille*."

However, in order to leave no stone unturned, I must note two things in this place:

The first is that since the offices of the Treasurers of France will survive, one can profit from a third of their salaries, it being certain that they will benefit greatly from the general reform of the kingdom if, when their salaries are reduced to two-thirds of what they were in the beginning, they are assured that no new taxes will be imposed on them.

The second is that by not eliminating the bonds issued by the city hall in the time of the late king, which are all created at 8.33%, this will be all the fairer since individuals currently can only get it at 5.55%, the possessors of the said bonds constituted on the city will benefit by 2.78% thanks to the king from those that they have of this same kind. And just as they will find this to their advantage, so will the king, in that the bonds with which the state is burdened will sell more easily than those of individuals, assuming that they are paid promptly with no reduction, as must be done in the public interest.

ᴮTo satisfy both the payment of these bonds and the wages of many officials who are either absolutely necessary or impossible to eliminate at the present time, I feel that of 45 millions by which the kingdom is now burdened, it is necessary to be satisfied with eliminating 30, leaving the rest for the payment of the burdens that will remain. Of 30 millions to eliminate there are almost seven that can only be reimbursed at 20%. The elimination will be made in seven and a half years as they come due.

The bonds currently at 20% come to exactly six million eight hundred thousand livres, to wit: six millions that were constituted from the eight million alienated from the *tailles* in the month of February 1634 and one hundred twelve thousand livres constituted by the Edict of March of the same year by the creditors de Moyssel and Payen

Of the other 24 there are still some that, since they only have to be reimbursed at 6.25%, which is the current price for such burdens, can be eliminated in eight years as they come due. But, as I have indicated above, considering that long-term plans are not too reliable in this kingdom, it is best to reduce all the desired eliminations to a number of years that does not exceed the limits of our patience.

To ensure that all the reimbursement that will be undertaken will be accomplished at the same time as the bonds that are sold at 20% are eliminated when they come due, it is necessary to create an extraordinary fund that is worth one-sixth of the current price of the said bonds, which amounts exactly to one payment of 7 millions for the elimination of that much debt.

To complete the elimination of the proposed 30 millions, there still remain 16 that must be reimbursed at the rate of 12.5% because that is the current price at which they sell.

Now, because the reimbursement of these 16 millions can only be made in twelve years by their due dates and it is desirable to shorten this time in order to reduce this elimination, just like the one of the 14 preceding millions,[286] to

---

[286] There is no previous mention of such a sum.

seven years, it is necessary to supplement three of its eight parts by extraordinary funds amounting to 48 millions.

Even though the greatness of this sum may initially seem astonishing, those who know how easy affairs of this nature are in this kingdom will have no doubt that it will be all the easier to find since it will only be necessary to find in seven years.

And there will no sooner be peace than the ordinary use of investments in order to find money will be abolished, and since those who have been accustomed to this kind of affairs cannot outgrow their first habits, they will willingly devote all their energies in the same old way to undo what they have done, that is to say, to extinguish and eliminate, by virtue of the new investments, the bonds, the duties, and the offices that they had once created.[B]

Thus the kingdom can be relieved of 30 millions a year from the ordinary burdens that is now carrying.

The people, effectively relieved of 22 millions from the *taille*, which is exactly half of what they are enduring, the revenue of the king will be 42 millions, as the following list confirms:

Receipts

From the *tailles*	22,000,000 livres
From the aides	4,000,000
From all the gabelles	19,000,000
From all the other tax farms	12,000,000
Total	57,000,000

Of which, having removed 25 millions for the payment of the burdens, there will remain 42 [*sic*] millions that will enter every year into the treasury, a sum so large that there is no state in Christendom that even raises half as much, after paying its burdens.

[B]If, subsequent to these eliminations, which will subject many people to paying the *tailles* without being able to complain about it, one also eliminates all the offices that are exercised by appointment or by a simple commission, if one limits the number of notaries, not only the royal, but in the ordinary jurisdictions, one would procure an immense relief for the people, both because they would be freed from all these leeches by this means and because, besides, since there would be more than one hundred thousand officials of this kind to curtail, those who would be deprived of their ordinary employment would be compelled to resort to war, commerce, or farming.

If one subsequently reduces all the exemptions of the nobility and of the boarders in the royal household, it is certain that since the cities, the communities with exemptions, the sovereign courts, the offices of the Treasurers of France, the elections, the salt stations, the officials of waters and forests, of the domains and tithes, the intendants and receivers of the parishes, comprise more than one hundred thousand exemptions, this would relieve the people of more than half of their *tailles*, since it is also certain that the ones who should pay the most are the ones who pay to become exempt.

Well do I know that it is easy to draw up such projects, similar to those of Plato's *Republic*, which are chimerical.

But I venture to say that this plan is not only reasonable but so easy to execute that if, by the grace of God, the king will soon have a peace in this kingdom, which will last along with his servants, among whom I am one of the least, instead of leaving this advice by a testament I hope to be able to carry it out.[B]

EIGHTH SECTION

Which shows in a few words that the power of princes must depend on their possessing the hearts of their subjects

[B]Philippe de Valois[B]

[B]Ammianus Marcellinus Bks. 16 and 17[B]

If the finances are handled as calculated above, the people will be entirely relieved. The king will be powerful by possessing the hearts of his subjects, who, in return for his caring for their welfare, will be led to love him by their own interest.

Former kings have put such a premium on the hearts of their subjects that they have preferred to consider themselves kings of the French than kings of France, and, indeed, this nation has formerly been so famous for adoring its princes that ancient authors have praised it for its readiness to sacrifice its blood and its wealth in their service and for the glory of the state.[287]

Under the kings of the first, second, and third race until Philip the Fair, the only public treasury that was kept in this kingdom was the treasury of hearts.[288]

[B]This policy was based on the saying of a great prince who, although he was deprived of the true light of our faith, did not fail to see so clearly by that of reason that he felt that he would never be lacking for money in case of need if he was loved by his people. Cyrus and Xenophon, Book 5 of his *Institutes*[B289]

Well do I know that the past times have no relationship to present, that what is good in one century is often out of place in another. But, certain as it is that the treasury of hearts will no longer suffice, it is just as sure that gold and silver are almost useless without the first. Both are necessary, and whoever has only one will be needy in the midst of prosperity.

---

[287] Ammianus Marcellinus in *Rerum gestarum libri* XXXI.

[288] Philip IV. See note 140 above. Not exactly the most lovable.

[289] Xenophon, *Cyropaedia*, more like Bk VIII.

Chapter X

Which concludes this work by demonstrating that its message will be completely wasted if princes and their ministers are not so devoted to governing the state that they do everything possible to fulfill their obligations without abusing their power

To conclude this work on a happy note, it only remains for me to indicate to Your Majesty how, since kings are obliged to do many more things than private persons, they cannot avoid committing more sins of omission than private persons can ever commit. This is also the case for those on whom sovereigns discharge a part of their load, since this honor subjects them to the same obligations.

Both, considered as private persons, are subject to the same faults as other men. But with regard to the public policies that they administer, they are subject to many more, seeing that they could not be wanting without sinning against the obligations of their ministry. Considering this, someone might be good and virtuous as a private individual and be a bad magistrate and sovereign by his negligence in fulfilling the obligations of his post.

In a word, if princes do not do everything that they can to regulate the different orders in their states, if they are negligent in the choice of a good council, if they disdain good advice, unless they are not particularly careful to let their example speak for them, if they are lackadaisical in instituting the reign of God, reason, and justice at the same time, if they fail to protect the innocent, to reward the good services that are rendered to the public, and to punish the disobedience and the crimes that disturb the order, discipline, and safety of states, if they do not dedicate themselves as much as they must to foresee and prevent the evils that can happen and take careful precautions to deflect the storms that the clouds bring from afar when one least expects them, if favoritism does not keep them from making good choices of those whom they honor with important posts and the principal employments in the kingdom, if they don't keep a firm hand on maintaining the power of the state at the level where it must be, if, on every occasion, they do not prefer the public interest to particular ones, even though they may otherwise be virtuous, they would be much guiltier than those who actually sin against the laws and commandments of God are by committing the sin, since it is certain that not doing what one should and doing what one should not do is the same thing.

I must also indicate to Your Majesty how if princes and those who serve under them in the highest dignities have great advantages over private persons, they possess such a benefit on demanding terms, since they are not only subject by their omissions to the faults that I have outlined, but there are still others by commission that are particular to them.

If they use their power to commit some injustice or some violence that is denied to private persons, they commit a sin for which, as princes and magistrates, they are even more responsible and for which the King of Kings will demand a full accounting on the day of judgment.

These two kinds of faults particular to princes and magistrates must give them food for thought. They are much more serious than those of private individuals because, as universal causes, they spread disorder everywhere. Many private individuals can still be forgiven, whereas public persons will be damned.

One of the greatest of our neighbor kings cried out before dying that he was less fearful of the sins of Philip than he was of those of the king. This was a truly pious thought, but he would have been much more useful to his subjects and to himself if he had kept this in mind during the heyday of his greatness and his administration instead of only realizing its importance when he could only reap the fruit for his salvation.[290]

I beseech Your Majesty to start thinking right now about what this great prince, perhaps, did not think about until the hour of his death, and in order to induce you to do it by my own example, I promise you that I will never stop thinking about the public affairs that it pleases you to place in my charge.

---

[290] Philip II (1527–1598), King of Spain from 1556. What a revealing statement!

Appendix

Continuation of the Succinct Narration

[with Richelieu's own hand additions in script]

1639

Even though the year 1639 was a combination of roses and thorns, I am sure that posterity will judge that the ones and the others have contributed equally to your glory.

You had designated three armies to be employed in Picardy and Champagne at the frontiers of the enemies, so that two would act one after the other and the third would always be in reserve.

Feuquières, who commanded one of them, had orders to attack Thionville, but first of all he had to see what Piccolomini intended to do. His instructions were to oppose him if he tried to enter into Flanders and, if he withdrew, to attack the stronghold.[291]

In his enthusiasm, this courageous and ambitious gentleman rushed to attack this stronghold in the hope of drawing in Piccolomini and then advancing toward him in order to take him by surprise. But, unfortunately for him, this carefully laid plan did not work.

Instead of forestalling his enemy, he was taken so completely by surprise that he did not have a chance to come up with all his forces, and he was obliged to fight piecemeal at a great disadvantage, which he did, however, so firmly that, had it not been for the unconscionable cowardice of his cavalry, he would probably have avoided his misfortune.[292]

Thus you began the campaign with the loss of a battle. But aside from the enemies having been given this victory rather than having won it fair and square, the firmness with which you kept the results of such an awful tragedy from being ruinous to your state made having lost the battle better than winning it.

---

[291] Manessès de Pas (1590–1640), Marquis de Feuquières, Governor of Verdun. Ottavio Piccolomini (1599–1656) was one of the Holy Roman Emperor's best generals. Thionville was a key Imperial stronghold on the Moselle River, about fifty-one miles north of Nancy in Lorraine.

[292] The battle took place on June 7, 1639. More than the French cavalry was at fault, as Richelieu himself admits.

Puffed up by his victory, Piccolomini attacked Mouzon, a frontier city that no one took very seriously, so neglected up to then that it was hardly included among the strongholds that could be defended. However, not only was he unable to take it, but he lost the flower of his army in trying.[293]

By taking it too lightly, it proved too strong for him, and by trying to overrun it by assault instead of digging trenches, two thousand men died on the spot, and this butchery of his best soldiers discouraged the others so that the fear of a setback similar to the one that poor Feuquières had received obliged him to raise the siege in the face of Marshal de Châtillon, who came up to him with the third of your armies.

You took Hesdin, nicknamed "the strong," because it actually is, all the more important to Your Majesty since it covers much of your frontier and protects half of Picardy from raids and ravages.[294]

You took it in the face of the Cardinal-Infante and Piccolomini, who, after having won and lost, now had one more chance to try their luck.

From Picardy, you moved into Champagne, where you found a fresh army that was waiting for the result of the attack on Hesdin, with which you took Ivoy, a stronghold whose location and strength was a threat to Champagne. This city was no sooner in your hands than it was razed by your orders so as to teach the Spanish to honor their treaties, that of [Vervins] requiring them to demolish this stronghold.[295]

After taking Hesdin and razing the city of Ivoy, you proceeded to Grenoble to stop the headlong rush of your sister Madame by moderating her imprudence.

While you were on this voyage, Marshal de La Meilleraye defeated the enemies twice, once so completely that he overran the camp of their Croats, where more than 400 of them died on the spot, and once, even though he only had one-half of his troops, besides remaining master of the field, he killed more than a thousand men on the spot and captured three of their cannons, and if one of his principal regiments had done its duty, he would have defeated their entire army.[296]

---

[293] Mouzon is a small town in the Ardennes about six and a half miles southeast of Sedan. Châtillon relieved it on July 20, forcing Piccolomini to withdraw the next day.

[294] Hesdin was a very strategic Spanish stronghold in Picardy, about fifty-one miles south of Calais. Charles de La Porte (1602–1664), Marquis, later Duke, de La Meilleraye, was a cousin of Richelieu and, like all of Richelieu's relatives, highly touted by him in his writings. He laid siege before Hesdin on May 20, 1639. After he was joined by Louis XIII, it capitulated on June 29.

[295] Ivoy-en-Champagne, a small town about twelve miles southeast of Sedan. Châtillon took it on August 2. The expressions "razed" and "demolished" refer to the tearing down of the fortifications, not to the destruction of the town.

[296] The battle against the Croats took place on August 2, but it was little more than a skirmish. Meilleraye then went on to attack the nearby Fort Saint-Nicolas, where he won a more serious engagement, but as Richelieu leaves us to guess, he did not take the fort.

Since your sister Madame's misconduct deprived her in a short time of something that she should have prized more than her own life, namely, the respect of her subjects, it went from contempt to hatred and from hatred to revolution, which in the space of three months put more than two-thirds of Piedmont in the hands of the Spanish, which they had never been able to initiate by force during the life of Dukes Charles Emmanuel and his son Amadeus, though they had tried it many times.[297]

Even the city of Turin, the capital of this state, was not exempt from the misfortune of this princess.[298]

Even though the presence of their sovereigns is a citadel for the strongholds where they reside, even though she had two thousand men in Turin, most of whom were Swiss and Piedmontese, Prince Thomas did not fail to capture the stronghold with twelve hundred men, something unheralded and almost unbelievable even to those who were watching. And this was done so quickly that this unfortunate princess hardly had the time to withdraw to the citadel, where she would have died in two days for lack of everything if your armies had not come to her rescue. In this miserable state she was compelled to put this stronghold in your hands at a moment when she could neither defend it nor could anyone expect you to do it for her. If she had only listened to reason previous to this emergency, if she had only allowed her principal strongholds to be guarded by your forces, she would not have lost any of them, but it was never possible to get her to distrust her enemies and to put her trust in Your Majesty.[299]

She preferred to be despoiled of not only part of her state but the keys to all the rest through the loss of Nice and Turin rather than to assure herself of all of it by the consignment of these two strongholds, which would have ruined the plans of her enemies and confirmed the security of the mother, the son, and the state all together.

The example of Philibert Emmanuel, grandfather of her children, who saved his state by this means after he had lost most of it, could not induce her to use this remedy.[300]

Even though this was then necessary for her salvation, even proposing it was a crime, and whatever one did to get her to listen to reason on this subject, the best that one could do was the consignment of Carmagnola, Cherasco, and

---

[297] Diego Felipe de Guzmàn (1580–1655), Marquis de Leganéz, Spanish governor of Milan, and Prince Thomas invaded Piedmont around March 23, 1639, and succeeded in overrunning a great portion of it.

[298] By April 14 they were threatening to besiege the capital, Turin.

[299] This incident occurred on July 27.

[300] Philibert Emmanuel (1528–1580), Duke of Savoy from 1553, who managed to maintain his independence from the French and the Spanish.

Savigliano, which, even though they were in very bad shape, were saved notwithstanding the various schemes of Prince Thomas to capture them.[301]

The repeated appeals of your sister Madame, after she was despoiled of Piedmont, for Your Majesty to come to her aid gave you some hope that she wanted to give you the means to bail her out.[302]

As soon as she had joined Your Majesty in Grenoble, you tried in all sorts of ways to get her back on the right track. But she demonstrated to her detriment that the weakest minds are the most resistant to reason.[303]

You did everything possible to stop her craziness and the bad advice of those who were contributing the most to her ruin, but she was too stubborn, and the others were either too ignorant to recognize what was good for them or too malicious to go along with it or too timid to interfere.

Various considerations kept you from punishing them.

And even though they were well aware of the reason and the power that you had to do it, their knowledge of your prudence and your goodness kept them from fearing their just deserts and gave them grounds to continue their original conduct insolently.

If the mind of a woman had been capable of taking advice, yours would have liberated her from the disdain of her subjects, while your armies would have protected her from the aggression of the Spanish and the ill will of her brothers.[304]

The only way she could still save herself was by the consignment of Savoy, which would have obliged her brothers to fear that if the young duke should die, she would turn against them.[305]

---

[301] The desperate Cristina had allowed the French to garrison these three strongholds by a treaty signed on June 1, 1639. This entire description of events in the Duchy of Savoy appears to have been written under extreme emotional strain, if one observes the way in which Richelieu is jumping around chronologically.

[302] On August 5 Cristina left the citadel of Turin, leaving her supporters to conclude a truce with Prince Thomas. She finally ended up in Momigliano, from where she reluctantly decided to meet personally with Louis XIII and Richelieu in France, but she was terrified, among other things, that they would imprison her confidant, Filippo d'Aglié (1604–1667), and take possession of her son, the little Charles Emmanuel II.

[303] She was in Grenoble from September 25 to about October 15.

[304] Strictly speaking, her brothers-in-law.

[305] Richelieu, who had admitted in the Second Part, Chapter VI, that marriage alliances were of only limited value in diplomacy, now railed at the idea that Cristina considered herself a mother first and a sister second and was doing her best to follow the traditional policy of the dukes of Savoy, which was to maintain their independence as much as possible against all comers. All too human perhaps, but this tells us volumes about the double standard by which he perceived the world.

The ties of blood, your reputation, and all the imaginable safeguards that you offered should have quieted her own fears, but she would always find a pretext to stick to decisions that could only lead her to her ruin.

It was submitted to her that Your Majesty and his predecessors had repeatedly restored Piedmont when you had every justification to retain it, so that it would have to be crazy to fear that you intended to take it over perfidiously now.

Even though the final advice that she received from her husband was to put her trust in Your Majesty and in his creatures, he had no sooner breathed his last than she completely rejected it.

The Jesuit Monot, whom, while her husband was alive, she had disliked so much that the coils of his character should never have given her any confidence in his fidelity, now became her favorite because she thought he was faithful to her other favorites.[306]

This miserable monk gave her so much poison in the form of medicine that there were not enough antidotes against it.

Thus the only effect of your voyage was to save Susa, Avigliana, and Cahours from the general devastation of Piedmont, which was not capable of stopping the course of her ruin as long as her misconduct continued.[307]

The extravagance of this princess was such that, to her everlasting shame, she behaved toward Your Majesty as if she were dealing with her enemies. You did not see her son.

In these straits, you considered over and over again whether you should abandon such an irresponsible person.

It was advantageous to do this in order to excuse the misfortunes against which it seemed impossible to protect oneself. But this decision would have been so harmful to this miserable woman, who could not be abandoned by you without being abandoned by everybody, that Your Majesty preferred to jeopardize your reputation rather than to precipitate the ruin of a person whom nature had made your sister, even though she was unworthy of her brother.

In fact, instead of abandoning her, you reinforced your army in Italy and sent the Count d'Harcourt to command it with orders that gave him the opportunity to conclude this campaign gloriously.[308]

---

[306] The Jesuit Pierre Monod (c. 1586–1644) was another one of her confidants. In January 1639 Richelieu had pressured Cristina into arresting him, and in 1640 Richelieu pressured her into letting him be imprisoned in a French fortress where he died.

[307] Cristina came out of the trip with some concessions to Louis XIII and Richelieu, but they failed to browbeat her into allowing them to garrison the stronghold of Momigliano.

[308] Henri de Lorraine (1601–1666), Count d'Harcourt. Now Richelieu is getting ahead of himself, since he should have told us that the Cardinal de La Valette, who commanded in Italy, had died (see note 311 below) and that Louis XIII had appointed Harcourt to replace him.

The stinging wounds inflicted by your sister Madame were aggravated by the death of the Duke of Weimar, a prince whose merit and reputation made his loss almost irreparable.[309]

Your Majesty reacted to this incident in keeping with your reason and your virtue.

Even though after this misfortune the officers of the army of the late duke volunteered to serve Your Majesty, who had always maintained them at your expense, there were so many difficulties in concluding a new treaty that it took no little doing for Your Majesty to overcome them.

Your open enemies and those who acted as if they were your friends obstructed you as much as they could but in vain.

The stronghold of Breisach was of such importance that everybody wanted it. Your reputation and your own good required that it remain at your disposal.

It was necessary for you to deal tactfully with these contenders, and yet it was necessary to be very firm with them in various situations in order to keep them from acting too high and mighty.

You played it by ear, and you ended up with much greater control of this army than you had previously, and the stronghold of Breisach and many others that the Duke of Weimar claimed as his own, even though they were not, were now entirely assured to you.[310]

You had barely stopped drying your tears over the death of this great captain when the death of the Cardinal de La Valette started them flowing again. His loss touched Your Majesty all the more since his fidelity, his zeal, and his desire to gain honor by serving well were the real cause.[311]

He was so saddened by the treason of his brother the Duke de La Valette that he never recovered after acknowledging that this bad man had previously plotted to put Metz into the hands of the Spanish along with his person.

And since the misconduct of Madame left him no means of successfully leading your armies, he was so outraged at seeing the loss of Piedmont that even though no one is responsible for the actions of others, particularly when it is not possible to stop them, those of this princess finished him off, right after a siege that should have encouraged him since he had beaten the enemies and taken the stronghold in their presence.[312]

---

[309] Bernard of Saxe-Weimar had died on July 18, 1639, so Richelieu is backtracking.

[310] This is one case where Richelieu is not exaggerating. The death of Bernard of Saxe-Weimar gave Louis XIII the opportunity to secure his own hold over Breisach.

[311] The Cardinal de La Valette had been commanding in Piedmont since April 1638. He died on September 28, 1639.

[312] Richelieu is now backtracking to the fact that La Valette had managed to keep Prince Thomas from taking the citadel of Turin.

Since misfortunes, no less than good luck, often come in bunches, the loss of Salces, one of the last acts of this campaign, followed these two unfortunate incidents. However, since it is common knowledge that you had just overrun this stronghold a few days previously, along with other nearby ones that remained in your hands, it may truly be said, given what has happened in Spain, that you had better luck than your enemies. If those who commanded your armies had been as intelligent as they were well intentioned, they would not have shown how much better they were at making conquests than at keeping them, which is characteristic of the French.[313]

Either too many men had been put in this stronghold to defend it or too few victuals to keep them supplied. Enough troops as were needed would have been left inside it if the outworks had been defensible. But since they were not, in two months the number of regiments in it only served to eat up the victuals that should have lasted more than four if only as many as were necessary had been left there to defend it.

Thus the besieged, who could not be captured by force, fell prey to their hunger, and the effort to relieve them was carried out so negligently that it did more to hasten their ruin than anything else.

They could have avoided this mistake by always keeping your army close to the enemies in order to cut off their victuals, discomforting them in different ways, or attacking their circumvallation in time. Your Majesty did not fail to give the orders, and if you did not reap the fruits of your prudence, this was because they were not executed.

This setback was compensated for by what may have been the most remarkably successful battle in the annals of history. While the Count d'Harcourt was in Grenoble, Your Majesty had ordered him to occupy the post of Chieri in order to impede the enemy from seizing it and thereby break the communication with Chivasso or with the citadel of Turin, and then to attack it if he could. After remaining there for as long as he could feed his army, he decided to go into winter quarters across the Po.[314]

He was well aware that the Marquis de Leganéz was close by at Poirino with twice as many men. He could not be avoided.

He knew that Prince Thomas could come out of the city of Turin with five or six thousand men to block his passage.

---

[313] Salces in Roussillon had been taken July 29 by the Prince de Condé. The Spanish attempted to retake it, and Condé made extraordinary efforts in order to force them to raise their siege. However, on November 2, the Spanish, under the great Ambrogio Spinola, routed the French, producing another disaster reminiscent of Fontarabia in 1638.

[314] October 17, 1639.

But since necessity obliged him to abandon a position where he could no longer survive, he had no other choice but to try to get out of there so secretly that the enemy would not have the time to cut him off.

After having taken every possible precaution to hide his intention, he left Chieri at the crack of dawn with what troops he had left, which was barely 5,000 foot and 3,000 horse, the rest being near Coni to oppose the troops of the Cardinal of Savoy. If the inhabitants of Chieri had not been a bunch of spies for the enemy, your army could have passed without trouble, but Leganéz and Prince Thomas had been carefully warned of the departure of the Count d'Harcourt. The first elements of his advance guard were no sooner on the banks of the creek of Rotta, preparing to build a bridge in order to cross it, than 3,000 horse and 500 dragoons detached from the main body, which was composed of 10,000 foot and 5,000 horse, charged the rear guard commanded by La Motte-Houdancourt, forcing him to defend himself instead of thinking about crossing.

At the same time Prince Thomas hurried out of Turin with 1,000 horse and 4,000 foot and attacked the advance guard under your general, who put up such a fight that he stopped him in his tracks and left his troops in such disarray that he himself admitted that if the night had not fallen, he would never have come out alive.

Following this success, the Count d'Harcourt rushed to build a bridge on which his advance guard and all the baggage of his army could cross, while La Motte-Houdancourt gradually withdrew under cover of darkness in order to reach it. That night passed in continual skirmishes, while Leganéz waited for the arrival of his artillery in order to have a general battle with all his forces the next day. But La Motte foresaw his intentions so that before daybreak all his infantry joined the Count d'Harcourt on the other side of the creek of Rotta under cover of two lines of musket fire, which gave his cavalry and his dragoons a chance to cross safely.

This action was all the more glorious since the enemies had 20,000 men against 8,000 of yours, who could not get through without marching between them and were still victorious after being attacked on both sides, so that Prince Thomas was routed with much bloodshed, and the Marquis de Leganéz lost 2,000 men, while the dead and wounded on your side were not more than 300.[315]

Thus, even though this campaign began badly, it can be said that it ended well, and reason demands that it be put among your most fortunate, since you took various strongholds from your enemies, and by stopping the course of the ruin of your sister Madame, insofar as she would allow you do it, you profited by your prudence from the death of a prince that could have been harmful.

---

[315] Battle of La Rotta, November 20, 1639.

If one also considers the noteworthy naval battle that the Dutch won against the Spanish in the English Downs, no one can deny your good fortune in this year and your contribution to this action, not only because of the financial support that States receive every year from Your Majesty but also because of the particular assistance that they received on this occasion from the Governor of Calais, without which their admiral acknowledged that not only could he not have won but he could not have fought.[316]

1640

The preparations for the year 1640 will undoubtedly astonish posterity since, when I recall them, they have the same effect on me, even though I was their principal author under your authority.

All the expenses of the war of the preceding years that had been made with extraordinary funds were converted this year into ordinary ones.

All the troops that had been previously levied at the end of the campaigns to make up for the deterioration that armies always undergo after they have been on foot for a while had winter quarters like all the rest so as to be ready to serve in the spring.

Thus from the beginning of the year, you had some 100 regiments of infantry in the field and more than 300 companies of cavalry.

This year you doubled the subsidy that you had been accustomed to give to the Dutch so that the Prince of Orange could augment his troops by 10,000 foot in order to execute his proposal to attack Dam and Bruges together.[317]

Even though this augmentation was considerable, the month that your troops on the Meuse lost in order to attract the enemies and give the Prince of Orange, who had asked you do to it, a better chance to carry out his plan cost even more.

The interests of the common cause were so dear to you on this occasion that you preferred them to your own, and since you believed that if your allies hit them hard, your enemies would be more receptive to peace for fear of something worse, your troops on this occasion overcame the discomforts

---

[316] The Battle of the Downs, on October 21, 1639, won by Admiral Maarten Tromp over the Spanish admiral Antonio de Oquendo, was a kind of death knell for the Spanish navy, although it did manage, at great loss, to disembark most of the troops that it was transporting. The Governor of Calais was Louis de Béthune (1605–1681), Count de Charost. He had, on orders from Louis XIII, furnished Tromp with four hundred cannon balls and four mills of powder, and on October 19, Tromp distributed them to his ships.

[317] Richelieu had made this promise to Frederick Henry as far back as November 22 and 24 of the previous year.

of a barren countryside, of a late season, and of a rainy spring for an entire
month so that the oldest-timers who were still alive admitted that they had
never seen anything like it.[318]

Foreseeing that since the beginning of the war, the enemies had not been
able to do anything against your armies except by catching them unawares,
they might begin the campaign in Italy before a large enough body of your
troops could cross the mountains in time to resist them, and also because
your sister Madame had never wanted to give them winter quarters in her
states, you made so many efforts to overcome the difficulties of nature, of the
season, and of the malice of the bad characters who corrupted this princess
that, at the same time that your enemies might have felt secure in Italy in
the absence of your principal forces, enough were found to give the Count
d'Harcourt the opportunity to relieve Casale for the third time and to punish
for the third time the nefarious scheme of your enemies.

The first time, *since you achieved this glorious effect without even
leaving Susa,* you had *relieved* this stronghold with your shadow, the
second by the presence of your armies, which dumbfounded your enemies
without fighting them, and God permitted it to be saved for the third time *by
their* effect, which *was such* that it might truly be said *to be* unexampled.
Scarcely will there ever be a captain who has earned so much glory by a
single action as the Count d'Harcourt by such an ingenious plan and such
a great success.[319]

Your army consisted of no more than 8,000 foot and 3,500 horse; the enemies outnumbered it by more than 6,000 men. They were so well entrenched
that the Marquis de Leganéz spoke confidently of taking Casale, had assured
the king his master of it, and was counting his chickens before they were
hatched. However, the blessing of God, the firmness, the ambition, and the
effectiveness of the general of your army in Italy, of his principal officers,
and the courage of your entire army validated your entire undertaking and
convinced everyone that victory depends more on the courage and virtue of
men than on their number. The Count d'Harcourt attacked his enemies so vigorously that even though he was repulsed the first time, he overran *them* the
second so completely that they lost *all their artillery, their munitions,
and nearly all their baggage,* many flags and standards. The dead and
prisoners numbered 6,000.[320]

The result of this noteworthy victory was not only the salvation of Casale
but the taking of Turin, all the more glorious since this action was the cause.

---

[318] Which adds up to the fact that the Prince of Orange had an attack of gout and did practically nothing during the entire campaign.

[319] For the first two times, see notes 27 and 31 above.

[320] Harcourt's great victory over the Spanish before Casale was on April 29, 1640.

After provisioning Casale with everything necessary, the Count d'Harcourt lost no time in establishing his quarters before Turin, fortifying them, and working at the circumvallation. *And even though before it could be* completed, the Spanish, who are naturally firm in their plans and not liable to be easily discouraged, hurried to keep it, *he did not fail to achieve his purposes.*

This siege *was* all the more remarkable in that there were more than 5,000 soldiers in the stronghold, aside from that many inhabitants under arms. Considering this, it was noteworthy for its various sorties and clashes in which your army always got the upper hand. In one of these, the enemies made a general attack in which even though they made it to the camp, they received such a warm welcome that more than 4,000 died on the spot. *Which gives occasion to say truthfully that since the besiegers had to defend themselves from two armies, they had to make a countervallation to protect themselves from those inside as well as a circumvallation against those outside*

Yours distinguished themselves not only by their valor but also by the hardships that they endured without a murmur, hunger for twenty-two days while the army of the enemies had taken two posts that cut them off entirely from their victuals. All this time, they survived with a handful of rice on one day, that many peas on the next, and eight ounces of bread on the third, while waiting for help from France to arrive. The efforts of Your Majesty to give the Count d'Harcourt the means of carrying out such an ambitious plan are incredible. Aside from more than 20,000 recruits that you sent there, the commons and the nobility of Dauphiné, the twenty regiments of infantry and six of cavalry drawn from your armies in Languedoc, Provence, and Brittany kept relieving and strengthening your armies in Italy until Prince Thomas, who had no gunpowder left besides what the Marquis de Leganéz could fire into the city inside some cannon balls, made one last try *just as unsuccessfully* with a massive sortie seconded by the Marquis de Leganéz and, *by an invention as prodigious by its effect as by its novelty*

after having defended the city for four and one half months,

~~surrendered it~~ [*sic*] with a great deal of honor to himself for his great resolution, and the besiegers could only have done more if they had captured the person of the prince along with the stronghold.[321]

---

[321] The siege of Turin was distinguished by the use by the Spanish outside the French lines of missiles, each one carrying ten pounds of gunpowder and salt in order to resupply the garrison, and by the death during a sortie by the garrison of a German woman who had risen to the rank of captain in the cavalry. Despite these innovations, Prince Thomas had to surrender the city on September 24.

Your orders carried expressly that providing the prince could be captured along with the stronghold, even if the siege would be prolonged by a month, this was the thing to do. The stronghold was entirely out of gun powder and had only three weeks of victuals. They had it in them to carry out your intentions, and if they did not, since their courage and zeal is known by everyone, they can only be faulted for not realizing the importance of capturing this prince, without whom the Spanish could not wage a successful war in Piedmont, or for the incapacity of the French to overcome the natural impatience with which they are born.

While your armies were campaigning so gloriously in Italy, they were not idle in Artois, where Arras was besieged and taken in less than two months with a great deal of glory. This undertaking was all the more glorious since it was noteworthy from start to finish.

It was begun in the face of the enemies, who had the time to assemble their forces because your armies had lost at Charlemont.

The circumvallation, which was five leagues in length, was entirely finished in 20 days, and in fifteen more days the siege works had advanced to the point that nothing had ever been seen like them.

Your forces were constantly confronted with not only a powerful army but also the person of the Cardinal-Infante, that of Duke Charles of Lorraine, and the Imperial general Lamboy, who were all actively engaged in keeping this undertaking from being successful.

The Battle of Sailly, the defeat of the Count de Buquoy near Bapaume, and the defense of the circumvallation when it was attacked are not to be taken lightly.

If one considers that of twelve convoys that were sent to the camp, including two of 4,000 carts each, the enemies, even though they were masters of the field with the most powerful army that the Low Countries had seen since they have been under the obedience of Spain, could only intercept a single one of 250 carts that they ran into by chance, it can be seen, I am sure, that the king knew what he was doing and that God was on his side.

It is hard to fathom how the siege began almost in the face of the enemies and the capitulation was signed with their army in battle formation within cannon shot of your camp, without recognizing that God had permitted it in order to add to the glory of Your Majesty.[322]

Instead of the other armies of Your Majesty campaigning only on the banks of the Rhine as they had in previous years, this one saw them in the heart of Germany under the command of the Duke de Longueville, without whose

---

[322] The siege of Arras took place between June 12 and August 10, 1640.

junction I am sure that your allies would admit that they would have had great difficulty that year in resisting the efforts of the Empire.[323]

The great successes that the armies of Your Majesty have had on land have been followed by the one that the Marquis de Brézé achieved at sea near Cadiz, where he had gone to wait for the sailing of the great fleet that they send to the Indies every year, and even though he only had twenty warships and the enemies had forty, including ten great royal galleons, he did not fail to attack and fight them so successfully that *in the heat of battle* two galleons were sunk by gunfire and two others, *one being the Admiral,* so badly damaged that they sank in the Bay of Cadiz in spite of all the efforts to salvage them.[324]

Three considerations make this victory noteworthy. The first is that even though this fleet had on numerous occasions been attacked by the English and the Dutch, it had always been victorious, for which reason it was named after the virgin.

The second is the cost of the four lost ships, estimated with their cargo at almost two millions in gold.

The third, that to interrupt and postpone the sailing of such a fleet puts it in great risk of sailing at the wrong time.

This victory would have been greater if some of the commanders of this armada had not been more intimidated by the size of the ships they had to fight and the bent of their crews than they were inspired by the opportunity of serving you.

Catalonia[325] *Philips*[326]
What the Count d'Harcourt will do[327]

I do not speak of the revolt of Catalonia because it happened without Your Majesty having contributed anything to it. Admittedly, since these people had recourse to your protection, your war against Spain gave you all the more reason to promise them

---

[323] Henri II d'Orléans (1596–1663), Duke de Longueville, had succeeded to the command of the army of Bernard of Saxe-Weimar. Despite Richelieu's optimism, all Longueville could do was keep his own army and the French party in Germany from breaking up.

[324] The battle took place on July 22, 1640. The Spanish did lose one galleon and one small boat, but Brézé did not keep their fleet from sailing to America.

[325] It would appear as if Richelieu intended here to go into detail on the revolt of Catalonia, and it then occurred to him that such a discussion was inconsistent with the aim of the Succinct narration, after which he decided to mention it briefly.

[326] Saint-Philippe was a Spanish fort halfway between Calais and Dunkirk. On July 17, 1640, the Count de Charost (see note 316 above) carried out a daring raid in the vicinity of the fort, which netted over 1,000 sheep, 60 mares, and 155 cows, although Richelieu seems to have thought better about listing it among the great actions of Louis XIII.

[327] In all probability Richelieu intended to illustrate here the instructions for the Count d'Harcourt, who was to reestablish a chastened Cristina in Turin under French protection.

your assistance, since what they were begging of you was a very good means of inducing your enemies to make peace.

~~If this disturbance has not had the result that might have been expected, the frivolity of these people, who are as easy to please as they are to displease is the cause (cause)~~[328]

Since it is honorable for Your Majesty to take advantage of whatever comes your way even though it may not be honorable to ask for it, the coolest heads praise you for having lent an ear to the enemies of your enemies instead of going out of your way to oppose them.[329]

It is to my great regret that this year what everyone with any intelligence had been expecting from the previous one finally happened.

The insolence of a miserable Piedmonter, as presumptuous as he was cowardly, who could not be kept in line by warnings from you, by the pleas of his own parents, and by all his friends, and who outraged an entire country by his misconduct, finally obliged you to remove him from the company of Madame so as to deprive her of his pernicious counsels.[330]

The benefits that the enemies of this princess gained from this bad character were so harmful that it was impossible for you not to decide to resort to force. You hesitated to do it, but it was not humanly possible to save the states of your nephew the duke without ruining this scoundrel, who was the principal cause of all the advice that had put them in jeopardy.

The public safety, combined with the particular interests of your family, tipped the balance and made you resolve what necessity required both from your wisdom and from your conscience.

There are certain occasions in which one cannot but disdain the tears of women without becoming the cause of their ruin. They are usually so unsuited for the government of states that not following their opinions is usually goodness and justice all together. You regretted on this occasion to have to act against the wishes of your sister Madame, but you were gratified by the support of everyone for doing something that was not only useful but totally

---

[328] The line through this paragraph makes us privy to a moment of pique against the Catalans by Richelieu, which he quickly got over. See the next note.

[329] Louis XIII had lent much more than an ear, since on September 7, 1640, he had signed a treaty of assistance with the rebels and on January 23, 1641, the Catalans proclaimed him Count of Barcelona. This passage shows three things: (1) Richelieu had little sympathy for these rebels, (2) he was prepared to sell them out in order to make a quick peace, and (3) he crossed out his derogatory statements sometime in the course of 1641 when he had reconciled himself to a long war. Curiously, however, the crossed-out passages are not reproduced in the printed versions of the continuation of the Succinct narration.

[330] Filippo D'Aglié (1604–1667), distinguished nobleman and patron of the arts, lover of Cristina, who advised her to resist the pressures of France. He was arrested in Turin on December 31, 1640, and quickly transferred to the château of Vincennes, from which he was only released after the death of Richelieu.

necessary. And you should be thankful to God that not only was this action reasonable but He has justified it by its outcome.

1641

You began the year with a treaty between Your Majesty and Prince Thomas, who had no sooner apologized for his bad conduct than you were prepared not only to forget it but to treat him as if he had always been attached to the interests of his house and to yours.[331]

He received your money but only executed the treaty he had concluded with Mr Mazarin on this one point.

If the favor of Your Majesty on this occasion did not produce its desired result, the frivolity of this prince was the only cause.[332]

He had enough sense to know what was good for him but not enough firmness to do it, and his turnabout is all the more remarkable in that he took up arms against Your Majesty on the same day that he promised to take them up for you, without the slightest pretext whatsoever.

In spite of this drawback, your armies did not fail to take Moncalvo in the middle of winter, even though the undertaking would not have been attempted without the assurance of the said Prince Thomas that he would support it.[333]

In the month of February a part of the naval forces that Your Majesty had in the Mediterranean Sea took five enemy vessels loaded with wheat for Roussillon, two Spanish galleys, and some boats destined for the same end.[334]

You permitted the Duke of Lorraine to come to Paris after he had repeatedly asked you to do so. You pardon [*sic*] him and restore [*sic*] his possessions to him, retaining only what you felt to be totally necessary in order to keep him in line in the future.[335]

---

[331] It was more of an offer than a treaty that the Duke de Longueville, the Count d'Harcourt, Jules Mazarin, and the French ambassador De la Court made to Prince Thomas in Turin on December 2, 1640. It offered to acknowledge his rights of succession, to promote his reconciliation with Cristina, to allow him to send a gentleman to Spain in order to retrieve his wife and children, and to give him a hefty pension in return for coming himself to France and joining the French against Spain.

[332] This is an interesting dating reference indicating that the negotiations continued, since Prince Thomas finally came around to joining the French by a treaty that he signed on July 1, 1642.

[333] The future Marshal de Turenne took this stronghold on March 5, 1641.

[334] This action took place on March 18, 1641, in the Bay outside Rosas, preventing the resupply of the Spanish garrisons in Roussillon and Catalonia.

[335] This act was signed in Paris on March 28, 1641, between Richelieu and Charles IV, sworn to by him in Saint-Germain-en-Laye in front of Louis XIII on April 2 and ratified by the duke back in Lorraine on April 29. The variation in tenses indicates that the process was still ongoing.

Marquis de los Velez,[336] the
Prince di Nocera[337]

You relieve Barcelona against two armies of the King of Spain and defeat them with only a few troops.

The Sieur de La Motte, who commanded your armies in Catalonia, trapped 12,000 men and 2,000 horse in Tarragona and destroys them with 8,000 of yours. A first attempt to relieve them with forty galleys is repulsed by your naval armada with fifteen of theirs being taken, burned, or run aground.[338]

If this same armada made up of 18 galleys, 20 warships, and many fire ships was not so successful against the second attempt that the enemies undertook with 29 galleys and 35 ships, public opinion blames its commander for this failure, which might be attributed to the difference in the number of ships if your armada had given battle as it should have instead of seeking its security in a quick retreat, which saved your ships but not the reputation of their commander.[339]

You took Aire, a stronghold particularly well fortified since it can only be attacked at one point. You captured it in 54 days notwithstanding all the efforts of the Cardinal-Infante, who never abandoned a single league of circumvallation.[340]

This siege was all the more noteworthy in that you continued it notwithstanding the rebellion of the Count de Soissons, the revolt of the Dukes de Guise and Bouillon, and the loss of a battle that these rebels won in combination with the armies of the Emperor, more through the bad conduct of yours

---

[336] Pedro Fajardo Zuñiga y Requeséns (1601–1647), Marquis de los Velez, was the Spanish viceroy of Catalonia when the revolt of Catalonia broke out. He was attempting, by a combination of reassurances and terror, to advance on Barcelona.

[337] Francesco Maria Carafa (1580–1642), Duke di Nocera, viceroy of Navarre, who came to the support of Los Velez with a small contingent.

[338] Philippe de la Motte-Houdancourt (1605–1657) had arrived in Catalonia in the middle of February with a mere twenty soldiers and began to build up both his French and his Catalan army. Joined by a French fleet under Sourdis, on July 4 Houdancourt undertook the siege of Tarragona, a seaport some sixty-one miles southwest of Barcelona. In a fierce naval battle between July 4 and 6, Sourdis kept Garcia de Toledo (1579–1639), Duke de Fernandina, from revictualing the stronghold.

[339] This second naval battle of Tarragona (August 20–25, 1641) was won by a bigger Spanish armada under Fernandina and José de Cardenas (1584–1644), Duke de Marqueta, over the blockading French fleet. Notwithstanding the skill of Sourdis in extricating his armada in the face of a superior enemy, the French had to abandon the siege of Tarragona, and the dashing of Richelieu's hopes for a quick peace is clearly evident in his disparagement of Sourdis's rearguard action.

[340] Aire was a Spanish stronghold on the Lys River some thirty-six miles southwest of Calais. The Marshal de La Meilleraye undertook to besiege it on May 19 with a large army and succeeded in taking it by July 26, but the French did not hold it for long. See note 355 below.

than through their own valor, and though they had more dead than we did, all of your infantry was either dissolved or taken prisoner.[341]

The defection of the Duke of Lorraine, who was obliged to join his troops to your army, was in no small way responsible for this incident, in which, however, God demonstrated that He is on your side since this battle resulted in the death of the Count de Soissons, who was the leader not only of this revolt but apparently of many others and who was irreplaceable.[342]

Your Majesty, who always keeps the interests of your state in mind, had no sooner heard of this disaster than you resolved to go personally to where it had happened in order to remedy it. And you had no sooner arrived than the armies of the Emperor withdrew without any other wages for their victory than the city of Donchery, which held out for three days against your army even though they had left there a garrison of 1,500 men.

No sooner was this stronghold retaken than the Duke de Bouillon came to terms, and Sedan changed from a haven for the discontented to a place of obedience, to the great joy of the inhabitants, who, during the defection of their lord, were constantly showing their zeal for France.

Only the Duke of Lorraine did not return to his duty, even though he was obliged to do so. His fear of retribution and the solicitations of the enemies made him forget his word, his faith, his reputation, and his interests. He went to Flanders to join your enemies, but he was so unbalanced that he could do good neither for himself nor for anyone else.

Since you were occupied in Champagne, the appeals in Flanders for the Cardinal-Infante to take advantage of this opportunity made him decide to keep Aire from being reprovisioned and to defeat the army that had made this conquest, hoping in one way or the other to retake it. But your absence and all their efforts did not keep Marshal de La Meilleraye from getting four months of victuals into the stronghold and from offering a battle before withdrawing, which they avoided with good reason because if they had lost it, the loss of their country would have been inevitable.

The news of their plan did not keep you from sending 6,000 men into Lorraine in order to retake by force what you had willingly restored to the duke,

---

[341] During the siege of Aire, Frédéric-Maurice de la Tour d'Auvergne (1605–1652), Duke de Bouillon, a former Protestant who was sovereign in the Principality of Sedan, joined with the Spanish, with Henri II, Duke de Guise (1614–1664), and with Louis de Bourbon (1604–1641), Count de Soissons, who had already participated in a plot to assassinate Cardinal Richelieu in 1636, in another revolt against his ministry. The rebels roundly defeated a French army sent against the rebels under Gaspar de Coligny on July 6, 1641, at the Battle of La Marfée outside Sedan.

[342] Charles IV promptly proceeded to ignore his treaty, and by August the French had reoccupied his territories.

and this undertaking was so successful that in six weeks you reconquered everything that you had restored with the exception of La Motte, which was too far from the body of Lorraine to be important for your affairs at present.

Those of Champagne were no sooner terminated than Your Majesty headed back to Picardy.

You learned along the way that, since it would have consumed all the victuals for the stronghold if the Marshal de La Meilleraye had taken the time to demolish most of the circumvallation of Aire, the enemies had once more besieged it.

You might have tried to attack the trenches, but it had been so easy to repair and strengthen them that those who were to undertake it considered it rash.

Their advice was to think about some powerful diversions. Your Majesty decided on this and had no sooner given them the order than with the reinforcement of part of the troops that you had brought with you from Champagne, they took Lens and La Bassée and devastated most of the countryside.[343]

They would have subsequently taken over the populous and rich city of Lille had not the time that was needed in order to prevent these two strongholds from being overrun permitted the Cardinal-Infante to throw so many troops into Lille that it was decided to take your armies elsewhere.

For this purpose, they retraced their steps. They attacked Bapaume, a stronghold as important for excluding the invasion of France as it was for facilitating that of the Low Countries. It threatened the entire frontier and had up to then been considered impregnable due to the lack of water.[344]

It was so vigorously attacked that even though it was perfectly fortified with seven bastions, a good counterscarp, six half-moons, and a palisade in its trench, it was captured in eight days, even though the besieged would only surrender after a mine had blown up one of their bastions.

Your armies were successful not only in Flanders, since those commanded by the Count d'Harcourt in Italy took the fort of Ceva, stubbornly defended by the Spanish and Germans, restored all the Lansleburgo, the Moncenisio, and the nearby valleys to the obedience of the Duchess of Savoy and to the duke her son, and took the very strategic stronghold of Coni with all the more glory in the face of great resistance.[345]

The various efforts of Prince Thomas to disrupt this siege with different diversions make it all the more noteworthy in that they were unsuccessful.

---

[343] Brezé and La Meilleraye attacked and took Lens and La Bassée on September 20, 1641.
[344] Brezé and La Meilleraye attacked it on or about September 11, 1641, and it surrendered on September 18.
[345] Coni was about fifty miles south of Turin, near the frontier with the Republic of Genova. Harcourt besieged its fort late in July. I have spelled these places according to their Italian names, although the first two are now part of France thanks to Benito Mussolini.

The loss of 1,600 men, including a quantity of officers, killed in his attack on Cherasco only adds to the result of this undertaking.[346]

His attempt to take Chivasso by surprise, which was repulsed with losses, is another example.[347]

That of the Spanish on Rosignano, where they were welcomed in the same way as Prince Thomas was by those two strongholds, only adds to its brilliance.[348]

If they take Moncalvo, the fact that they then raze the stronghold shows that their conquest is not great.[349]

The surrender of the strongholds of Demonte and Revel, which secure all the valleys that are on border with France, can truthfully be said to be a result of the loss of Coni, which covered them. It crowns the glory of your armies in Italy and points out how much your sister Madame has gained by giving up her ill-advised policies.[350]

Those who commanded your armies in Roussillon took a number of small strongholds in order to keep Perpignan from being reprovisioned and did everything they could to weaken this stronghold so it would fall into your hands.

If Germany, which has been the most famous theater of the war during the last twenty years, does not furnish historians with as much material about your armies as about those of your allies this year as in previous ones, it has not failed to leave posterity with the winning of two great battles, all the more important in that they happened at a time when your enemies were about to invade France with a part of their forces and that your army and that of the Swedes were without their generals, the Duke de Longueville because of an illness that obliged him to return to his native land and Banér, who had commanded the Swedish army since the Battle of Nördlingen, because of his death.[351]

---

[346] Cherasco was about thirty-one miles southeast of Turin. Between August 21 and September 24, Prince Thomas made two attempts to divert the French by attacking it without success.

[347] Chivasso was about twelve miles northeast of Turin. Prince Thomas tried to attack it during the siege of Coni.

[348] A city in Monferrato, some fifty-two miles east of Turin, held by troops loyal to Cristina. The Spanish, in support of Prince Thomas, attempted an attack on it and failed.

[349] Prince Thomas laid siege before it in September and took it, an indication of how difficult it was to gain complete control of the entire territory of the state.

[350] Demonte was about fifty-six miles southwest of Turin. It fell on October 18. Revel was about sixteen miles northeast of Turin.

[351] Richelieu is referring to Jean-Baptiste Budes (1602–1643), Count de Guébirant's victory with the support of the Swedish general Königsmark at Wulfenbeutel over the Austrians under the Archduke Leopold and Piccolomini on June 29, 1641, and to the skirmish near Hessendam on August 24, also with the support of the Swedes. Johan Banér (1596–1641), the right-hand officer of Gustavus Adolphus in the Thirty Years' War, had died on May 20.

What should have caused you a great deal of harm, on this occasion, proved of no little advantage to you, since the only thing that made the enemies decide to fight was their overconfidence in the face of enemies who were without leaders.

Since the King of Portugal, restored to the throne of his fathers by the zeal of his subjects, beseeched Your Majesty to help him with a naval armada, even though the bulk of your forces were occupied in the Mediterranean Sea, you did not fail to send another, made up of 30 ships, which would have done great things if those who had promised this prince to follow his example once they felt strong enough at sea had been as religious in keeping their word as they were resentful of the government of Spain. If their change of mind deprived this armada of part of the glory that it might have acquired, it did not keep the King of Portugal from profiting greatly from it since it arrived precisely at a time when he needed it to enforce the exemplary punishment of a conspiracy by some of his principal subjects.[352]

Even though it is well known that the dominance of Spain is due to the fact that while its rulers may change, its policies never do, there is no one, I am sure, who would not acknowledge that the death of the Cardinal-Infante at the end of this year, either from sadness at seeing the bad state of the king his brother's affairs or from his constant efforts at trying to restore them in Flanders, was ordained by God in order to deprive Spain of a prince who was of immense use in retaining the obedience of the people whom he was governing.[353]

Monaco[354] *If you lose Aire*[355] *Spanish galleys lost in a Storm*[356] *Distribution of Benefices*[357]

---

[352] This plot was led by Sebastião de Matis de Noronha (1586–1641), Archbishop of Braga from 1635 and partisan of Spain, who collected some fellow conspirators. He and his accomplices were arrested on July 28, 1641, and his accomplices brutally executed on August 29, the archbishop dying in captivity one month later.

[353] He died in Brussels on November 9, 1641.

[354] Honoré II Grimaldi (1597–1662), Prince of Monaco from 1604, had abandoned Spain and admitted French troops into the city, according to the *Gazette* of November 30, 1641, and several others that followed.

[355] The Spanish retook it on December 7. The loss was casually reported in the *Gazette* on December 14, 1641.

[356] Announced in the *Gazette* on December 21, 1641.

[357] Reported in the *Gazette* on December 14, 1641.

Bibliography

MANUSCRIPTS

Original Manuscripts of the *Political Testament*

OM¹ Most of the original manuscript of the *Political Testament* is missing, but it is possible to obtain a good sense of its evolution from an analysis of its eighteen copies, which I have designated either as Text A or Text B, as well as from the printed edition first published by Henri Desbordes in 1688. Richelieu began composing what has come down to us as Text A around September 1640 with the assistance of his secretary, Pierre Cherré. They were adding practically all of Text B by the end of the year, but Cherré continued to perfect it into the 1680s.

OM² Bibliothèque Nationale *Ms. Cinq Cents Colbert* 2. This is the only portion of the original manuscript that we still possess. It is an attempt to continue the Succinct narration beyond 1638. It was begun in the course of 1641 and covered 1639, 1640, and most of 1641. It was given up in December 1641.

Manuscript copies of the *Political Testament*

During Richelieu's Life

(in order of composition)

Text A Bibliothèque Nationale *Ms. Français* 23247, *Testament Politique ou les Maximes d'Estat de Monsieur le Cardinal de Richelieu.* This is an excellent (though imperfect) eighteenth-century copy of another lost copy

229

donated to the Sorbonne in 1646 by Michel Le Masle, one of Richelieu's principal confidants. The students who made it carefully noted its differences from B[6], the copy in the French Ministry of Foreign Affairs, in the margins.

Text B[1]   Bibliothèque de l'Arsenal *Mss.* 3561–3562, *Testament Politique De L'Eminentissime Armand Cardinal de Richelieu pair Et grand admiral de France premier ministre d'Estat durant Le Regne de Louis Treize~ du nom Roy de France Et de navarre.* This is a copy made in the eighteenth century of a missing manuscript of the first copy that we have of Text B. It was originally made between the end of 1641 and the beginning of 1642 and bound in the arms of Louis Henri de Bourbon-Condé (1692–1740), grandson of the Great Condé and minister to Louis XV. It was acquired by the Arsenal from the Condé collection in Chantilly.

Text B[2]   Bibliothèque Municipale (Médiathèque) de Rennes *Ms.*154*bis*, *Testament politique ou Les maximes d'etat du Cardinal de Richelieu.* This is the first copy that we have that was made in the seventeenth century. It was probably made between the end of 1641 and the beginning of 1642. Its present home at the library in Rennes is suspiciously close to the city of Saint-Malo, whose bishop in the seventeenth century, Achille de Harlay, had been a close collaborator of Cardinal Richelieu in his *Histoire.*

Text B[3]   Bibliothèque de l'Institut *Ms.* 5819, *Testament Politique, Cardinal de Richelieu.* This is a copy made in the eighteenth century of a missing manuscript of the third copy that we have of Text B. This copy was acquired by Jacob Friedeman von Werthern, Saxon ambassador to the court of France between 1769 and 1772. The original of this copy was probably made between the end of 1641 and the beginning of 1642.

Text B[4]   Bibliothèque Nationale *Ms. Français* 10219–10220, *Testament Politique de l'Eminentissime Armand Cardinal duc de Richelieu, Pair et grand Admiral de France, Premier Ministre d'Estat sous le Regne de Louis XIII du nom Roy de France et de Navarre Premiere partie 1642 Seconde Partie 1642.* This copy appears to have been prepared, along with the next two texts, between March 21 and May 26, 1642, in Narbonne, right after the cardinal fell so seriously ill that he proceeded to dictate his will.

Text B[5]   Bibliothèque Nationale *Ms. Français* 6561, *Testament Politique de l'Eminentissime Armand Cardinal Duc de Richelieu Pair et Grand Admiral de France, Premier Ministre d'Estat Sous le Regne de Louis XIIIe du Nom Roy de France et de Navarre Premiere Partie 1642 Seconde Partie 1642.* This is the second of the Narbonne texts, showing signs of being prepared in a great hurry.

Text B[6]   Archives des Affaires Etrangères, Mémoires et Documents *France 82, Maximes d'Estat Ou Testament Politique de l'Eminentissime Armand Cardinal Duc de Richelieu Pair et Grand Admiral de France, Premier Ministre d'Estat Sous le Regne de Louis XIII du nom Roy de France et de Navarre.* Though lacking a date in the title, this copy shows great continuity with its two predecessors and equals if not surpasses B[5] in its peculiarities. It was obtained by the French Ministry of Foreign Affairs in 1705 after the death of the second Duchess d'Aiguillon.

Text B[7] Bibliothèque Mazarine *Ms.* 2130, *Maximes d'Estat Ou Testament Politique de l'Eminentissime Armand Cardinal Duc de Richelieu Pair et Grand Admiral de France, Premier Ministre et chef du Conseil d'Estat Sous le Regne de Louis XIII Roy de France et de Navarre, commandeur des ordres du Roy Evêque de Lusson, Cofondateur et bienfaiteur de la maison et société de Sorbonne pour servir à la reformation, police et gouvernement de France et à la conduite particulière d'un état*. One of the cleanest and most elegant copies that we have, which was, I believe, prepared in Tarascon, where Cardinal Richelieu resided for nearly two months between mid-June and mid-August 1642, celebrating some sort of remission from his illness and the forthcoming execution of the king's favorite, the Marquis de Cinq-Mars, for high treason.

Text B[8] Bibliothèque Nationale, *Ms. Français 23248, Maximes d'Estat Ou Testament Politique de 'Eminentissime Armand Jean du Plessis, Duc de Richelieu, Pair et grand Amirail de France, Premier minister et Chef du Conseil d'Estat sous le regne de Louis XIII Roy de France et de Navarre, Commandeur des ordres du Roy, Evesque de Luçon, Confondateur et bienfacteur de la maison et societé de Sorbonne*. This is simply an eighteenth-century copy of B[7], disregarding its paragraphing.

Text B[9] Bibliothèque Nationale, Réserve *Ms.* Morel de Thoisy 54, fols. 23–144, *Maximes d'estat du* [sic] *testament politique de L'Eminentissime Armand du plessis Cardinal Duc de Richelieu, Pair et grand Amiral de France Ier Ministre et Chef du Conseil d'Estat Sous le Regne de Louis XIII Roy de France et de Navarre, Commandeur des ordres de Sa Maiesté, Evesque de Luçon* fondateur [sic] *Confondateur et bienfaiteur de la Maison et Societé de Sorbonne*. This is a copy undertaken in the eighteenth century, for an indefatigable collector of documents, of a seventeenth-century copy possibly also prepared in Tarascon.

Text B[10] Bibliothèque de l'Arsenal *Ms.* 3739, *Maximes d'Estat Ou Testament Politique de l'Eminentissime Armand Cardinal Duc de Richelieu Pair et Grand Admiral de France, Premier Ministre et chef du Conseil d'Estat Sous le Regne de Louis XIII Roy de France et de Navarre, commandeur des ordres du Roy Evêque de Lusson, Cofondateur et bienfaiteur de la maison et société de Sorbonne*. Notice the spelling of "Lusson"! This is an eighteenth-century copy in deceptively uninspiring condition, but hiding behind its missing folios and sloppy table of contents is the final condition of the *Political Testament* prior to the death of Cardinal Richelieu.

After Richelieu's Death

(in order of composition)

Text B[11] Bibliothèque Municipale, Carpentras *Ms.* 721, *Testament Politique ou Maximes d'Estat De L'Eminentissime Jean Armand Du Plessis Cardinal Duc De Richelieu Premier Ministre Sous le Regne De Louis XIII d'heureuse memoire*. As the title implies, this was composed after the

death of both Cardinal Richelieu and Louis XIII. As an added bonus, it
was written entirely in the hand of Richelieu's secretary, Pierre Cherré.

Text B[12]   Bibliothèque Sainte-Geneviève *Ms.* 808, *Testament Politique ou Maximes
d'Estat De L'Emnentissime Jean Armand Du Plessis Cardinal Duc De
Richelieu.* This copy not only, in the title of its Second Part, refers to
Louis XIII as being of "heureuse memoire" but was also clearly com-
missioned by Cherré since it incorporates a portion of the authoritative
changes that he made on his own copy.

Text B[13]   Bibliothèque Nationale *Ms. Français* 10221, *Testament Politique ou les
Maximes D'Estat Du Cardinal de Richelieu Divisé en deux Parties.*
This is the first of the five texts that claim there was a peace between
France and its enemies in 1639, and each of these texts contains clear
continuities with Cherré's own B[11]. These five texts were all done con-
currently, but, still, there are clear elements of continuity between them.

Text B[14]   Bibliothèque Royale de Belgique *Ms.* 9941, *Testament Politique ou Les
Maximes d Estat de l'Eminentissime Jean Armand du Plessis, Cardinal
Duc de Richelieu.*

Text B[15]   Bibliothèque Municipale, Châlons-sur-Marne *Ms.* 225, *Testament Politique, ou les Maximes d'Estat du Cardinal de Richelieu.*

Text B[16]   Bibliothèque Municipale, Rouen *Ms.* 2759, *Testament Politique, ou Les
Maximes d'Etat du Cardinal de Richelieu.*

Text B[17]   Bibliothèque Municipale, Nantes *Ms.* 1118, *Testament Politique ou les
Maximes d'Estat du Cardinal de Richelieu.*

Manuscript Versions of Desbordes's Editions

Musée Condé (Chantilly) *Ms.* 924.
Bibliothèque de l'Arsenal *Ms.* 3853.

EDITIONS OF THE *POLITICAL TESTAMENT*

(in order of publication)

Desbordes, Henri, ed. *Testament politique d'Armand du Plessis, cardinal duc de
Richelieu.* Amsterdam, 1688, 1689, and 1690. The fourth edition (1691) adds
some lengthy "Observations Historiques sur le Testament Politique du Cardinal
de Richelieu," which Desbordes claims he has just received and continue to be
included by him and his successors in four more editions until 1740.

Griffet, Henri. *Histoire du règne de Louis XIII.* 3 vols. Paris, 1758. Vol. 3, 617–635,
contains the first printing of the continuation of the Succinct narration.

Foncemagne, Etienne Lauréold de, ed. *Maximes d'Etat, ou testament politique
d'Armand du Plessis, cardinal duc de Richelieu.* Paris: Imp. de Le Breton, 1764.
Contains a Text B, the "Observations Historiques sur le Testament Politique du

Cardinal de Richelieu," and a "Lettre écrite de Dijon en 1765 aux auteurs des Journal de Trévoux."

Recueil des Testamens politiques du cardinal de Richelieu, du duc de Lorraine, de M. Colbert & de M. de Louvois. 4 vols. Amsterdam: Chez Zacharie Chaterain, 1749 (with "Observations," 1769).

André, Louis. *Cardinal de Richelieu, Testament Politique.* Paris: Robert Laffont, 1947.

Hill, Henry Bertram, ed. *The Political Testament of Cardinal Richelieu, the Significant Chapters and Supporting Sections.* Madison and London: University of Wisconsin Press, 1961.

Dessert, Daniel. *Testament politique ou Les maximes d'Etat de Monsieur le cardinal de Richelieu.* Paris: Robert Laffont, 1990.

Hildesheimer, Françoise, ed. *Testament politique de Richelieu.* Paris: Société de l'Histoire de France, 1995.

Richelieu. *Testament politique.* Edited by Arnaud Teyssier. Paris: Perrin, 2011.

COMMENTARIES ON THE *POLITICAL TESTAMENT*

(in chronological order)

Aubery, A. *Histoire du cardinal duc de Richelieu.* Paris, 1660.

Montesquieu. *De l'esprit des lois.* Ch. V, Bk. 5.

Le Long, Jacques. *Bibliothèque historique de la France.* Paris, 1719.

Voltaire. *Mensonges imprimés du Testament politique du cardinal de Richelieu,* printed at the end of his play *Sémiramis.* Paris, 1749.

Voltaire to Frederick II, December 30 or 31, 1749, Voltaire to Frederick II, February 5, 1750, Frederick II to Voltaire, April 1750, in any good edition of their correspondence.

Foncemagne, Etienne Lauréold de. *Lettre sur le Testament politique du cardinal de Richelieu* (1750).

Ménard, Léon. "On peut se souvenir de ce que nous disions dans nos mémoires de février, I, Vol. Art. XX." *Mémoires sur l'Histoire des Sciences & des Beaux Arts* (May 1750): 1133–1145.

Ménard, Léon. *Réfutation du sentiment de M. de Voltaire, qui traite d'ouvrage supposé le testament politique du cardinal de Richelieu* (1750). Reprinted in *Mémoires sur l'Histoire des Sciences & des Beaux Arts* I, Art. XX (1750): 344–360.

Voltaire. *Des mensonges imprimes, dans Oreste tragedie.* Paris: Le Mercier, 1750.

Voltaire. *Remarques pour servir de supplément à l'Essai sur les moeurs et l'esprit des nations et sur les principaux faits de l'histoire depuis Charlemagne jusqu'à la mort de Louis XIII* (1763).

Foncemagne, Etienne Lauréold de. *Lettre sur le Testament politique du cardinal de Richelieu, imprimée pour la première fois en 1750 et considérablement augmentée dans cette seconde édition.* Paris: Le Breton, 1764.

Voltaire to d'Argental, November 2 and 14, 1764, and to Etienne Noël Damillaville, November 5, 7, and 23, 1764, in any good edition of his correspondence.

Mercier, Barthélémy, Abbé de Saint-Léger, "Lettre de M*** aux auteurs des Mémoires pour l'Histoire des Sciences & des Beaux-Arts, touchant les nouveaux écrits sur le véritable auteur du Testament politique du cardinal de Richelieu . . . Dijon ce 5 février 1765 (1765). Reprinted in *Mémoires sur l'Histoire des Sciences & des Beaux Arts* (March 1765): 650.

Voltaire (anonymous). *Arbitrage entre M. de Voltaire & M. de Foncemagne* (1765).

Voltaire. *Doutes nouveaux sur le testament attribué au cardinal de Richelieu*. Geneva and Paris, 1765.

Bibliothèque de l'Arsenal, Ms. 7577, fols. 157–180. Correspondence between Jean-François Gamonet, Charles Michel du Plessis-Villette, and Voltaire regarding the *Political Testament*, 1754–1755, published in the André edition, pp. 488–506 and in Besterman, *Correspondence*, Oxfordshire, Banbury, 1968–2018, XVIII, D11268, D12307, D12337.

Voltaire. "Etats, gouvernements, quel est le meilleur?" In *Dictionnaire philosophique portatif*. London, 1765.

Voltaire. *Questions sur l'Encyclopédie* (Geneva, 1771).

Hanotaux, Gabriel. *Maximes d'État et fragments du cardinal de Richelieu*. Paris, 1880.

Hauser, Henri. "Autour du testament politique de Richelieu." *Bulletin de la Société d'Histoire Moderne*, 8ᵉ série, no. 3 (avril 1935): 34–76, to which Edmond Esmonin responded in the same journal, no. 15 (janvier 1937): 214–216.

Stengers, Jean. Review of André's edition of the *Testament politique. Revue Belge de Philologie et d'Histoire* 26, no. 3 (1948): 650–660.

Mousnier, Roland, "Le *Testament politique* de Richelieu." *Revue Historique* 201 (1949): 55–71.

Esmonin, Edmond. Review of "A propos du *Testament politique* de Richelieu," by R. Pithon. *Revue Suisse d'Histoire* VI (1956): 177–214, in *Revue d'Histoire Moderne et Contemporaine* 5, no. 1 (1958): 74–77.

Avezou, Laurent, "Autour du *Testament politique:* A la recherche de l'auteur perdu (1688–1678)." *Bibliothèque de l'École de Chartes* CLXII (2004): 421–453.

Sonnino, Paul. "The Dating of Richelieu's *Testament politique*." *French Studies* XIX, no. 2 (2005): 262–272.

Sonnino, Paul. "Testament politique." In *Dictionnaire Richelieu*, edited by Françoise Hildesheimer and Dénes Harai, 357–358. Paris: Champion, 2015.

KEY PRIMARY SOURCES ON RICHELIEU

Richelieu, Armand Jean du Plessis de. *Lettres, instructions diplomatiques et papiers d'état du cardinal de Richelieu*. Edited by Georges d'Avenel. Collection de documents inédits sur l'histoire de France, ser. 1. 8 vols. (Paris, 1853–1877).

Richelieu, Armand Jean du Plessis de. *Les papiers de Richelieu*. Monumenta Europae Historia. Paris: A. Pedone.

Section politique interieure, correspondance et papiers d'état:
I.   1624–1626 (1975). Edited by Pierre Grillon
II. 1627 (1977). Edited by Pierre Grillon
III. 1628 (1979). Edited by Pierre Grillon
Index Vols. I–III (1980). Edited by Pierre Grillon
IV. 1629 (1980). Edited by Pierre Grillon
V.   1630 (1982). Edited by Pierre Grillon
VI. 1631 (1985). Edited by Pierre Grillon
Index Vols. IV–VI (1997). Edited by Marie-Catherine Vignal

Section politique exterieure, correspondance et papiers d'état: Empire allemand
1626–1629 (1982). Edited by Adolf Wild, Anja Victorine Hartmann
1630–1635 (1997). Edited by Anja Victorine Hartmann
1636–1642 (1999). Edited by Anja Victorine Hartmann
Index Vols I–III (2003). Edited by Aurélia Berger

Richelieu, Armand Jean du Plessis de. *Mémoires du cardinal de Richelieu*. In *Collection des mémoires relatifs à l'histoire de France*. Edited by Petitot and Monmerqué (Paris, 1819–1829), ser. 2, XXII–XXX, or in *Nouvelle collection des mémoires pour servir à l'histoire de France*. Edited by Michaud and Poujoulat (Paris, 1836–1839), ser. 2, VII–IX, or the incomplete modern edition published by the Société de l'Histoire de France (1907–), 10 vols.

PRINCIPAL SECONDARY SOURCES ON RICHELIEU

(in order of publication)

Hanotaux, Gabriel. *Histoire du cardinal de Richelieu.* 6 vols. Paris: Firmin-Didot and Plon, 1893–1947.
Hauser, Henri. *La pensée et action économiques du cardinal de Richelieu.* Paris: Presses Universitaires de France, 1944.
Wedgwood, Cicely Veronica. *Richelieu and the French Monarchy.* London: English University Press, 1949.
Tapie, Victor. *La France de Louis XIII et de Richelieu.* Paris: Flammarion, 1952.
Ranum, Orest. *Richelieu and the Councillors of Louis XIII: A Study of the Secretaries of State and Superintendents of Finance in the Ministry of Richelieu.* Oxford, UK: Clarendon Press, 1963.
Bergin, Joseph. *Cardinal Richelieu: Power and the Pursuit of Wealth.* New Haven, CT: Yale University Press, 1985.
Hildesheimer, Françoise. *Richelieu.* Paris: Flammarion, 2004.
Ranum, Orest. *Les bienfaits, la gratitude et l'action politique: une analyze du don et du pouvoir dans le Testament politique de Richelieu.* Paris: Pages d'Histoire, 2018.

Index

CPSIA information can be obtained
at www.ICGtesting.com
Printed in the USA
LVHW042240260623
750879LV00019B/86